Lecture Notes in Networks and Systems

Volume 277

The series "Lecture Notes in Networks and Systems" publishes the latest developments in Networks and Systems—quickly, informally and with high quality. Original research reported in proceedings and post-proceedings represents the core of LNNS.

Volumes published in LNNS embrace all aspects and subfields of, as well as new challenges in, Networks and Systems.

The series contains proceedings and edited volumes in systems and networks, spanning the areas of Cyber-Physical Systems, Autonomous Systems, Sensor Networks, Control Systems, Energy Systems, Automotive Systems, Biological Systems, Vehicular Networking and Connected Vehicles, Aerospace Systems, Automation, Manufacturing, Smart Grids, Nonlinear Systems, Power Systems, Robotics, Social Systems, Economic Systems and other. Of particular value to both the contributors and the readership are the short publication timeframe and the world-wide distribution and exposure which enable both a wide and rapid dissemination of research output.

The series covers the theory, applications, and perspectives on the state of the art and future developments relevant to systems and networks, decision making, control, complex processes and related areas, as embedded in the fields of interdisciplinary and applied sciences, engineering, computer science, physics, economics, social, and life sciences, as well as the paradigms and methodologies behind them.

Indexed by SCOPUS, INSPEC, WTI Frankfurt eG, zbMATH, SCImago.

All books published in the series are submitted for consideration in Web of Science.

More information about this series at http://www.springer.com/series/15179

Daniel Raposo · Nuno Martins ·
Daniel Brandão
Editors

Advances in Human Dynamics for the Development of Contemporary Societies

Proceedings of the AHFE 2021 Virtual Conference on Human Dynamics for the Development of Contemporary Societies, July 25–29, 2021, USA

Springer

Editors
Daniel Raposo
CIAUD & School of Applied Arts
Polytechnic Institute of Castelo Branco
Castelo Branco, Portugal

Nuno Martins
ID+ & Design School
Polytechnic Institute of Cávado and Ave
Barcelos, Portugal

Daniel Brandão
CECS/Institute of Social Sciences
University of Minho
Braga, Portugal

ISSN 2367-3370 ISSN 2367-3389 (electronic)
Lecture Notes in Networks and Systems
ISBN 978-3-030-80414-5 ISBN 978-3-030-80415-2 (eBook)
https://doi.org/10.1007/978-3-030-80415-2

This Springer imprint is published by the registered company Springer Nature Switzerland AG
The registered company address is: Gewerbestrasse 11, 6330 Cham, Switzerland

Advances in Human Factors and Ergonomics 2021

AHFE 2021 Series Editors

Tareq Z. Ahram, Florida, USA
Waldemar Karwowski, Florida, USA

12th International Conference on Applied Human Factors and Ergonomics and the Affiliated Conferences (AHFE 2021)

Proceedings of the AHFE 2021 Virtual Conference on Human Dynamics for the Development of Contemporary Societies, July 25–29, 2021, USA.

Advances in Neuroergonomics and Cognitive Engineering	Hasan Ayaz, Umer Asgher and Lucas Paletta
Advances in Industrial Design	Cliff Sungsoo Shin, Giuseppe Di Bucchianico, Shuichi Fukuda, Yong-Gyun Ghim, Gianni Montagna and Cristina Carvalho
Advances in Ergonomics in Design	Francisco Rebelo
Advances in Safety Management and Human Performance	Pedro M. Arezes and Ronald L. Boring
Advances in Human Factors and Ergonomics in Healthcare and Medical Devices	Jay Kalra, Nancy J. Lightner and Redha Taiar
Advances in Simulation and Digital Human Modeling	Julia L. Wright, Daniel Barber, Sofia Scataglin and Sudhakar L. Rajulu
Advances in Human Factors and System Interactions	Isabel L. Nunes
Advances in the Human Side of Service Engineering	Christine Leitner, Walter Ganz, Debra Satterfield and Clara Bassano
Advances in Human Factors, Business Management and Leadership	Jussi Ilari Kantola, Salman Nazir and Vesa Salminen
Advances in Human Factors in Robots, Unmanned Systems and Cybersecurity	Matteo Zallio, Carlos Raymundo Ibañez and Jesus Hechavarria Hernandez
Advances in Human Factors in Training, Education, and Learning Sciences	Salman Nazir, Tareq Z. Ahram and Waldemar Karwowski

(continued)

(continued)

Advances in Human Aspects of Transportation	Neville Stanton
Advances in Artificial Intelligence, Software and Systems Engineering	Tareq Z. Ahram, Waldemar Karwowski and Jay Kalra
Advances in Human Factors in Architecture, Sustainable Urban Planning and Infrastructure	Jerzy Charytonowicz, Alicja Maciejko and Christianne S. Falcão
Advances in Physical, Social & Occupational Ergonomics	Ravindra S. Goonetilleke, Shuping Xiong, Henrijs Kalkis, Zenija Roja, Waldemar Karwowski and Atsuo Murata
Advances in Manufacturing, Production Management and Process Control	Stefan Trzcielinski, Beata Mrugalska, Waldemar Karwowski, Emilio Rossi and Massimo Di Nicolantonio
Advances in Usability, User Experience, Wearable and Assistive Technology	Tareq Z. Ahram and Christianne S. Falcão
Advances in Creativity, Innovation, Entrepreneurship and Communication of Design	Evangelos Markopoulos, Ravindra S. Goonetilleke, Amic G. Ho and Yan Luximon
Advances in Human Dynamics for the Development of Contemporary Societies	Daniel Raposo, Nuno Martins and Daniel Brandão

Preface

The AHFE 2021 International Conference on Human Dynamics for the Development of Contemporary Societies focuses on how human factors and ergonomic principles impact on quality of life and society lifestyles through interactions between academia, industry and government. We understand that research and design should be centered on people without considering them as the center of the universe, but rather as people who participate in a society and world.

The objective of this conference is to promote research on human factors and ergonomic principles in the context of the design of artifacts and systems (human, social, symbolic, technological, economic and cultural) that impact on health, wellbeing, safety, sustainability, food, enjoyment, accessibility, interaction, education, intelligibility, integrity, democracy and place development.

The conference welcomes submissions of original papers, case studies or research papers reporting on new models, practices and processes with an impact on the development of society considering people, companies, government bodies and the world. This book covers five unique yet overlapping design areas such as:

- Human dynamics for social cohesion
- Arts and creativity in education
- Co-creation perspectives
- Creativity and complexity
- Design and human–computer interaction
- Design for equality and human rights
- Design for health
- Design for sustainability
- Design for welfare
- Human dynamics and urban planning
- Identity, citizenship and mobility
- Media arts and socio-cultural factors
- Food design
- Transdisciplinary design wayfinding

A total of three sections are presented in this book:

1. Sustainability and Ecodesign
2. Human Interaction and Communication in Industry
3. Human Dynamics for Social Cohesion

Each section contains research papers that have been reviewed by members of the International Editorial Board. Our sincere thanks and appreciation to the Board members as listed below:

We hope that this book, which presents the international state of the art in the field of industrial design, will serve as a valuable source of theoretical and applied knowledge enabling human-centered design of a variety of products, services and systems for global markets.

July 2021

Daniel Raposo
Nuno Martins
Daniel Brandão

Contents

Sustainability and Ecodesign

Dryas as a Model for Lighting Products Design

Liliana Soares[1](✉), Ermanno Aparo[1], Rita Almendra[2], Fernando Moreira da Silva[2], João Teixeira[3], and Jorge Passos[4]

[1] Instituto Politécnico de Viana do Castelo, Portugal & CIAUD, Lisbon, Portugal
lsoares@estg.ipvc.pt
[2] Universidade de Lisboa, Faculdade de Arquitetura, CIAUD, Lisbon, Portugal
[3] Cadeinor, Fafe, Portugal
[4] Double Concept Bar-Drink & Design, Viana do Castelo, Portugal

Abstract. This study is part of an ongoing research project addressing the design of lighting products, comprising human, historical and semantic references to requalify and update previous concepts. The authors propose the concept of dryas as design model, considering dryas as an organism that embodies nature (as environment), medium (as process), art and persons. Methodologically based on a mixed practice, the study supports the cooperation between different agents to enable new symbolic paths and produce alternative, hybrid design projects. Permeable and adaptative, the design process involved the academic environment, the productive sector and the entertainment industry. The tangible result was a musical show with new floodlight devices designed by Altempo Design Research Group and produced by Furnor and Corticeira Amorim. Contingent on global public health issues, the intangible result is the improvement of the quality of life through network systems and a design approach focused on synergy, human factors and sustainability.

Keywords: Network system · Design method · Sustainability – human factors

1 Introduction

Stage lighting design enhances and balances all the components of a performance. Lighting is an essential component for any live stage event, and light design is an example of synergy as interaction giving rise to a whole that is greater than the sum of the parts. This paper aims to contribute to the design and development of systemic lighting products that embody human, historical and semantic references, requalifying previous concepts into an updated existence as design requirements [1], contingent on the current global public health concerns. The very concept of liquid reality [2] calls for constant inquiry in the light of new developments, challenging designers to create holistic and sustainable products. Associated with Greek mythology, Dryas are tree spirits or nymphs, who are born and die with their specific trees. The dryas' concept includes nature (as an environment), medium (as a process), art and people, to foster a renewed, more sensible design for a more responsible and critical society. This study supports the production

D. Raposo et al. (Eds.): AHFE 2021, LNNS 277, pp. 3–8, 2021.
https://doi.org/10.1007/978-3-030-80415-2_1

of deterritorialization [3] in a given timeframe, to enable alternative, hybrid and symbolic paths. The paper presents a new perspective for the rapport between the academic environment, the business world and the performing arts. The introduction of new creative processes involving design, teaching, crafts, industry, music and theatre intends to effectively improve the show business, favouring the environment and society as a whole. The creation of a local network system included a lighting appliances company, a raw material company and different entities connected to the entertainment sector. The goal was to create the prototypes for four lighting fixtures, through alternative semantic paths, conveying impressions and knowledge to improve the product design, use and performance. The lighting appliances sector is characterized by new technological applications fitting requirements of low consumption and high efficiency. New products require new semantic values to strengthen the poetic function of lighting dark spaces. The performance of light, such as sound, may be an art form. Light waves create moods and craft atmospheres for a performance.

Following the foregoing considerations, the research question was: To what extent can the modus operandi of design, combining enterprise, craftsmanship and design, which is always a redesign [4], contribute to an effective improvement of the performances produced in the show business?

2 Background

Considering the research problem, this study aims to build a local network system in the North of Portugal, combining the synergy from different professionals from different fields. In academic terms, master's dissertations from the Polytechnic Institute of Viana do Castelo have direct application at the level of set, stage and prop design, costume design, and musical instruments. Over the past seven years, such dissertations have produced prototypes for scenarios, costumes, scene props and musical instruments. Students have reached solutions accepted by directors of theatre companies and by musicians. This creative action was developed with the local professional theatre company (Teatro do Noroeste - Centro Dramático de Viana do Castelo – CDV), a local music school (Escola Profissional Artística do Alto Minho – ARTEAM) and several other companies. The validation of results was achieved in the academic field. All students collaborated with different local artisans. On the one hand, students developed scenographic solutions, costumes and stage props for specific plays proposed by the theatre companies. On the other hand, the students designed parts of musical instruments, connecting the productive local knowledge and the experience of music teachers and Lutiers. In collaboration with these entities, the students created a process of values [5] to develop their design projects. Another cornerstone for the present study were the projects developed with groups of students from the IPVC Integrated Design Master's Programme (MeDeIn). Specifically, in 2016, the project entitled "Alice in Viana das Maravilhas" [6] produced an event in the city of Viana do Castelo as a result of the synergy between different local entities, companies and institutions. The urban scale cultural event brought added value from the involved partners. The project included 15 students and 3 teachers from the IPVC, the ceramic manufacturing company Fábrica de Cerâmica Artística do Vale do Neiva, the Teatro do Noroeste - Centro Dramático de Viana do Castelo (CDV), ARTEAM (Escola

Profissional Artística do Alto Minho), and other local enterprises. The event allowed the creation of prototypes bringing together about 250 people. Finally, the entire creative process was published on social networks to publicize the action. Other research projects in the scope of music were the Almada trumpet (2018) designed by Ermanno Aparo [7] and the Shatron mute for trumpet (2019) designed by Altempo Design Research Group [8]. The outcomes of these projects were innovative products, combining different areas of knowledge and manufacture, creating systems of territorial networks characterized by synergy through the presence of partners from different areas, highlighting the Altempo Design Research Group, ARTEAM and Furnor.

This study aims to demonstrate that the synergy from different areas of knowledge constitutes an opportunity for innovation.

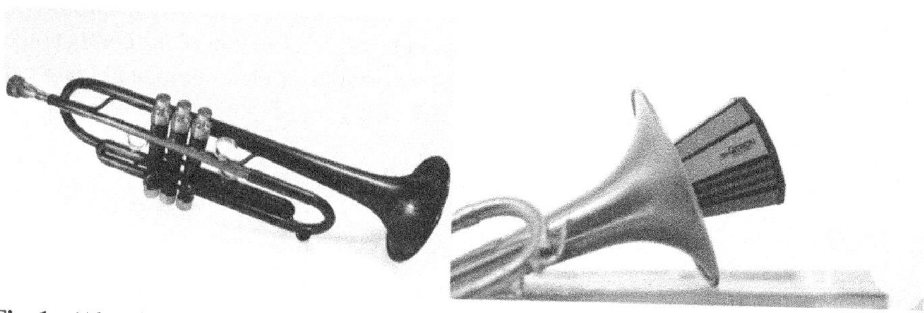

Fig. 1. (Almada Trumpet and Shatron mute for trumpet). Source: Ermanno Aparo and José Melo.

3 Objectives

The objectives of the present ongoing research are the following:

1. To build a local network system, relating different professionals from different fields, producing synergy. The project comprises academic partners, namely Altempo - Research Design Group[1], the Polytechnic Institute of Viana do Castelo and the Research Centre for Architecture, Urbanism and Design (CIAUD)[2], partners from the entertainment sector, such as the local theatre company Teatro do Noroeste - Centro Dramático de Viana do Castelo – CDV[3], the Escola Profissional Artística do Alto Minho – ARTEAM[4], a musical training institution that contributes to the strategic cultural and artistic development of the region. The study also involved Furnor, a company located in the city of Vila Nova de Famalicão, "(…) dedicated to the manufacture and finishing of metallic components and parts, which can be incorporated in its bathroom accessory lines, in its lighting lines (…)"[5] and Amorim

[1] https://competition.adesignaward.com/designer.php?profile=270118.
[2] http://ciaud.fa.utl.pt/index.php/en/
[3] http://centrodramaticodeviana.com/
[4] http://www.fam.pt/pt/escola/sobre-nos.
[5] http://www.furnor.com/_empresa.

Isolamentos, cork insulation company from the municipality of Santa Maria da Feira, in the district of Aveiro, with extensive work in research and development of new products. The project also adds low-technology and handicrafts, which characterize the manufacturing fabric of the northern region or Portugal [9].

2. To highlight the impact of business innovation applied to the entertainment sector. The cooperation between different areas of knowledge may contribute to rethink and test innovative ways of using lighting fixtures. In the long run, this presents an opportunity to create new businesses, contributing to sustainability and improving competitiveness. In addition, a complex system that considers human factors included in the whole environment may present a solution to design products with social responsibility. To design lighting products is not only based on the previous know-how from Furnor, but also on the future scenic impact of lighting.
3. Based on the case studies, research questions and proposed objectives, the following hypotheses are considered: The modus operandi that combines drawing competence, artisanal culture and entrepreneurial initiative presents a methodological approach with a creative, experimental and innovative role towards knowledge transfer and product design.

4 Methods

This study is based on a mixed methodology, integrating both quantitative and qualitative methods. The theoretical stage included the collection and analysis of concepts, case studies, and literature review. This allowed identifying the research hypothesis and triggered multidisciplinary brainstorming, so that the partners could produce mutual processes in a holistic strategy. Previous experience and different practices promoted the creation of effective paths. In the interventionist stage of research, an active investigation was carried out, including fieldwork and experimentation. Finally, in the stage of practical application of the project, the formulated research hypotheses will be verified or validated. Design method is understood as an attitude towards new design thinking foundations, based on the peculiar "designerly ways of knowing" [10].

5 Research

The music teachers of the ARTEAM (Escola Profissional Artística do Alto Minho) presented the musical program for 2021, giving the first step for a new product design – in this case, four different stage lighting instruments. The program included: 1) Ferenc Farkas (1905–2000); 2) Gustav Holst (1874–1934); 3) Claude Debussy (1862–1918); and 4) Antonín Dvořák (1842–1904). The concepts related to Mythology, Nature and the Environment were analysed by Altempo Design Research Group, in particular the concept of the tree nymphs or Dryas (common to different cultures). The next step was the analysis of the musical themes to cover the project. Considering the current pandemic situation and the conditions that affect the articulation of such a project, the first meeting with Sílvia Cancela and Ana Vieira from ARTEAM determined it would be better to limit the project to small ensembles or chamber music ensembles. Subsequently, the Altempo design team chose a string quartet (two violins, a viola and a cello) and a wind quintet (an oboe, a bassoon, a clarinet, a flute and a horn). After hearing the pieces that would be performed, the design group chose the following pieces:

Table 1. Chosen composers, pieces and musical training for the Dryas project.

Composer	Piece	Musical training
Ferenc Farkas	Early Hungarian dances from the 17th century (1959)	Wind Quintet
Gustav Holst	A-flat Op. 14 (1903)	Wind Quintet
Claude Debussy	Rêverie (1890)	Wind Quintet
Antonín Dvořák	F major, Op. 96, nicknamed the American Quartet (1893)	String Quartet

This choice identified common elements among the pieces, summarized as follows:

1. Ferenc Farkas' work alludes to Hungarian music and the presence of deities linked to the concept of the tree. Due to the strong presence of the Baroque tradition, it seemed important to highlight the reference to the tablature. Elements such as rhythm and circular dance movements were identified, interpreting the male dancers in this piece as modular design elements.
2. Gustav Holst refers to the English context, in particular, the "English madrigals" and the cult of nature. The figure and work of this English composer are also related to the Indian tradition, namely the figures of the "shalabhanjika", the Goddesses of the trees.
3. Claude Debussy reveals a strong relationship with Impressionism (Renoir), Romanticism (Mallarmé) and the proximity to natural elements and mythology used as decoration both in the visual arts and in architecture.
4. Finally, the bohemian musician Antonín Dvořák was very connected to his Czech origins and deities of Nature such as the Celtic and Greek. Dvořák's trip to the United States - to a small town inhabited by a strong Bohemian colony - places this composer in direct contact with the reality of Nature conveyed by a bird (the Scarlet Tanager) that characterizes the 3rd movement of the play "American".

The second stage of the design process consisted of storytelling and interpretation of the composers' message. Simultaneously, the company Amorim Corticeira produced the first cork blocks available for the design team to start the first tests. In addition, some doubts about production issues concerning metallic parts were clarified together with Furnor company. Still in this second stage, it was decided that the most suitable setting for the performance in the city of Viana do Castelo would be the atrium of the Church of São Domingos. Regarding the filming of the rehearsals and the possibility of attending such rehearsals, the previewed dates would be around January 2021.

6 Conclusions

The Dryas project indicates that a design process involving multiple players poses an opportunity for innovation and to support local industry, namely the entertainment industry. Also, the design of stage lighting fixtures constitutes an opportunity for partner companies to showcase new products in a setting that only the performing arts can offer. On the other hand, in the present pandemic context, audiences tend to prefer more intimate spaces such as open-air atria rather than large agglomeration venues such as concert-halls or stadiums. From the early lighting systems to illuminate theatrical productions in ancient Greece, the Dryas artifacts will propose stage lighting design for more intimate performances. The addressed case studies share the same synergy philosophy, adding value to the sum of the parts. For design research, this article advocates a collaborative, permeable design process, stimulating synergy from cross cultural fields, such as music, theatre, schools and the productive sector, promising social and economic gains. For design education, students are challenged to think about a complex and uncertain reality, including the prediction of the life cycle of a product and its impact on the lives of living beings and the environment. It is a holistic action in which human and environmental factors are essential to develop new products, in a responsible and eco-informed way.

Acknowledgements. This work was carried out with the support of CIAUD - The Research Centre for Architecture, Urbanism and Design of the Faculty of Architecture, University of Lisbon.

References

1. Gadamer, H.-G.: Philosophical Hermeneutics. University California Press, Berkeley (1976)
2. Bauman, Z.: Modernità liquida, Bari, Laterza (2005)
3. Deleuze, G., Guattari, F.: Difference & Repetition. The Athlone Press Limited, London (1994)
4. Latour, B.: A cautious prometheus? A few steps toward a philosophy of design' (with Special Attention to Peter Sloterdijk). In: Hackne, F., Glynne, J., Minto, V. (eds.) Proceedings of the 2008 Annual International Conference of the Design History Society – Falmouth, 3–6 September 2009, e-books, pp. 2–10. Universal Publishers (2008)
5. Mari, E.: Autoprogettazione? Edizioni Corraini, Milano (2002)
6. Soares, L., Almendra, R.A., Aparo, E., Moreira Da Silva, F.: Design education for theatre regarding craft-design alliance. In: Almendra et al. (eds.) REDES 2019: People & Processes & Products & Philosophy. Taylor & Francis Group. CRC Press, pp. 226–273 (2020)
7. Aparo, E., Moreira Da Silva, F., Soares, L.: O design como método para a implementação de processos produtivos relacionados com a criação de instrumentos musicais em Portugal: a criação de uma campana de trompete. In: Zuanon (org). DAT (Design Art and Technology) Journal 2, 1, pp. 115–132 (2017)
8. Designer Press.: "Shatron Mute for Trumpet by Altempo Design Researh Group (Ermanno Aparo, Liliana Soares, João Teixeira, Jorge Passos). COBANLI, Onur Mustak (Coord.) A' Design Award - Product Winner Designs 2019–2020, Hardcopy Edition, vol. 35-p, Milan (2020)
9. Soares, L., Almendra, R.A., Aparo, E., Moreira Da Silva, F.: Much tradition about innovation: the creation of sceneries with craft-design cooperation. In: Monteiro, S., et al. (eds.) Tradition and Innovation, Taylor & Francis Group, CRC Press. Part III, London (2021)
10. Cross, N.: Designerly Ways of Knowing. Springer, London (2006). https://doi.org/10.1007/1-84628-301-9

Design, Plastics and Sustainability – Methodological Reflections

Dília Nunes[1](✉) and Joana Lessa[2]

[1] University of Algarve, Algarve, Portugal
a46526@ualg.pt
[2] Research Center for Architecture, Urbanism and Design, University of Lisbon, Lisbon, Portugal
jlessa@ualg.pt

Abstract. This paper intends to reflect on design methodologies applied to sustainability practices for the production and consumption of environmentally friendly products, and, to clarify misconceptions regarding ubiquitous materials like plastic and their impacts when compared to the alternatives available.

The results indicate that design methodologies are being adopted and implemented by stakeholders worldwide, some of which have significant participation in plastic pollution. Findings also suggest that misconceptions regarding plastics are enforced on consumers, although scientific evidence often proves otherwise. Consumer habits and behaviors represent a problematic use of these materials, thus sustainable design approaches that also contemplate the social dimension are a necessity. However, and although design methodologies seem to produce environmentally positive impacts with reliable outcomes, it was observed that future work in terms of creating an internationally uniform assessment tool could represent an important step for sustainable design approaches to be considered worldwide efficient metrics of sustainable ergonomic principles.

Keywords: Design for sustainability · Design methods · Plastics · Oceans · Circular economy

1 Introduction

For the past decades, humankind has deployed the planet's natural resources and produced an infamous amount of new manufactured materials at such a fast pace, that a new epoch, the Anthropocene, is now being widely discussed for recognition amongst scholars worldwide [1]. The Anthropocene relates to the time interval in which human factors and activities negatively impact Earth and its' ecosystems, causing significant climate changes like sea-level rise and habitat loss [2, 3]. Ubiquitous materials such as plastics are frequently referred to as a hallmark of these negative effects, not specifically because of the materials themselves, but because of their production methods, consumption patterns, and waste mismanagement [4, 5]. Studies evidence the nefarious impacts of plastic pollution on the Oceans [6, 7], where, if nothing changes, it is foreseen to exist

D. Raposo et al. (Eds.): AHFE 2021, LNNS 277, pp. 9–17, 2021.
https://doi.org/10.1007/978-3-030-80415-2_2

(by weight) more plastics than fish by 2050 [8]. Thus, aiming at the common good of both the people and the planet requires immediate action, where new approaches to the plastic marine litter problem are compulsory.

Design as a practice has been referred as an important catalyzer for the achievement of a more sustainable and healthier planet, especially when considering circular economy models and full life cycle analysis [9, 10]. Therefore, design methods and principles are foreseen as positive contributions to the development of products and services that tackle environmental threats and promote sustainability, a fundamental milestone currently acknowledged by the Design community, governments, and societies worldwide [11–13].

This paper intends to reflect on a set of design methodologies applied to sustainability practices, and also to clarify misconceptions regarding the production and consumption of plastics when concerning their inherent environmental impacts in comparison to the alternatives available.

2 Sustainability and Plastic Misconceptions

Sustainability as a concept sets on three pillars: Social (people), Environmental (planet), and Economic (profit) [14]. The balance between them is essential, and as stated in the Bruntland report, it "... meets the needs of the present without compromising the ability of future generations to meet their own needs (. ...) does imply limits - not absolute limits but limitations imposed ... on environmental resources and by the ability of the biosphere to absorb the effects of human activities." [15] However, consumerism values enforced by the growth of a capitalist economy, lead societies worldwide to unprecedented unevenness between these tripartite factors, where the Environment pillar has been severely penalized [16, 17].

Therefore, the need to develop new strategic tools that addressed the Environmental pillar is of great importance. The life cycle assessment (LCA) for example, is a well-known tool developed to assess the environmental aspects and potential environmental impacts of a product throughout its life cycle, from raw material acquisition to end-of-life considering production, use, treatment, recycling, and final disposal [18].

Back in 1959, when Sten Gustaf Thulin designed the plastic bag, he intended to create an alternative to paper bags, aiming to help the environment by reducing the cut down of forest trees needed for their production [19]. The idea was positive in essence because unlike paper, plastic is a lightweight, functional, resistant, and durable material with a cheap production cost [20] that can be reused a significant number of times. But consumerism patterns and consumption behaviours deviated from this environmentally friendly logic, and plastic bags became single-use plastic items, often wrongly discarded and a major source of plastic marine litter [6, 7, 20, 21].

Contradictory, paper has re-emerged as a more environmentally friendlier option to plastics, as well as other natural materials alternatives like cotton and bioplastics, but in fact, they may pose as even worse options than plastic when considering their full LCA [22, 23].

These misconceptions regarding plastic bags and other packaging items are frequently enforced on consumers, that commonly tend to perceive plastics as a non-environmental option, although scientific evidence often proves otherwise [22, 23].

These studies also show that the real problem with plastic pollution is not the material itself, but rather, and to a greater extent, its production and distribution methods, the consumer's unsustainable behaviours, and poor or non-existing waste management processes and facilities [4, 5].

Present governments, businesses, and societies began to understand the complexity of accessing the full life cycle of these new alternatives to the specific problem of plastics and the danger that both plastics and alternative options represent for both the planet and the people and started to act upon it so that sustainability risks and environmental threats such as plastic pollution can be mitigated [22–25].

3 Design for Sustainability Methodology

Presently, Sustainable Design is perceived as "a design practice, education and research that, in one way or another, contributes to sustainable development" [26]. However, designers have long expressed concerns regarding sustainability and worked towards achieving a more environmentally driven planet. Sustainable design pioneers such as R. Buckminster Fuller, Victor Papanek, Vance Packard, or Dieter Rams, among others, have positively affected the design practice and shown that good design is creative, has a purpose, is made with intent, and offers sustainable simple solutions to everyday problems and needs [27–31]. Their concepts, worries, and theories were disseminated even before the concept of sustainable development emerged in the 1980s [26], and are considered the references that laid the foundations for today's Design for Sustainability (DfS) methodology and approaches [31].

For the purpose of this study, and considering the limitations regarding length and timeframe, we will discourse and reflect on some of the most commonly acknowledged DfS approaches according to Vezzoli et al. (2014) four dimensions [26] and Ceschin and Gaziulusoy evolutionary framework of DfS [31].

3.1 Green Design and Eco Design

Green Design is considered to be the first DfS approach and focused predominantly on the product level of sustainability [31]. It aimed to lower the environmental impact of products through the redesigning of their individual aspects, by reducing the amount of materials used, reusing parts of the products to create new ones, or by replacing virgin materials with recycled ones [32]. But although this was a positive step towards DfS, the practice lacked depth because it only focused on the individual product and its singular environmental performance, consequently promoting green consumerism, which ultimately maintained unsustainable patterns of consumer behaviours, thus not providing a significant capacity for environmental gain [31].

Eco Design addresses the environmental dimension of sustainability, focusing on the product and its environmental performance, just as Green Design [31]. However, there is an important difference between these initial DfS approaches, defined by their scope of action. Eco Design considers the product's full life-cycle, from the extraction of the raw materials to its final disposal, thus promoting its eco-efficiency [31]. This approach provides a comprehensive Life Cycle Assessment (LCA) that enables designers to have a more holistic understanding of the impacts of their design decisions [26]. When "it is estimated that over 80% of all product-related environmental impacts are determined during the design phase of a product" [33], smarter ecologically driven choices are desirable, and unlike Green Design, Eco Design can develop precise approaches to target specific stages on the life cycle of the products that have a greater impact on their environmental footprint [31]. However, as much as Eco Design is an important sustainable design approach, it still relates essentially to products and their technical cycles and does not contemplate other important dimensions of sustainability like consumer behaviour patterns, that sometimes represent greater product environmental impacts than all the technical phases of a product [31].

3.2 Biomimicry and Cradle to Cradle

Biomimicry (BM) and Cradle to Cradle (C2C) are two DfS approaches inspired by nature. The first mimics the models and processes of nature to addressed design problems, while the second creates regenerative systems of closed loops for technical nutrients and open loops for biological nutrients [31, 34, 35].

C2C is based on three principles: Waste equals food, eco-effectiveness, and respect for diversity [35]. The first principle, Waste equals food, divides nutrients into two categories: biological or technical, where all waste materials are productively re-incorporated into new production and use phases [34], with open loop environmental cycles for the biological nutrients and closed loop industrial cycles for the technical ones. Eco-effectiveness aims to increase the positive impacts of the materials and products, rather than eco-efficiency used in Eco Design, which only tries to minimize the negative impacts of a product. Respect for diversity, the third principle, seeks to include not only biodiversity but also diversity of place, culture, desire, and need so that an interdependent relationship is created, contributing to the construction of healthy and thriving natural systems [34]. Limitations for this design approach have been discussed in terms of being narrow as its focus mainly promotes the shift from a waste paradigm to a resource one. By doing so, it disregards complementary aspects beyond the scope of implementation, and lacks accurate assessment due to the limited assessment scope of LCA, that doesn't consider other environmental impacts [31], (Niero et al. (2018) and Bach et al. (2018), as cited in Ceschin and Gaziulusoy, 2019, p. 73).

BM as its name states, mimics nature to tackle design problems [35]. Its principles also lay under three premises, although they differ from the C2C approach. BM advocates for the use of nature as a model, by imitating or taking inspiration from nature's models to solve human problems; the use of nature as a measure, by applying nature's ecological standards to measure what works, what is appropriate, and what lasts; and the use of nature as a mentor, based not on what we can extract from the natural world, but on what we can learn from it [35]. For Cohen and Reich, (as cited in Ceschin and Gaziulusoy, 2019, p. 78) BM design is defined as 'an intended emulation of nature life solutions for solving contemporary challenges". Scalability, material constraints, manufacturing constraints, irrelevant design constraints, and accurate environmental assessment, are some of the limitations researchers indicate this approach needs to address [31].

3.3 Emotionally Durable Design and Design for Sustainable Behaviour

Both approaches emerged from the understanding that human behaviour has an important role in the environmental impacts of products where there is a need to contemplate more than the LCA and the development of extended lifespan of products by considering the social dimension of DfS [31].

EDD aims to create a bond between the consumer and the product so that social aspects like psychological obsolescence, (a term created by Chapman) [36], could be delayed or avoided and a reduction of consumption patterns, intrinsically linked to sustainability, could be achieved. On another perspective, Norman's emotional design approach [37] is divided in three different attachment levels (visceral, behavioural, and reflective), that grasp aspects from appearance and aesthetics to function, performance, meaning, and cultural characteristics of users, which can theoretically enhance the emotional relationship between consumers and their products.

Complementary, Design for Sustainable Behaviour (DfSB) is an approach that focuses on how design can shape or influence human behaviour [38]. It enables societal change, instilling sustainable behaviours and habits through a broader social perspective because it considers not only products but product systems, services, and the built environment [31, 38].

EDD and DfSB can be combined with the technical sustainability approaches that may balance their limitations. Subjectivity concerns, social and cultural aspects, and the constraints of a smaller range of products are limitations debated in EDD [30]; and ethical concerns, lack of metrics, and lack of evidence-based examples are the most common limitations attributed to DfSB [38].

4 Practical Applications of DfS Approaches

Some of the most studied DfS approaches were described previously and both benefits and limitations of each approach were expressed. It was made clear that sustainable design approaches vary between the technological focus dimension (Green Design, Eco Design, C2C, and BM), and the social focus dimension (EDD and DfSB).

As for the evolution of the approaches, it is possible to observe that in the Green Design approach the design scope was essentially limited to making the materials and components of a product less harmful to the environment. This approach had serious sustainability limitations and soon evolved to Eco Design [31]. Eco Design is an efficient method commonly employed to improve the LCA of products, and it is frequently used by worldwide companies like The Coca-Cola Company®, Unilever® or Nestlé®, some of the world's biggest plastic pollution producers [39]. But although it is undeniably an important approach, it lacks the broader view of the environmental implications beyond a product's life cycle [31]. In this regard, it is acceptable to consider that, if interchanged with a social design approach like EDD or DfSB, we believe it has the potential to develop improved integrated solutions that may address design problems with a more holistic approach.

C2C and BM are nature-inspired design approaches that seem to contribute to a wider understanding of design-related problems because they contemplate the effectiveness of natural flows and processes. C2C developed its own certified standards, the Cradle to

Table 1. Design for sustainability approaches and practical applications with plastics.

DfS Approach	Application	Description
Eco Design	Coca-Cola bottles (Trademark brands) 	Made from 100% recycled PET, these bottles use recyclable materials and less plastic. When correctly discarded, they are fully recyclable.
Cradle to Cradle	Carnegie Xorel Yarn 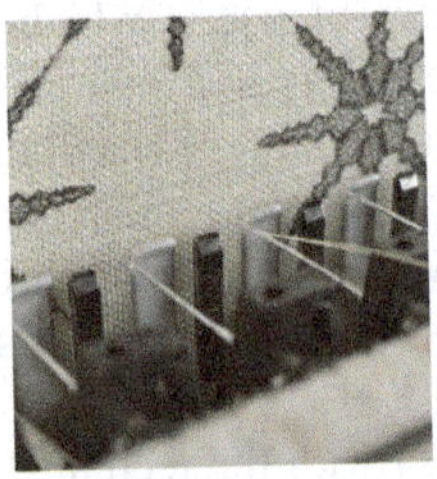	A 100% solution-dyed polyethylene, free of chlorine, plasticizers, heavy metals, toxic dyes, and ozone-depleting chemicals. Its design properties make it inherently colorfast, stain-resistant, durable, antibacterial, and non-absorbent.
Biomimicry	Biomimicry 3d printed sofa 	A soft seating chair inspired on plant cell structures that can be locally produced, adaptable to personal needs, and contains all functions made out of only one material.
EED	Fill it Forward APP 	An app that promotes environmental and social responsibility together with innovation that inspires sustainable initiatives and empowers people to make an impact through actions around the world.
DfSB	Loop Packaging 	A system where consumers make a 100% refundable deposit to borrow the packaging, that is professionally cleaned and reused once consumers finish using them.

Cradle Certified™, where products are assessed for environmental and social performance across five sustainability categories based on different accredited achievement levels. Carnegie, Stabilo®, and C&A, are some renown worldwide frontrunners brands that hold this certificate [40].

As stated earlier, plastic pollution is a problem that stands on the opposite end of sustainability. We consider that to understand the practical applications of the analysed DfS approaches concerning the mitigation of plastic pollution by tackling its first stage design problems, it is important to look at specific cases. Table 1 provides examples of products, systems, or programs that use DfS approaches to promote a sustainable use of plastics.

The above referred cases, show that DfS approaches are being adopted and implemented by stakeholders worldwide, some of which (like The Coca-Cola Company ®) have a significant participation in plastic pollution [39]. We consider that the examples also show that consumer habits and behaviours represent a social design dimension that is not taken into consideration by the technical DfS approaches because they are greatly focused on the improvement of the products and services, rather than on consumer behaviours and practices.

Results also seem to demonstrate the inexistence of worldwide recognized metrics to evaluate and define standards of implementation and assessment on the outcome of DfS approaches. LCA may vary depending on the indicators evaluated [20–22], and C2C certifying standards, although globally recognized, account only for their own defined metrics [41]).

Furthermore, when considering the scope of the DfS approaches analysed in this study and their applications (see Table 1), it is noticeable that they are pertinent for Circular Economy (CE) models [31]. According to the Ellen MacArthur Foundation (EMF), CE is defined as "one that is restorative and regenerative by design and aims to keep products, components, and materials at their highest utility and value at all times, distinguishing between technical and biological cycles" [42]. This definition by itself evidences the role that Eco Design, C2C, and BM have in the core of CE development, but also reinforces the dominance that the technical DfS approaches have over the behavioural ones. We consider that this opens an opportunity to further research, where an interconnection between approaches may result in a more holistic system of design thinking for environmentally friendly solutions to human problems.

5 Conclusions

The economic growth of a capitalist system created the need for products and services that didn't consider the environment and deployed Earth's natural resources, while the consumer habits and behaviours reinforced these negative environmental impacts. We consider that plastic pollution evidences this problem, and shows that current consumerism patterns and consumption behaviours have led to climate change, with the planet and its resources reaching a dangerous and unsustainable condition. DfS approaches appear to be fundamental if we wish to invert this destructive trend and pursue a sustainable path that allows the preservation of natural resources and the fulfilment of human needs, as promoted by the CE model. The practical applications of DfS approaches shown in the study suggest that the design community and worldwide companies are committed to this change.

The results also suggest that DfS technical and behavioural combined approaches are a viable strategy that should be pursued and followed up, which opens and opportunity for future research.

Although design methodologies seem to produce environmentally positive impacts with reliable outcomes, findings indicate that the metrics to assess them are scarcely established and lack uniformization (ex.: C2C defines its own specific standards). We therefore consider that future work in terms of creating an internationally uniform assessment tool could represent an important step for DfS approaches to be considered worldwide efficient metrics of sustainable ergonomic principles.

References

1. Waters, C., et al.: The Anthropocene is functionally and stratigraphically distinct from the Holocene. Science **351**(6269), aad2622 (2016)
2. Subcommission on Quaternary Stratigraphy, http://quaternary.stratigraphy.org/working-groups/anthropocene/
3. Zalasiewicz, J., Waters, C., Williams, M., Summerhaeys, C.: The Anthropocene as a Geological Time Unit. Cambridge University Press, Cambridge (2019)
4. World Economic Forum, Ellen MacArthur Foundation, and McKinsey & Company. http://www.ellenmacarthurfoundation.org/publications
5. Plastics Europe Organization, https://www.plasticseurope.org/en/resources/publications/4312-plastics-facts-2020
6. Plastics Oceans International, https://plasticoceans.org/plastic-pollution-research-papers/
7. Our World in Data, https://ourworldindata.org/plastic-pollution
8. Ellen Macarthur Foundation, https://www.ellenmacarthurfoundation.org/assets/downloads/news/New-Plastics-Economy_Background-to-Key-Statistics_19022016v2.pdf
9. European Environment Agency: Circular by Design - Products in the Circular Economy. Report No 6/2017. Publications Office of the European Union, Luxembourg (2017)
10. Ellen Macarthur Foundation, https://www.ellenmacarthurfoundation.org/circular-economy/concept
11. United Nations Association: Design for Sustainability, https://www.sustainablegoals.org.uk/design-for-sustainability/
12. Wilson, G., Bhamra, T.: Design for sustainability: the need for a new agenda. Sustainability. **12**(9), 3615 (2020)
13. Ideo, https://www.ideo.com/
14. Purvis, B., Mao, Y., Robinson, D.: Three pillars of sustainability: in search of conceptual origins. Sustain. Sci. **14**(3), 681–695 (2018). https://doi.org/10.1007/s11625-018-0627-5
15. United Nations, https://sustainabledevelopment.un.org/content/documents/5987our-common-future.pdf
16. Trentmann, F.: Chapter I – Introduction. The Oxford Handbook of the History of Consumption. Oxford University Press, Oxford (2012)
17. Nova-Reyes, A., Muñoz-Leiva, F., Martínez, T.: The tipping point in the status of socially responsible consumer behavior research? A bibliometric analysis. Sustainability **12**, 3141 (2020)
18. ISO, https://www.iso.org/obp/ui/#iso:std:iso:14040:ed-2:v1:en:fn:2
19. BBC News, https://www.bbc.com/news/av/science-environment-50043369

20. Alam, O., Billah, M., Yajie, D.: Characteristics of plastic bags and their potential environmental hazards. Resour. Conserv. Recycl. **132**, 121–129 (2018)
21. United Nations Environment Programme, http://hdl.handle.net/20.500.11822/7720
22. Ministry of Environment and Food of Denmark, https://www2.mst.dk/udgiv/publications/2018/02/978-87-93614-73-4.pdf
23. United Nations Environment Programme, http://hdl.handle.net/20.500.11822/31932
24. United Nations, https://sustainabledevelopment.un.org/?menu=1300
25. United Nations Climate Change, https://unfccc.int/process-and-meetings/the-paris-agreement/the-paris-agreement
26. Vezzoli, C., et al.: Product-Service System Design for Sustainability. Greenleaf Publishing, Sheffield (2014)
27. Fuller, R.B.: Operating Manual for Spaceship Earth. Southern Illinois University Press, Carbondale (1969)
28. Papanek, V.: Design for the Real World, 2nd edn. Academy Chicago Publishers, Chicago (1984)
29. Packard, V.: The Hidden Persuaders. D. McKay Co., New York (1957)
30. Vitsoe: Ten principles for good design, https://www.vitsoe.com/eu/about/good-design
31. Ceschin, F., Gaziulusoy, I.: Design for sustainability. A multi-level framework from products to socio-technical systems. (Open Access) (2019). https://doi.org/10.4324/9780429456510
32. Burall, P.: Green Design. Design Council, London (1991)
33. EU Science Hub, https://ec.europa.eu/jrc/en/research-topic/sustainable-product-policy
34. McDonough, W., Braungart, M.: Cradle to Cradle: Remaking the Way We Make Things. Vintage, London (2009)
35. Benyus, J.M.: Biomimicry: Innovation Inspired by Nature. Perennial, New York (2002)
36. Chapman, J.: Emotionally Durable Design: Objects, Experiences, and Empathy. Earthscan, London (2005)
37. Norman, D.: Emotional Design. Basic Books, New York (2004)
38. Niedderer, K., et al.: Design for behaviour change as a driver for sustainable innovation: challenges and opportunities for implementation in the private and public sectors. Int. J. Design **10**(2), 67–85 (2016)
39. Break Free from Plastic, https://www.breakfreefromplastic.org/wp-content/uploads/2020/12/BFFP-2020-Brand-Audit-Report.pdf
40. C2C Center Companies and Organisations, http://www.c2c-centre.com/companies-and-organizations
41. Cradle to Cradle Products Innovation Institute, https://www.c2ccertified.org/get-certified/product-certification
42. Ellen MacArthur Foundation, https://www.ellenmacarthurfoundation.org/assets/downloads/TCE_Ellen-MacArthur-Foundation_9-Dec-2015.pdf

Fostering Sustainability on Campus: Design of an IoT-Enabled Smartbottle for Plastic Reduction in the Academic Environment

João Mendes[1], Ana Curralo[1,2](✉), António Curado[3], and Sérgio I. Lopes[1,4]

[1] ADiT – Instituto Politécnico de Viana do Castelo, 4900-347 Viana do Castelo, Portugal
jmiguelmendes@ipvc.pt, {anacurralo,sil}@estg.ipvc.pt

[2] ID+ – Instituto de Investigação em Design, Media e Cultura, Aveiro, Portugal

[3] Prometheus – Instituto Politécnico de Viana do Castelo, 4900-347 Viana do Castelo, Portugal
acurado@estg.ipvc.pt

[4] IT – Instituto de Telecomunicações, Campus Universitário de Santiago, 3810-193 Aveiro, Portugal

Abstract. Public higher education institutions have a particular moral responsibility in increasing the awareness, knowledge, skills and values required to create a fair and sustainable future. Through sustainable design, the Project Refill_H20 aims to eliminate the use of plastic water bottles in the 6 schools of the Polytechnic Institute of Viana do Castelo (IPVC), respective bars, canteens and halls of residence A survey of the academic community will identify the set of physical, aesthetic and functional features to create the product specifications for the Smartbottle and Water Refill Station. ICT and IoT technologies will encourage autonomy, pedagogically helping users to acknowledge, identify and reduce their environmental footprint. Applying the principles of circular economy, this academic project promotes the reduction of plastic consumption, production and waste. Contributing towards a paradigm shift, sustainable design canvasses conditions to reduce plastic in the oceans, improving the environment and the quality of life on Earth.

Keywords: Sustainable design · Smartbottle · IoT · RFID · Sustainability · Campus

1 Introduction

Sustainable development allows meeting the needs of the present without compromising the ability of future generations to meet their needs. This principle combines sustainable design and technological innovation to promote new models of behaviour while producing ecological awareness, action, and economic results. In the intersection between design, technology and sustainability, the tangible target of the "Refill_H20" project is to eliminate the use of plastic water bottles on the IPVC Campus (Polytechnic Institute of Viana do Castelo), a higher education institution aiming to play a leading role in sustainable development.

D. Raposo et al. (Eds.): AHFE 2021, LNNS 277, pp. 18–25, 2021.
https://doi.org/10.1007/978-3-030-80415-2_3

The IPVC is a higher education institution that in addition to investing in innovation, research and knowledge, assumes a proactive role in the sustainable development of the Alto Minho region in the north of Portugal. Although often overlooked, higher education institutions play a key role towards sustainability as a whole and specifically in the reduction of plastic waste. Reducing the consumption of plastic water bottles would constitute a change in the consumption habits of the IPVC academy: students; teachers and employees, favouring the reduction of disposable waste, subsequently reducing the energy consumption and greenhouse gases emission from the recycling process.

This article presents a case study on the development of sustainable products through a project approach oriented towards the search for innovation. The study addresses a multidisciplinary methodological approach based on the intersection of complementary tools. Based on the concept of Participatory Design, the bottle as interactive artifact stems from a previously defined methodology [1], including user participation in the design process. The cooperation between sustainable design and technological innovation in the context of Information and Communications Technologies (ICT) and the Internet of Things (IoT) allows developing an interactive Smartbottle that 'communicates' with a water refill station. This is intended to foster more eco-friendly attitudes from users, students, teachers and employees, contributing to a paradigm shift in plastic consumption and waste. The new habits will favour waste reduction, particularly plastic water bottles, on campus and beyond.

The Smartbottle is equipped with a radio frequency identification (RFID) chip, integrated with the refill station management system, enabling an automatic filling process with no physical contact with the equipment, an estimated average amount of water consumption through a mobile application, an estimated amount of averted plastic waste, energy saving from overall waste reduction, reduction of greenhouse gas (GHG) emissions and information on users' environmental footprint.

The search for innovation through sustainable design and new technologies may be profitable and promote systemic changes in the behaviour of individuals. Also, the mitigation of environmental imbalances on campus will have off-campus impact. Design thus offers answers to protect the environment and improve the quality of life.

2 Sustainable Design and Academic Environment

Etymologically, the term sustainable derives from the Latin *sustinere* (hold up, hold upright; furnish with means of support; bear, undergo, endure). Sustainability is the ability of consumers or companies to remain in a given environment without violent damage to that environment. It requires strategies so that resources may be available in the future.

Human activities do not require disrupting the natural recovery cycles of the planet. Also, they don't require weakening the natural heritage of future generations [2]. Sustainability should reach all levels and areas of knowledge, for global unabridged application in contemporary society [3]. Human well-being is a social construct that takes shape over time, considering different factors. The notion has evolved since the industrial revolution, with successive changes following the evolution of society. Although it constitutes a dynamic and articulate set of perspectives, expectations and evaluation criteria, there is a persistent characteristic: to combine the perception of well-being with an increasing availability of products and services [4]. Therefore, identifying the unsustainable nature of many of the current practices will allow building a more conscious society, economically viable, socially just and ecologically correct, based on deep and complex sustainable approaches [5].

In fact, the principles of several universes, including the academic world, are delayed regarding what happens in the "real" world. This delay subsequently hinders the development of a lifestyle that is consistent with current issues, considering education an interactive process in which the environment changes the student, and the student changes the environment. As such, it is imperative to foster new relationships outside the comfort zone, learning new ways to participate and guide projects, improving citizens' ability to engage in meaningful dialogues about the environment, promoting new rapports between makers and users.

3 The Smartbottle Ecosystem

The Smartbottle Ecosystem was designed to achieve the main goal of the Refill_H2O, an EEA Grants Portugal environmental project [6], that aims to eliminate the use of plastic water bottles on the IPVC Campus, through the design and development of an interactive Smartbottle that 'communicates' with a Smart Water Refill Station to foster more eco-friendly attitudes among local users such as students, teachers and employees, thus contributing to the reduction of plastic consumption in bars, canteens and halls of residence in the IPVC campus. Figure 1 depicts the overall Smartbottle ecosystem, presenting two examples of use of the Smart Water Refill Station.

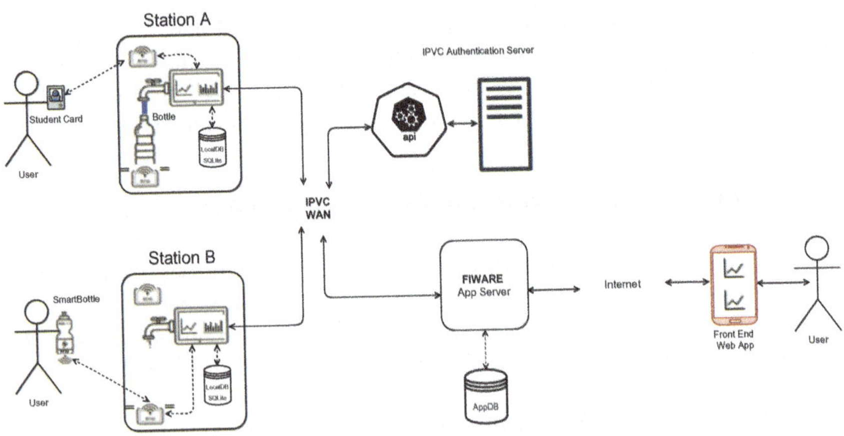

Fig. 1. Smartbottle ecosystem with two smart water refill stations, and core blocks of the ICT infrastructure.

The proposed ecosystem includes five main components: 1) the Smartbottle (interactive artifact); 2) the deployed IoT Edge Devices (Smart Water Refill Station) that communicates with the Smartbottle using RFID technology and the Student ID Card for user authentication; 3) the IPVC Wide Area Network, i.e. the ICT infrastructure that will perform backhaul communications; 4) the IPVC Authentication Server (that can be accessed in a "as-a-service" approach); 5) the FIWARE Application Server handles all communication between the IoT edge devices, data storage, and the client app through a context broker [7], whose architecture is described in detail in [8].

The Smartbottle is equipped with a radio frequency identification (RFID) chip, that integrates with the Smart Water Refill Station, enabling the following features:

- automatic filling process (no physical contact with the equipment);
- estimated average amount of water consumption through a mobile application (number of refills per time period);
- estimated amount of averted plastic waste (considering different metrics: temporal, cumulative, individual or referring to colleges, classes, etc.);
- energy saving from overall waste reduction and reduction of greenhouse gas (GHG) emissions;
- information on users' environmental footprint.

To use the refill station, the user must provide valid authentication by placing the Smartbottle [1] in the refill station or by placing an ID Card with native RFID technology and placing a conventional water bottle in the refill station.

The client application is based on responsive web technologies with visual analytics tools and dashboard-based technologies such as Grafana, towards a powerful interface to display useful information in a clear, user friendly way. The user interface includes three main functional areas: i) a dashboard that will display relevant metrics (number of refills per time period, estimated average amount of water consumption, estimated amount of averted plastic waste, energy saving from overall waste reduction and reduction of greenhouse gas (GHG) emissions); ii) specific key performance indicators (KPI's) and information on users' environmental footprint; An Authentication Area enables user authentication, allowing the application to change accordingly to the user; and iii) a user and system administration area to support backoffice operations regarding user management and system administration tasks.

This will allow the use of the refill station without a Smartbottle. When using a Smartbottle, the refill station dispenses water until the maximum capacity of the bottle or until the ID Card disconnects from the RFID reader. After disconnection, the station will trigger an event that will store data on a local self-contained transactional light-weight database engine, serverless and featuring zero-configuration, with no setup or administration requirements.

The Smart Water Refill Station features an application for user interface, for real-time display of different metrics and indicators concerning the contribution towards waste reduction, reduction of greenhouse gas (GHG) emissions and other relevant information. Gamification is used to promote user motivation and engagement [9], applying game features to a non-game context. This will allow open competition, selecting who contributes more towards the reduction of the GHG, or who shows healthier behaviours concerning water drinking, and the subsequent advantage is to promote a cleaner and more sustainable campus.

4 Prototype Candidates Design

From a methodological point of view, the Refill_H2O project involved an exhaustive survey at the scale of the IPVC (schools, bars, canteens and halls of residence), to identify the consumption habits of the resident population (students, teachers and staff) concerning plastic water bottles. This early survey is a determining factor in the entire follow-up of the project as it assesses and provides answers for the research questions that arise during the design process, informing and enriching the research conclusion.

In the survey, the resident population was invited to identify a set of physical, aesthetic and functional requirements to allow the identification of design specifications for a new environment-friendly water bottle. The appropriate materials, automatic opening and closing, easy to fill, adequate volume, durability and aesthetic appearance. Subdivided in three stages, the Consumer, the Bottle and the Service, the survey collected data to be used as input for the Smartbottle design and the quality of the future service.

In the first stage, the questions focused directly on the daily water intake of the IPVC population, the preferred locations for regular water collection and the number of bottles purchased weekly at the institution. Subsequently, the survey inquired on the opinion about the bottle, to define essential characteristics for the development of the future product. The questions assessed the bottle volume, factors to take into account in the development of the sustainable bottle, the material and relevant characteristics of the product. Service-oriented questions focused on understanding if the technological factor associated to the bottle and the refill station was appealing to the user, if it should be interconnected with an application and what data to present the user, the price the user would be willing to pay, the payment methods, the type of water, if the product was regarded as useful to reduce plastic in the planet, and if the user would actually be willing to use it.

Through the participation of 536 consumers, it was possible to identify the gender, age group, education level and occupation, predominantly (80%) students. Although a similar percentage of respondents drink water frequently, more than 90% agree it is useful to monitor the daily water intake. Concerning reusable bottles only 412 users declare to have one, corresponding to 10% of the total users. This project targets 5000 consumers. It was also identified that 96.1% of the respondents prefer a reusable bottle instead of a disposable plastic bottle. Concerning size, the preferred capacity was between 0.50 cl and 0.75 cl.

Aspects such as Functionality, Materials and Cost were considered the most significant for the sustainable bottle. Among a variety of environmentally friendly materials, the preferred were Stainless Steel, Recyclable Plastic, Bamboo and Glass. Other selected aspects were easy washing, absence of smell or taste in the water, easy to carry and thermal insulation.

With regard to service, that is, the relationship between the Smartbottle and the filling station, it was possible to understand (Table 1) that users are interested in a system with communication between the machine, the bottle and an application (app), displaying information such as volume of water intake, contribution to overall ecological footprint, and cost comparison.

More than 97% of the respondents consider the refill station & the reusable bottle are an adequate strategy to prevent plastic use in the IPVC community. However, according

Table 1. Important information to be provided by the application (Source: Authors).

1	Amount of water intake	436 (81,3%)
2	Contribution for ecological footprint	335 (62,5%)
3	Comparison of average weekly expense	261 (48,7%)
4	Number of daily refills	258 (48,1%)

to Table 2 below, approximately 85% of the respondents declared they would prefer the new system instead of purchasing disposable bottles provided the school provided a refill source at a low cost. About 90% of the respondents declared they would use the local filling station provided a good drinking water quality.

Table 2. Answers concerning the use of the refill station (Source: Authors).

Questions:	Answers:	Percentage:
If there was a low-cost refill source at school, would you prefer it to purchasing new disposable bottles?	Yes	84.70%
	No	15.30%
Would you use the refill station?	Yes, but only with the guarantee of high-quality water	46.80%
	Yes, however, I want high quality water at a low cost	47.60%
	No. Tap water or bottled water is good enough for me	5.6%

The participation of target users in the process of developing a product that aims to reduce plastic in the oceans allows the designer to understand and assimilate what target consumers think. This is useful to align the constituting features and create a product that will fulfil its function and purpose.

5 Results - Prototypes

The following stage was bottle drawing. To innovate and create an attractive bottle that would simultaneously raise awareness towards endangered marine species, a specific shape of a marine mammal was considered. Although all marine life is in decline due to ocean pollution, in the next 30 to 50 years the Orca may lose more than half of its population due to hazardous substances on seawater. Toxic chemicals weaken the Orca's immune system, affecting its reproductive capacity. Parents may also eventually transmit the pollutants during birth or during the breastfeeding period, causing the species to gradually reduce. Hence, the shape of the bottle was based on the physical and morphological traits of the Orca.

Fig. 2. Prototype A, B and C (Source: Authors).

The cylindrical, aerodynamic body of prototypes A, B and C, inspired by the shape of an Orca, as portrayed in Fig. 2, present curves that constitute an ergonomic handle, facilitating bottle use and transportation. Different raw materials were proposed to meet the survey results. The material for prototype A was recyclable plastic, highlighting the contrasting colours of the Orcas. The stopper of prototype B is made of recyclable plastic and the body of the bottle is in aluminium, and prototype C is entirely in aluminium.

The reliefs in prototypes B and C add friction to the bottle curves. The first relief was inspired by the white spots of the Orca, the second is based on the new brand image of the IPVC campus. The projection at the base is intended to add stability to the bottle when placed on a surface. That will be the place of the technological chip that will communicate with the filling station. All prototypes were designed to include an RFID tag in the bottom for easy interface with the Smart Water Refill Station.

6 Conclusion

The Smartbottle is intended to improve the environmental status of marine waters and coastal areas, by helping to reduce the use of plastics and plastic waste. The Smartbottle & Refill Station system constitutes an awareness raising initiative targeting students, teachers and workers of the IPVC campus. The system design is intended to raise awareness of the negative impact of plastic production on life on the planet.

A hybrid methodology allows designers to prioritize the development stages, focusing on the needs of target users. The inclusion of ICT and IoT technologies enables the creation of an interactive Smartbottle that 'communicates' with a Smart Water Refill Station. A survey of the academic community identified a set of physical, aesthetic and functional features to create the product specifications. Innovation through sustainable design and new technologies may be profitable and promote systemic changes in the behaviour of individuals and their communities. Hence, the mitigation of environmental imbalances on campus is expected to produce off-campus results.

The prototypes will be subject to a usability test performed near the target users, to identify and solve problems, improving product usability. This test will assess the different tasks involved in the Smartbottle use, such as grabbing, drinking, carrying and refilling. Through prototyping and usability testing it is possible to understand the users' performance and relationship with the Smartbottle and Refill Station.

Design projects are able to change the way of life of consumers. As key transformer of society, design is able to develop new social propositions and influence attitudes.

Allied with the axiom that human needs do not include environment degradation, the power to increase social awareness allows designers to improve the world.

Acknowledgments. The authors wish to thank the Program Environment, Climate Change and Low Carbon Economy, created following the establishment of a Memorandum of Understanding between Portugal and Iceland, Liechtenstein and Norway, under the EEA and Norway Grants 2014–2021, for the program areas of Environment and Ecosystems (PA11), and Climate Change Mitigation and Adaptation (PA13), for financing the project 10_SGS#1_REFILL_H20. The project was selected in the scope of the notice of funding opportunity Small Grant Scheme # 1, concerning projects for the prevention and awareness-raising for the reduction of marine litter. This Project contributes to the execution of Objective no. 1 of the Environment Program, which is to increase the application of the principles of Circular Economy in specific sectors, and the Output 1.3 of the Program, through the promotion of Circular Economy through the Reduction of plastic in the Oceans, originated from terrestrial activities, following the Annex I of the Program Protocol signed May 27, 2019.

References

1. Mendes, J., Curralo, A., Curado, A., Lopes, S.I.: The sustainable smartbottle: a proposed design methodology to minimize plastic pollution. In: Martins, N., Brandão, D. (eds.) Advances in Design and Digital Communication. Digicom 2020. Springer Series in Design and Innovation, vol. 12. Springer, Cham (2020). https://doi.org/10.1007/978-3-030-61671-7_27
2. Manzini, E., Vezzoli, C.: O desenvolvimento de produtos sustentáveis: os requisitos ambientais dos produtos industriais, EDUSP, São Paulo (2005)
3. Rodrigues, J., Bellio, L., Cavalcante, C.: Sustentabilidade no design: a transversalidade das teorias filosóficas e suas articulações na contemporaneidade complexa. In: ModaPalavra E-periódico, Ano 6, No. 9, pp. 95–115. UDESC, Santa Catarina (2012)
4. Manzini, E.: Design para a inovação social e sustentabilidade. Comunidades criativas, organizações colaborativas e novas redes projetuais. In: Cadernos do Grupo de Altos Estudos, vol. 1, Programa de Engenharia de Produção da Coppe. UFRJ, Rio de Janeiro (2008)
5. Papanek, V.: Design for the Real World Human ecology and social change. . Thames and Hudson, London (1972)
6. EEAGrants Refill_H20 Project: https://tinyurl.com/4coeemhx
7. FIWARE Foundation: https://github.com/FIWARE/catalogue
8. Martins P., Lopes S.I., Curado A.: Designing a fiware-based smart campus with IoT edge-enabled intelligence. In: Rocha Á., Adeli H., Dzemyda G., Moreira F., Ramalho Correia A.M. (eds.) Trends and Applications in Information Systems and Technologies. WorldCIST 2021. Advances in Intelligent Systems and Computing, vol 1367. Springer, Cham (2021). https://doi.org/10.1007/978-3-030-72660-7_53
9. Alsawaier, R.: The effect of gamification on motivation and engagement. Int. J. Inf. Learn. Technol. **35**(1), 56–79 (2018)

Fashion Design Education Towards Transition: Circularity and Biobased Materials

Gabriela Forman(✉)

CIAUD, Lisbon School of Architecture, Universidade de Lisboa, Rua Sá Nogueira, 1349-063 Lisbon, Portugal

Abstract. Decisions made at the creation process are crucial, requiring great awareness. Aesthetics, careful assessment of materials, production and recovery are key aspects when designing Fashion within a Circular Economy framework. This paper analyses Design practices and Material preferences through a mixed methods approach to infer on the level of success of implemented curricula (undergraduate), using diverse strategies aimed at circularity. Overall outcomes confirm the relevance of a student-centered classroom and adopted content transfer approaches (e.g., critical thinking, active/interactive learning, dual-ideation process, collaborative learning, experimental/exploratory), facilitating higher engagement from pupils and problem-solving; informed decisions, planning for longevity, fitting processes, awareness of material flow and values, resulted also in a massive increase on bio-based and natural materials application (production from varied waste streams, textile and non-textile residues) as well as a decrease on synthetic dyes and virgin fibers. Although not exhaustive, this analysis may benefit future related briefs or teaching/learning adjustments.

Keywords: Product design education · Circular economy · Bio-based materials · Creative process · Learning methodology · Experimental-base practice

1 Introduction

Broadly, Design refers to how something is planned and made; it may also refer to the outcome itself, the composition of artistic elements arranged in a certain form, revealing different levels of complexity in aesthetics, functionality, construction, material resilience [1]. The object is then a palpable expression of the entire thought process of the creative, his main decisions and values.

Many studies comment on the issues associated with poorly developed products or planned obsolesce and fast-paced trends, particularly at the cost of the environment and social equality, prompting the increasingly growing efforts towards a circular approach to design goods. Fashion Design education, guide students to integrate informed decisions in creation, materialized in the form of clothes/fashion accessories. Artistic elements are central to the subject, however, current economy and environmental concerns added layers to these, pressing paradigms within the fashion system. Creation needs to skilfully

D. Raposo et al. (Eds.): AHFE 2021, LNNS 277, pp. 26–34, 2021.
https://doi.org/10.1007/978-3-030-80415-2_4

balance aesthetics, identity, functionality, craft and sustainability. Finance should also be added, as commercial success is a decisive factor.

Intended to facilitate the transition from challenging linear practices of designing goods to a circular system envisioning objects holistically, a new program was implemented at the undergraduate level in *Fashion Design Course,* pupils transitioning from students to young professionals; besides intending to join the workforce of one the most problematic industries of the world regarding sustainability, this is a generation with particular characteristics (e.g., instant gratification tendency, self-directed, observed as independent, visual, multitasked, with specific communicational codes and ambitions [2–4]. Design educational programs must evolve to account for exercises tailored to improve skills such as critical thinking, self-awareness, pluralism, team-work and collaboration, empathy and other abilities needed to problem-solving, creativity and innovation. To be far reaching and attractive, it must also be implemented in a manner that better suits such cohort of students [5].

This paper presents an analysis on Design practices and Material preferences towards a circularity mindset to design products. It studies the students dynamics and their fashion design projects, discusses their involvement, views and proficiency through the experience. Decisions at the creative stage were analysed to infer on the level of success of implemented strategies in the curricula, subsequent outcomes, concepts and content integration, material application or chosen processes.

2 Methodology

2.1 Sampling and Methods

Sample group of 30 undergrads (ranging 20–22 years old), cohort *Generation Z*, studying Fashion Design Project (3rd year, first semester, classroom A, *Fashion Design Course 2020–2021),* thus transitioning from students to young professionals. The study took place in the *School of Architecture, Universidade de Lisboa*, Portugal.

For this study, a mixed methodology approach was used. The comprehensive scientific literature (e.g., scientific articles, books) was crucial to analyze in depth multidisciplinary topics and equally to reinforce transferred knowledge and support strategies and access to tools, then applied during the assignments. A preliminary study to the class (covertly observational, participant approaches and informal semi-structured interviews) revealed they showed varied gaps in knowledge, mainly associated to sustainability in fashion and related key concepts - circularity specific design strategies and material aspects (properties, production, related technologies, recovery). Furthermore, these interviews informed on primary interests, concerns, preferences.

The Circular Economy (CE) tenets were presented, introducing the main aspects of loop systems and their flows (slow and fast), the significance of raw material, technical and biological nutrients of each loop and the importance of designing out waste; multiple case-studies were examined, generating ideas exchange and concepts learning through debate, helpful to observe and clarify misconceptions.

The discussion (and consciousness) on the role of the contemporary designer, acting within society as an agent of change, was of high level relevance.

Varied Circularity and Design Strategies (e.g., *TED's Ten*) and tools (e.g., *Critical Thinking, Design Thinking, Playful Learning, Collaborative Learning, Experimental/Exploratory* approaches) [6–9] were introduced to initiate practice-led fashion projects. Progress was evaluated by looking closely into decision-making processes and analyzing the varied methodologies applied and outcomes.

Observation (witnessing to behaviour and interactions, first-hand) and constant enquiries were crucial during the whole study, helping to perceive the extent of concept assimilation as well as guidance, needed be. Descriptive analysis methods were also used to identify incidence on categories of material and/or practices and processes; multiple projects (60 in total, fashion products for slow and fast cycles of utilisation) were examined in order to understand if patterns would emerge, which challenges arose and the adopted solutions. This was of help to recognise engagement, and form quantifiable complementing data on the subject, equally important to grasp the pertinence of the program.

3 Results and Discussion

3.1 Strategies Supporting Improved Curricula

The dual-ideation process (intuitive and reflective) [9] was mostly positively received with a back-and-forth of thoughts and views on, and for, specified targets, where the attachment/detachment of ideas played an important role towards innovation and to attain set objectives (shared, common-goal).

Visual and concise content and image-based knowledge transfer were better embraced by students as methods for learning (e.g., concepts through infographics, mind mapping, case-studies through photography, videos) as well as experimentation, hands-on approaches, target-oriented applications and sense of mission.

When guided towards a playful, yet solid, experimental-practice methodology to problem-solving, results indicate that students appreciate not only the discovery process and serendipity element that comes from exploring, but also the sense of unleashed creativity or originality. A trial-error method was noticed to be equally essential to growth and assimilation of content. Exploratory exercises were key for some pupils, to whom projects were organic, spontaneous developments (in their perspective, desirable for richer understanding of real possibilities of application); through experimentation, uncovering the potential of natural and innovative materials, for instance, some students remarked that materiality preceded the design creation directing it (usually the opposite occurs), which also provided for an overall stimulating effect. This may be a reason for the feeling of *creative freedom* noted by some undergraduates.

Assignments through collaborative learning approaches had twofold responses: some students enjoyed the process and stated that different views improved ideas and projects; in stark contrast, part of the students identified difficulties, dealing with peers not willing to work or to whom ideas would differ and clash, jeopardizing the whole creative process and adding stress.

3.2 Circularity and Outcomes

Surprisingly, and for the first time in the course, 63% of the sample group opted for innovative biobased materials, such as bioplastics, mostly derived from varied waste streams, textile and non-textile residues (e.g., algae, bacteria, food, starch, paper, wood, etc.); these were explored by not only studying resources but also by developing materials, under guidance of the professor. The study also shows 20% of the students applied synthetics and 100% of them resourced to natural fibres, organic cotton was applied to all projects. Higher percentages of lyocell (57%), alpaca wool (53%) and hemp (37%) were observed.

Some of the chosen processes and strategies towards circularity include multifunctionality, genderless clothing, zero-waste processes (e.g., knitwear, 3D Printing, biofabricating), natural dyeing or absence of it, reprocessing of fibers, biodegradability for super-fast cycles of utilization, slow fashion strategies to render longevity to fashion items, co-creation, material production from waste, emergent technologies (e.g., wearables, biotechnologies), amongst others.

3.3 Content Assimilation

For educators, the comprehensive scientific literature was of relevance to strengthen transferred knowledge and to support strategies and the access to tools applied during the assignments. Another important aspect was grasping on how these would be implemented and worked through the projects, i.e., which practices to apply to better meet the needs of this group of late adolescents (19–21 age), a generation that experiences the world in a very different way, compared to previous generations [10, 11].

Generation Z, shaped by the societal changes occurred in recent years (e.g., digital technologies, political dual views), often displays higher levels of stress and anxiety [12, 13], which may compromise effective learning [14], besides the underdevelopment of the prefrontal cortex, responsible for the regulation of emotions as well as attention, flexibility, high-level problem-solving skills, amongst others such as delay of gratification [15]. A deficiency in interpersonal socialization and cognitive skills linked to self-regulation, impacts on how to navigate emotions, attention to the task at hand, persistence, confidence towards effort for positive outcomes, plasticity [15]. These are crucial factors in terms of attaining goals and perseverance in face of adversity. Therefore, a sensible educator, and suitable practices, accounting for these characteristics is likely to cultivate feelings of empathy, support, responsiveness, guidance, social significance and overall success, particularly in terms of problem-solving and informed decision-making [5]. Consequently, image, interaction with peers and collaborative learning, ideation, exploratory experimental work and an holistic and playful approach to things were practices promoted for content assimilation and to try and push forward a critical thinking mindset and, hopefully, creativity/innovation.

Despite the obvious limitations of the study (e.g., COVID-19 pandemic context, sensitivity of interveners, creativity degree of students) through observational methods and the analysis of both qualitative and quantifiable results collated, implemented strategies had different levels of accomplishments.

Content through the usage of images and infographics tend to get more attention than, for instance, handed articles to read. Nevertheless, students still presented open-mindedness to use varied sources of information, or multitasking and *DIY* undertakings, as described by the literature review as characteristics of this cohort [2, 4].

Regarding focus and effort to organize assignments and related tasks, overall results indicate issues, particularly with managing deadlines, although in most cases due to their enthusiasm with learning new subjects, taking time to emerge on them until full completion. This might also be explained by several authors, for whom *Generation Z* is noticeably more self-direct in terms of learning [2]. Another reason could be related to their habits of learning, also documented in research literature as unsuitable; as an easily distracted generation they tend to find themselves taking more time to learn outside the classroom as the full content tend to be disregarded with distractions, such as constant texting, internet, technological devices in the classroom [4].

Concerning assignments, exercises occurred to foster collaborative learning (interaction aiming at the combination of skills and perspective adjustment); this offered mixed results, requiring close attention from tutors. Negative outcomes described by some students were indeed associated with *competence status*, *free riding* and *lack of collaborative skills* as outlined by research as possible outcomes of this approach [16]. An underlying issue associated with lacking interpersonal social skills mentioned might also be the inability to connect or flexibility, not only with team members but, also, with end-users, stakeholders, etc., This is a key aspect to pay close consideration in the future and in need of further analysis; how students perceive design and pluralism or (observed) tendency to design from their own individual perspective (own taste or standards) is a concern, as it may compromise creation in general, even the eventual user-centered, co-creation or participatory design strategies.

3.4 Circularity-Driven Program

The CE tenets were introduced followed by detailed info on what constitutes importance on the different loops of this business framework - the technical and biological nutrients, the distinctive flows that products/materials might travel and the importance of designing out waste at the creative stage of product development (predicting outcomes in the production/utilization/recovery journeys) [17, 18]. In terms of designing in an informed plausible manner, future designers must grasp the full significance and consequence of material application, and values attached to products; this is particularly relevant for fashion items as they are considered *fast-moving consumer goods*, dropping in value very quickly [18]. Multiple case-studies were presented, examined through discussion; the consciousness of diverse existing perspectives and conversations on the role of the contemporary designer were imperative.

Classic critical thinking strategies (e.g. *Bloom's Taxonomy*), the *5 W's and the 1 H* revealed to be largely favorable; equally applied to the assignments (where reflection, deep analysis and subsequent problem solving occurred), proving to be effective. Awareness and Circularity Design Strategies (and tools) application and progress were evaluated by looking closely into the executive process of the students, albeit the complexity of decision-making subject [19].

Informal interviews (semi-structured) and careful observation to sample students, suggested that their main drivers for real change in the fashion system and design sector are linked to biodiversity/animal protection, climate change/pollution, followed by social and gender issues. Economics, an important aspect of this industry (and life), was not always clearly understood; students revealed little awareness of its implications at the design level or in terms of what it represents for sustainability. Misconceptions are linked to the belief that sustainability in fashion is solved only by avoiding, repressing the act of shopping altogether. Whilst statistics show fast fashion is not slowing down, consumerism must be considered. Moreover, COVID-19 Pandemic and restrictions makes clear that when economy stops, social equity plummet, as well as the sobriety of the planet. Sustainability requires balance, flexibility, in all fronts, from politics to finance to culture; a holistic view of the world is key.

Another challenging aspect was the perceived lack of knowledge on resources (possibilities, properties, technologies); most students stated frustration regarding materials subject as content was, in previous years, only delivered within a theoretical basis, with no context of real application or experimental approaches. Moreover, materials are varied and of extreme complexity, which makes their grasp harder. This led the program to an exhaustive research on raw materials, related technologies and processes (main characteristics and advantages/disadvantages) by examining critically deeply various fashion items; objects were dematerialized into their constituent raw materials (deconstructed and traced back to their origins and processes) and analyzed in depth. Following the interpretation and clarification of misconceptions, debates on the role of the contemporary designer - essentials and duties, the transfer of knowledge on the CE framework and design guidelines proceeded, as well as contemplating what time, flows and cycles represent for product development. Important to note that projects took two forms for most students - theoretical and practical.

Content was better embraced and understood through debate and case-studies delivered by image/video support, complemented with an experimental mindset, which is not surprising given the highly visual and technology-driven nature of the sample group. Imparting, simultaneously, CE concepts, problem/solution dynamics, overall rationale and impacts for the planet ecosystems, showed to be equally important, giving purpose to intentions and actions. Project solutions were considered according to target - slow or fast cycles: keeping the fashion products functionable/valuable for longer or, as in the case of super-fast cycles, the creation of products with relatively promptness to biodegrade/compost; applying fitting materials or *waste to value* and re-fibers; technologies, resources production and efficient recovery aspects assessment. Proving the depth of understanding, the increase and enthusiastic application and development of emergent materials from renewable sources and varied waste streams (e.g., bioplastics/bioleather, bananatex, pinatex, lyocell); this seems to confirm the *Generation Z* profile, as stated by many authors [10, 12], as resourceful, realistic, aware of real issues and seeking tangible pragmatic solutions to problems.

Most of the students searched alternatives to hide, hence the experimentation with bioplastics. This might be connected to the extreme awareness and philosophical importance of animal welfare for this generation as noticed by close observation, the interviews to students and extant literature reports [12]. However, some projects maintained the application of hide on the basis that, indeed, the aesthetics and functionality of real leather could not be surpassed by the alternative ones for now. Students remarks include: the peculiar way it gracefully ages, in structure and color, wear-and-tear resistance, the resilience of it makes it appropriate for slow and multiple cycles of utilization, clothing that tells stories, serving a long life of purpose and meaning. Results also reveal a decrease on synthetic dyes application or a total avoidance of dyeing; some projects opted for less harmful solutions to impart color to materials, or resourced to naturally colored fibers occurring in nature, as suggested through contemplated case-studies. For instance, the increase of Alpaca wool application, a versatile fiber in terms of color tones possibilities, was closely related to this aspect.

Students applying synthetics to their projects, such as recycled polyester, stated awareness on their possible production from PET plastics in general (e.g. bottles) and fiber recovery aspects making it a suitable and an applicable material for technical loops within the CE views.

4 Conclusion

The purpose of this mixed methods research study was to evaluate the effectiveness of the application of varied design strategies as a modality to increase awareness and knowledge about circularity. Additionally, curricula must always evolve and adapt to the specifics of each generation, societal demands and how students respond. Rapidly changing environment of social dynamics, must involve design that is able to provide sustainable solutions, that act towards users demands and means for their needed self-expression. Decisions at the creation process require awareness, enabling for a product to fit to purpose and resilient, preferably maintained indefinitely in a closed-loop of utilization (or safely discarded at the end of its life). For the success of Design, and a sustainable fair planet, the aesthetics, value, careful assessment of materials, production and recovery are key aspects to consider at the early creative stage.

Despite some of the minor constraints formerly outlined, analyzed gathered data, suggests that designing acknowledging the Circularity principles was largely successful; overall outcomes confirm the relevance of circular strategies/tools implemented and indicate a desire to counter the global production of virgin fibres. Additionally, it reveals an increased interest in learning in depth the emerging material structures and their particularities; an emphasis on these materials was noted. The latter occurs, in part, due to their emerging nature, unique aesthetics and properties, availability and *DIY* or *DIT* factor. The convenience to be transformed from waste to value, in a relatively approachable manner, is equally of importance. Moreover, the development of new material and the examination of unfamiliar techniques exposes ensuing challenges but also opportunities, particularly within the fashion design field and context.

Speculative or actual projects depict a real engagement and sense of mission to turn the issues of the industry around; pupils need context (real world impact, holist mindset and application) and complex content delivered in a playful but target-oriented manner. Recognizing the dynamics between theoretical and experimental practices may also be informative, helping to assess whether materials education benefits from a shift from the traditional technical and theoretical knowledge approach to an experimental-based one (with the playful component or the addition of other scientific subjects, craft and investigational methods). Although not exhaustive, this analysis may benefit future methodologies for materials/processes selection, pedagogic techniques or briefings/program adjustment. Regarding the projects, additional data is needed to analyse further key aspects of effective applicability (e.g., usability aspects, commercial success, perception on emergent materials, acceptance and appeal levels).

Acknowledgments. The author thanks the support from Fundação para a Ciência e Tecnologia and REDes, CIAUD, Lisbon School of Architecture – ULisboa.

References

1. Raizman, D.: History of Modern Design. Laurence King Publishing, London (2010)
2. Zimmer C.: Getting to know Gen Z: exploring middle and high schoolers expectations for higher education. Barnes and Noble College (2015)
3. Hughes, J. Communicating with generation Z: Everything you need to know. Keystone Academic (2018)
4. Bellur, S., Nowak, K.L., Hull, K.S.: Make it our time: in class multitaskers have lower academic performance. Comput. Hum. Behav. **53**, 63–70 (2015)
5. Darling-Hammond, L., Flook, L., Cook-Harvey, C., Barron, B., Osher, D.: Implications for educational practice of the science of learning and development. Appl. Dev. Sci. **24**(2), 97–140 (2020)
6. Earley, R.: The TEN: a tool for narrative prototypes. In: SHARE Handbook for Artistic Research Education, pp. 94–96 (2010)
7. Earley, R., Goldsworthy, K.: Playing for Time: Seven Practice-Led Workshop Tools for Making Design Decisions to Extend the Life of Fashion Textile Materials and Products. IOS Press Research in Design Series. PLATE Product Lifetimes and the Environment, pp.127–132 (2017). http://ebooks.iospress.nl/volumearticle/47856
8. Adamson, M.A., Chen, H., Kackley, R., Micheal, A.: LPC for the love of the game: game-versus lecture-based learning with generation Z patients. J. Psychosoc. Nurs. Mental Health Serv. **56**(2), 29–36 (2018)
9. Gonçalves, M., Cash, P.: The life cycle of creative ideas: towards a dual-process theory of ideation. J. Des. Stud. **72**, 100988 (2021)
10. Futurecast, F.J.: Getting to know genZ: how the pivotal generation is different from millennials (2017)
11. Twenge, J.M.: Why Today's Super-Connected Kids Are Growing up less Rebellious, More Tolerant, Less Happy—And Completely Unprepared For Adulthood—And What that Means for the Rest of us. Atria Books, New York (2017)
12. Fong, J., Lope, N., Lucchi, M., McDermott, P. Trench, B.: An Insiders Guide to Generation Z and Higher Education. University Professional and Continuing Education Association (2019)
13. Ulhs, Y.T., Ellison, N.B., Subrahmanyam, K.: Benefits and costs of social media in adolescence. J. Pediatr. **140**(2), 67–70 (2017)
14. Vogel, S., Schwabe, L. Learning and memory under stress: implications for the classroom. NPJ Sci. Learn **1**, 16011 (2016)
15. Siddiqui, S.V., Chatterjee, U., Kumar, D., Siddiqui, A., Goyal, N.: Neuropsychology of prefrontal cortex. Ind. J. Psychiatry **50**, 202–208 (2008)
16. Le, H., Janssen, J., Wubbels, T.: Collaborative learning practices: teacher and student perceived obstacles to effective student collaboration. Camb. J. Educ. **48**(1), 103–122 (2018)

17. Ellen MacArthur Foundation, Towards the circular economy: an economic and business rationale for an accelerated transition, vol.1 (2012)
18. Haffmans, S., van Gelder, M., van Hinte, E., Zijlstra, Y.: Products that Flow Circular Business Models and Design Strategies for Fast-Moving Consumer Goods. BIS Publishers, Amsterdam (2018)
19. Abadie, M., Waroquier, L.: Evaluating the benefits of conscious and unconscious thought in complex decision making. Behav. Brain Sci. **6**(1), 72–78 (2019)

Design and Science for the Valorisation of Residues and By-products of the Wine Industry

Elena Cioffi[1(✉)], Sonia Capece[1], Severina Pacifico[2], and Mario Buono[1]

[1] Dipartimento di Ingegneria, Università degli Studi della Campania "Luigi Vanvitelli", Via Roma, 29, 81131 Aversa, CE, Italy
elena.cioffi@unicampania.it

[2] Dipartimento di Scienze e Tecnologie Ambientali, Biologiche e Farmaceutiche (DISTABiF), Università degli Studi della Campania "Luigi Vanvitelli", Via Vivaldi, 43, 81100 Caserta, Italy

Abstract. In view of the urgent need to implement the transition from the "take-make-use-lose" industrial system to a circular and regenerative one, this study focuses on improving the sustainability of the wine industry, in particular the importance assumed by the management of residues and by-products of the wine production system from a circular economy and environmental protection perspective, from the planting of vines, to the production of grapes, up to the process of transformation and recovery of waste. There are management methods and limitations on alternative uses regarding by-products and residues deriving from winemaking, that are conditioned by precise regulations.

The study is intended as a thinking tool to investigate the possible results that these synergies can facilitate to reach definitions of solutions for the recovery, reuse, and valorisation of by-products and residues, thus transforming potential waste into a resource, reducing the environmental impact.

Keywords: Design · Science · Sustainability · Wine industry · By-products · Valorisation

1 Towards Globally Sustainable Models and Processes

This study investigates, through the themes of sustainability, the production processes of the wine industrial chain from which, on a large scale, new opportunities could arise. The systematic literature review relating to sustainability and innovation in the wine industry outline new strategies and directions for the sustainable management of processes and waste in the perspective of industrial symbiosis and oriented towards possible technology transfer interventions [1].

Traditional winemaking processes are carried out through practices with centuries-old traditions, this determines difficulties in the development of procedures for the valorisation and management of waste and residues and in the application of new technological solutions for the reduction of waste generated during the wine making process, at the

D. Raposo et al. (Eds.): AHFE 2021, LNNS 277, pp. 35–43, 2021.
https://doi.org/10.1007/978-3-030-80415-2_5

same time it is difficult to decrease the production of waste in wine production processes [2].

Since the end of the 90s, a more rigorous interpretation of sustainability, that urges to radical changes in production and consumption models, partially shifts the attention to design for the eco-efficient Product-Service System (PSS) [3].

The lack of awareness of how much the residues and by-products of the wine production industry can represent an inestimable source of products with high added value is the reason why several wineries do not always comply with the legislation, favoring an increase not only in the production of waste but also in the environmental impact resulting from their disposal (Dimou et al. 2015) and this is in complete contradiction with the goal of waste reduction provided for by ISO 14000 [4].

Product quality, sustainability and environmental protection are gaining increasing attention in the definition of programs, strategies and regulations. In this context, California holds a leading position among the most sustainable agricultural producing countries: Warner (2007) describes the efforts done by the Californian wine grape industry for reaching and educating growers about quality issues and sustainability. The New Zealand wine industry, instead, aims to be the first in the world to be 100% sustainable with the Sustainable Winegrowers New Zealand (SWNZ) program introduced in 1995. Both the Americas and Europe, Asia and Africa face similar environmental challenges but they strongly differ in terms of fertiliser usage, that is significantly lower in Europe. The 2006–08 European project "Bioactive-net" gave a detailed picture of the situation in Italy, France, Spain, and Greece about the yearly amount of grape processing residues and their current destinations based on current regulations [5].

2 Overview of By-products and Their Properties

During the winemaking process, by-products such as lees, pomace or marc and stalks are formed in huge amounts, and they could be applied in alternative production cycles (i.e. distilleries industry) or as an inexpensive source of high added-value ingredients (Ahmedna 2013). In this context, marc, which is a complex mixture of skins, seeds and any other solid material remaining after grape pressing, contains polysaccharides (30%), acidic pectic substances (20%), proanthocyanidins (15%), beyond lignin, proteins and phenols (Amendola et al. 2012; Devesa-Rey et al. 2011; González-Centeno et al. 2010; Minjares-Fuentes et al. 2014; Pine-lo et al. 2006). Bioactive compounds such as anthocyanins, and other flavonoids, as well as condensed tannins were also found in grape skins (Pinelo et al. 2006; Mendes et al. 2013a), stalks (Makris et al. 2007; Ping et al. 2011), and grape seeds. All these components are also an end-less reservoir of lipid and protein nutrients, fibers and minerals (Prozil et al. 2012a). Lignocellulose constitutes massively vine shoots, which, commonly generated during vine pruning, correspond to 93% of the waste obtained in viticulture (Sánchez et al. 2002), and wine lees. The latter, mainly formed during the fermentation and aging processes, and defined by Council Regulation (EEC) no. 337/79 as the residue formed in the lower part of the wine containers (Perez-Serradilla and Luque de Castro 2011), also consist in cellulose and hemicellulose, beyond phenols, lignin, proteins, organic salts (e.g. tartrate), and organic acids, such as lactic or acetic acid [4, 6, 7].

The leaves are the least studied and valued residue of the vine cultivation and the wine industry. It represents a production waste, massive especially in the early stages of winemaking and, in particular, in the destemming. Grape leaves are rich in organic acids, vitamins, stilbenes, anthocyanins and tannins with vascular-stimulating properties, with vaso-active and vaso-protective properties (Piccolella et al. 2019).

Phenols and polyphenols remarkably contribute to wine colour, flavour, and aroma (Pérez-Bibbins et al. 2015), and their extraction from the above-mentioned wastes and by-products is among the most studied aspects of wine production (Georgiev et al. 2014; Hixson et al. 2015; Hixson et al. 2016; Pinelo et al. 2006; Teixeira et al. 2014; Yu and Ahmedna 2013), the recent advent of green technologies favours their recovery in high yield, also overcoming environmental and health problems associated with the use of organic pollutant solvents (Fontana et al. 2013).

Green extraction technologies are supercritical fluid extraction (SFE), ultrasound assisted maceration (UAM), microwave assisted extraction (MAE), pressurized liquid extraction (PLE), and enzyme-assisted extractions are of actual interest (Alexandre et al. 2018) and are applied for recovering phenolic compounds from grape skin and seeds. These techniques are not time consuming, enjoy high extraction selectivity, are safe, and not toxic [8].

Attention to these compounds is not only aimed at highlighting their bioactivity but also and above all at defining new and more efficient extraction strategies. Many of these compounds, biosynthesized only by plants, have proven positive effects on human and animal health and show great application potential as ingredients in the food, nutraceutical, pharmaceutical and cosmetic industries.

However, in a nutraceutical scenario, the poor solubility of polyphenols, can often affect the achievement of their action. This requires the development of strategies, such as encapsulation or nano-formulation that foster the bioavailability and bioaccessibility.

The main economic products and processes suitable for winemaking by-products can be summarized as follows (Rebecchi et al. 2013): extraction of antioxidants and dyes, applications in the nutraceutical and cosmetic sector, extraction of antimicrobial compounds (against deterioration and populations pathogenic in food products, helping to extend the shelf life of products), food source for the livestock sector and use for traditional composting, extraction of bioactive compounds, energy recovery through thermochemical and biological treatments, production of fuels, special applications such as biosurfactants, biotechnological production of chemicals, texturing agents and biopolymers [4, 9, 10].

The marc antioxidant and antimicrobial properties are the basis of extensive research also in the biopolymers field. In this context, the pomace depleted of the phenolic fraction was investigated for the production of volatile fatty acids, which are biotechnological precursors of polyhydroxyalkanoates (PHA) (Martinez et al. 2016). Thus, marc is a highly renewable source for obtaining thermoplastic and biodegradable materials. Indeed, there are three processes currently investigated for obtaining bio-based polymers from the by-products of the wine industry: 1) direct extraction from biomass, 2) polymerization of constituent elements partially or totally derived from raw materials, 3) microbial synthesis (Nanni et al. 2021).

In recent decades bioplastics have gained a central role in fossil fuels replacement and/or for mitigating the plastic-induced pollution. However, in 2018 the production of bioplastics was only 2.1 Mt, which barely represents 0.6% of the total polymers produced. This limited production is mainly due to the low conversion yields and the technological barriers that exist for the chemical or biological transformations required. As the bio-based building blocks are mainly obtained from first generation raw materials such as wheat, corn, canola or sugar cane which, being food competitive, are expensive and ethically questionable, the possibility of using agricultural waste as different polymeric additives is interesting. In fact, although these products are usually mixed within plastics in small quantities, polymeric additives, such as stabilizers and plasticizers, are produced globally in large amounts and their ecological alternatives would be eco-friendly.

Wine by-products are potentially raw materials for producing bio-based building blocks or biopolymers, directly from microorganisms and for the manufacture of economical reinforcing fillers. Poly(lactic acid) (PLA), poly(butylene succinate) (PBS) and poly(hydroxyl butyrate) (PHB) could be favourably produced. Furthermore, as second generation (inedible) renewable raw materials, wine by-products, such as vine shoots, thanks to their lignocellulosic structure are tested as a carbon source for microbial production of polymer precursors such as bioethanol, lactic acid and succinic acid, as well as for direct PHA synthesis. Furthermore, tartaric acid generally extracted from wine lees, could be converted into succinic acid for the production of bio-polyesters [11].

3 Best Practices to Connect Communities, Models and Processes

It is necessary to pave the way for innovative areas of practice and intervention by defining perspectives that are advantageous in terms of sustainability and circularity of resources for the minimization of the impacts of the production system, due to the inefficiencies of an inadequate use of residues and by-products, and for the characterization, functionalization and study of the extraction processes of functional compounds and of the properties of the identified matrices. Production facilities must take actions in the context in which they operate, valorising local, social, cultural and material resources. The responsible use of local resources stimulates local development, prevents the relocation of production and the use of resources from outside, while maintaining the heritage of material culture on site. The systemic design, by taking action on processes with an orientation towards sustainability, in the perspective of an integrative relationship between community and territory, between natural and artificial, between human and ecosystem, shifts its focus towards a "human" dimension capable of sensitively and responsibly shaping a system of connections that involves places, communities, practices and processes.

The state of the art and the developments reported in the literature, regarding the use of waste from the wine industry, have allowed research to think about the definition of possible and further application scenarios.

Innuva, for example, is a platform that promotes the philosophy of reuse through the valorisation of wine production by-products and agricultural production waste to develop products and projects, enhancing territories, stimulating entrepreneurial activities in the agri-food sector and feeding a virtuous network of institutions, businesses, public administration, private sector and academia [12].

Among the valuable solutions, there is also Poliphenolia that, specialized in the study of polyphenols for tissue regeneration, transfers the properties of plant based polyphenolic molecules in the cosmetic field, within a cutting-edge scientific laboratory in the biomedical and cosmetic sector.

Fig. 1. Part of the industrial production process of Vegea plant-based leather: on the left is shown the coating and finishing of the mixture made of dried pomace to obtain fabrics; on the right a detail of the finished product.

Through the partnership with Innuva, Nobilbio company, which operates in oral implantology, is one of the first companies to have invested in research to study polyphenols extracted from pomace applied in the medical sector, and to create a product for the periodontal regeneration, enriched with polyphenols extracted from the Croatina pomace of the Alemat company [13].

Another emblematic case is represented by Caviro Group, which has adopted the cascade strategies for the valorisation of by-products of the wine industry, achieving self-sufficiency in energy consumption, obtaining renewable energy: from lees it produces biogas for electrical and thermal energy. While from the pomace thermal and electrical energy is produced through controlled combustion and through the best technologies for the treatment of emissions, as well as producing a wide range of products for the food and pharmaceutical industries, and for the agricultural sector. The contribution deriving from the extraction of polyphenols from grape seeds for oenological, food and nutraceutical use is also important; enocyanin, natural dye for food use and tartaric acid for oenological, food, pharmaceutical and construction industry use. Among the elements that characterize Caviro there is also the production of compost for organic crops. The analysis of environmental performance shows that Caviro recovers, to date, 99% of the waste produced [14].

The use of organic waste in production has played and continues to play an important role in enabling designers to overcome previous limits of feasibility [15]. The necessary transition towards a restorative and regenerative production model based on sustainable practices and lower environmental impacts is matched by the systemic production model. By borrowing behaviors already existing in nature, this approach considers the outputs of wine production as inputs for other production systems, redefining internal and external relations to the production process with an autopoietic thinking, allowing external systems to metabolize waste [16]. It is possible to realize an integration between production culture and design research, which takes into account environmental requirements by adopting the principles of eco-design and Product Life Cycle Design with the aim of reducing the input of materials and energy throughout the entire life cycle, bringing out connections and consistencies between production, reproductive and environmental processes towards efficient and sustainable scenarios. The Italian start-up Vegea (Fig. 1) also adopts these sustainable approaches for the production of innovative plant-based materials in the fashion, design, furniture, packaging, automotive and transport sectors. The company has developed and patented the system for the recycling of winemaking waste to obtain vegetable yarns, particularly similar to animal-derived leather in appearance and versatility. Furthermore, the patented physical and mechanical treatments allow specific and diversified finishes in order to give the leather different shades of weight, thickness, elasticity and color according to the different applications, conceived as a sustainable alternative to materials of animal origin and to all materials coming from non-renewable fossil sources [17].

The Valsovit project, then, is proposed as a propulsive and technological innovation tool for the valorisation of waste from wine industry and for the production of substances with high added value, using technologies with low environmental impact to promote sustainable approaches for the chemical and health industry. The research, carried out in scientific laboratories, involved the parallel development of studies for the velorisation of winemaking waste in the chemical and energy fields, in the nutraceutical, cosmetic, biostimulation and plant defense sectors.

In this context, the design of industrial processes represents a concrete realization of the circular bio-economy model since it aims to encourage the development of production technologies that can be integrated with already existing bio-refineries [18].

ValorVitis and ValorVitis 2.0 are the projects, involved in the reuse of residues and by-products of winemaking, ranging from the research and innovation phase to the realization of scale-up of the results and the involvement of companies, of the production context and the market, reaching the production scale, the civil society and the scientific community. This project promotes the recovery of winemaking residues, encouraging the production of flours based on grape skins and expanding the range of applications in the food, pharmaceutical and cosmetic sectors. The aim was the dissemination, among companies, of the innovative technologies developed by researchers to recover the by-products of winemaking through the production of new functional foods, useful for human health, with the possibility of extending the shelf life of the marc, overcoming the problem of the by-product accumulation seasonality [19, 20].

Another project, funded by the European Commission, through the European Social Fund, is CHEERS whose goal was to create prototypes of organic dye-sensitized solar cells, known as Gräetzel cells. The organic dye, extracted from the waste from the winemaking process, captures sunlight and injects electrons into the semiconductor, made up of porous titanium dioxide nanoparticles. The generated electron is able to travel through the external circuit, producing renewable and sustainable electricity. This solar cell is a molecular machine that works in the field of nanotechnologies, mimicking the process of chlorophyll photosynthesis, and represents an alternative to traditional systems (silicon cells) for economic advantage, thanks to the eco-friendly construction methods, which allow recycling with low environmental impact, and to the energy conversion efficiency in case of cloudy weather or artificial lighting [21].

4 Multidisciplinary Relations to Build Possible Application Scenarios

It is essential to have a detailed picture of the scenario on which to build new sustainable paths according to the Systemic Design approach. Descriptions of what and how much enters a system (input) and where it comes from, what and what happens inside it, and finally what and how much comes out with its destination or possible use (output) will be necessary. But it is also essential to identify the stakeholders involved, their nature, the knowledge and technologies they have at their disposal (Bistagnino, 2009).

The technological innovation available allows to obtain final products different from the traditional ones, but it is necessary to integrate the knowledge coming from the different scientific disciplines, passing through the environmental sciences, engineering, (bio) chemistry, bio (technologies), the logistics, economy and legislation of the wine sector. The collaboration of various professional figures allows to obtain new innovative / alternative integrated models of wine production [2]. To foster the dialogue between design and science, the recognition and appreciation of the role of scales (of size) becomes fundamental, from the macro to the microscale, of which science has a great understanding [22].

Scale-up is one of the main objectives of this study, design contributes to thoughtful concepts, provides indications and guidance while science and technology proceed in their evolution. Design not only makes products commercially usable, but adds value to them, influences politics and research without ever denying their poietic nature [22].

Bergdoll (2008) states that not only are designers interested in the latest scientific achievements, but scientists, engaged in the design process, have also found that design can help them master complexity and take advantage of new elements [22]. Ohmart (2008) argues, on the other hand, that the success of sustainable practices among winemakers depends mainly on two elements: the rigor of science and the actual results perceived by winemakers. Two issues with which can be understood, in part, the differences with which sustainable practices in viticulture are spread [23].

Indeed, although there is a large literature on environmental and biological practices in the wine industry, for the most part it focuses mainly on oenological and agronomic aspects and not strictly on management issues. The close relationship between academia and industry can provide benefits to the wine industry and improve sustainable processes and practices: research can help winemakers in adopting sustainable practices and can provide answers to some questions about process management [23]. Designers, between research and production, act as interpreters in interdisciplinary teams, configuring objects, scenarios and strategies [22].

Based on interdisciplinary approaches, this study encourages the rethinking of production and waste management models, introducing innovations and new applications of use through the principles and tools of the discipline of industrial design and chemical sciences. The design of products, services or processes can no longer consider exclusively its own specific field of action and be limited to a linear flow of information, know-how and production, but it must range in different fields of application with which to create relationships that allow an integrated and systemic development of processes, society, culture and territory [16].

Adequate procedures that enable targeted integration of these products through time-saving technologies for sectoral industries will provide successful results for phytochemical recovery and innovative products, which could contribute to the reduction of environmental pressure in wine areas from winemaking by-products [1].

References

1. Kalli, E., Lappa, I., Bouchagier, P., Tarantilis, P.A., Skotti, E.: Novel application and industrial exploitation of winery by-products. Bioresour. Bioprocess. **5**(1), 1–21 (2018). https://doi.org/10.1186/s40643-018-0232-6
2. Maicas, S., Mateo, J.J.: Sustainability of wine production. Sustainability **12**, 559 (2020)
3. Vezzoli, C., et al.: Design for sustainability an introduction. In: Designing Sustainable Energy for All, vol. 104 (2018)
4. Dávila, I., Robles, E., Egüés, I., Labidi, J., Gullón, P.: The biorefinery concept for the industrial valorization of grape processing by-products. In: Charis, M., Galanakis, E. (eds.) Handbook of Grape Processing By-products, p. 29. Academic Press, Cambridge (2017)
5. Spigno, G., Marinoni, L., Garrido, G.D.: State of the art in grape processing by-products. In: Charis, M., Galanakis, E. (ed.) Handbook of Grape Processing By-products, p. 9. Academic Press, Cambridge (2017)
6. Piccolella, S., Crescente, G., Volpe, M.G., Paolucci, M., Pacifico, S.: UHPLC-HR-MS/MS-guided recovery of bioactive flavonol compounds from Greco di Tufo vine leaves. Molecules, vol. 24 (2019)
7. Petti, L., et al.: Life cycle assessment in the wine sector. In: Notarnicola, B., et al. (eds.) Life Cycle Assessment in the Agrifood Sector, pp.125–126. Springer, Cham (2015). https://doi.org/10.1007/978-3-319-11940-3_3
8. Panzella, L., Moccia, F., Nasti, R., Marzorati, S., Verotta, L., Napolitano, A.: Bioactive phenolic compounds from agri-food wastes: an update on green and sustainable extraction methodologies. Front Nutr. **7**, 60 (2020)
9. Muhlack, R.A., Potumarthi, R., Jeffery, D.W.: Sustainable wineries through waste valorisation: a review of grape marc utilisation for value-added products. Waste Manage. **72**, 99–118 (2018)
10. Lavelli, V., Kerr, W.L., García-Lomillo, J., González-SanJosé, M.L.: Applications of recovered bioactive compounds in food products. In: Handbook of Grape Processing By-products. Sustainable Solutions, vol. 10, pp. 233–266. Academic Press, Cambridge (2017)
11. Nanni, A., Parisi, M., Colonna, M.: Wine by-products as raw materials for the production of biopolymers and of natural reinforcing fillers: a critical review. Polymers **13**, 381 (2021)
12. Innuva. https://www.associazioneinnuva.it
13. Poliphenolia. https://www.poliphenolia.com
14. Gruppo Caviro. https://www.caviro.com
15. Karana, E., Pedgley, O., Rognoli, V.: Materials Experience: Fundamentals of Materials and Design. Butterworth-Heinemann, Oxford (2013)
16. Bistagnino, L.: Design Sistemico. Progettare la sostenibilità produttiva e ambientale (in Italian), pp. 230–242. Slow Food Editore, Cuneo (2009)
17. Vegea. https://www.vegeacompany.com
18. Valsovit. http://www.valsovit.it
19. I risultati del progetto ValorVitis 2.0. https://www.progettoager.it
20. La ricerca e l'innovazione incontrano il mercato. http://www.valorvitis2.com
21. Al Vinitaly progetto di Ca' Foscari: energia pulita dagli scarti del vino. https://www.unive.it

22. Aldersey-Williams, H., Antonelli, P.: Design and the Elastic Mind, pp. 4–17. Museum of Modern Art (2008)
23. Santini, C., Cavicchi, A., Casini, L.: Sustainability in the wine industry: key questions and research trends. Agric. Econ. **1**, 9 (2013)

Human Interaction and Communication in Industry

Design and Development of a F-16 Fighter Pilot Training System Using Virtual Reality: First Insights

Nuno Martins[1(✉)], Rui Oliveira[2], Sílvia Faria[3], Vítor Carvalho[2,4], and Jorge Silva[5]

[1] Polytechnic Institute of Cavado and Ave/ID+, Barcelos, Portugal
[2] 2Ai Lab - School of Technology, Polytechnic Institute of Cavado and Ave, Barcelos, Portugal
[3] Polytechnic Institute of Cavado and Ave, Barcelos, Portugal
[4] Algoritmi Research Center, Minho University, Guimarães, Portugal
[5] Portuguese Air Force - Air Base 5, Monte Real, Portugal

Abstract. This project presents a study under development with the Portuguese Air Force in order to improve the ability of F-16 pilots to analyze post-flight data using virtual reality (VR) devices. The technology allows the simulator to be programmed and the design allows the study of the best location of the different data to be presented to the pilots. This paper focuses on the literature review and analysis of existing solutions in which the specification of the requirements for the practical development of the project has been completed.

Keywords: Portuguese Air Force · Design and Human-computer interaction · Virtual reality · Flight simulators · F-16 Aircraft · Interface design

1 Introduction

Portuguese Air Force[1] was created in 1952, it belongs to the national force system, as well as the Navy and Army, whose mission is to defend the Portuguese airspace, performing air operations and missions within the scope of international commitments. The F-16MLU is a multi-role fighter able to execute air-to-air and air-to-ground missions. The F-16 pilots, during the flight, use a Joint Helmet Mounted Cueing System that allows them to increase their performance sending data relative to what they are seeing at the flight moment. The collected data have a huge importance as it helps pilots to identify possible dangerous or warning situations for example. Real flights are carried out daily, but this is an expensive act and, therefore, there is a need for pilots to do "land" training simulations in order to improve their tactical and technical skills. Currently, an F-16 flight requires to undertake a briefing before and a debriefing after it in order to improve the abilities and skills of the pilot regarding what they are expecting during the flight and about their performed action during the flight. Debriefings have a significant impact on pilots' learning which are usually done with 2D technologies, which proves to be

[1] Information available at: https://www.emfa.pt/ 2020.

D. Raposo et al. (Eds.): AHFE 2021, LNNS 277, pp. 47–53, 2021.
https://doi.org/10.1007/978-3-030-80415-2_6

a major limitation, especially in close air combat missions (Dogfight). So, there is a need to improve debriefings tools and considering the literature review performed and the interviews with F-16 pilots the design and development of a flight simulator using virtual reality (VR) that allows with greater efficiency and accuracy the reconstruction of a flight (using collected data during real flights), with a customized interface in which the most diverse data can be presented in the most varied shapes and colors on the most diverse flight circumstances, will have a major importance. This tool should be able to simulate a flight with a panoramic view from outside the aircraft as well as a cockpit view presenting the flight dynamic variables such as velocity, altitude, among others. The current helmets of F-16 pilots present information and data using few colors and shapes. The project interface objective is to help the pilot to understand the most diverse data in an easy, intuitive, fast and effective way through the use of colors and symbols, where the system processing performance is also a major requirement.

This paper is organized in 5 sections. Section 2 presents the research methodologies used, Sect. 3 shows the state of art, Sect. 4 enunciates the project requirements and finally, Sect. 5 presents the final remarks.

2 Methodologies

The methodology used in the development of the simulator consists of an exploratory investigation sustained either in the review of scientific literature in the field or in the discovery and analysis of existing or ongoing solutions or technologies. Methods of semantic analysis of area images will be investigated. In order to create a solution that can answer the problem, scientific papers will be analysed in the scope of image processing to understand the best type of image, as well as the best resolution in order to obtain the best results. Methods to reference the data will also be reviewed, in order to understand if they should be stored in relational or non-relational databases. It will be analysed which are the best tools and those that are more suitable for the development of software for VR of this project. The methodology adopted was Design Thinking[2] as it is a practical and creative method designed for the user. This methodology was divided into five stages, which were not linear [1]. The first stage, Empathy, was characterized by the need to know users, problems and their needs. A semi-structured interview was conducted with a professional pilot from Portuguese Air Force. The questions asked were open questions so that the interviewee could deepen, for example, the improvements he considered relevant and the features that could be added. In addition to the interview, a set of reference interfaces were analyzed. The next steps were the definition and idealization in which the objective was to realize, through the interview and the analysis of the different interfaces, which functionalities should be improved and added, even if they did not exist in the real context. The Prototyping stage consisted of information architecture, wireframes and workflows in which the order of importance of the data was defined [2]. After this phase, it will be possible to proceed to the development of

2 Design Thinking – According to the book Guide to innovation, it is the "… set of methods and processes to approach problems, acquiring new information, and knowledge that later translates into new solutions. The premise behind this concept is to understand the methods and processes that designers use in order to raise the level of innovation" Porto Innovation Hub, s.d, Pag. 91.

usability tests by the pilots. It is intended to be an answer to the problems encountered in the interview. In this phase, observations will be made on the experience of using the prototype of the interface created. It is intended that this observation is structured and not participatory in order to understand how the pilot sees the interface and how it relates to it.

3 State of Art

This section is organized in 3 subsections, namely, Virtual Reality and Augmented Reality tools, Existing Simulators Analysis and Existing Helmets Analysis.

3.1 Virtual Reality and Augmented Reality

With the advancement of technology, VR and augmented reality (AR) become tools used to improve the experience of using games, but also in different areas such as aviation, medicine, construction or education [3]. Augmented reality arises when it is added to the real environment captured in real time, virtual content. In VR the user emerges only in the virtual environment, having no contact with the real environment. In the case of augmented reality and within the context of military aviation, the role of design is to allow the user to quickly and easily read new data, but at the same time it does not interfere with the environment and does not confuse the user. In the case of virtual reality, the role of design is to give the user the full experience of using a real flight. It is possible to consider the flight helmets used by pilots as augmented reality tools while flight simulators are considered VR. In this context, VR is an important tool for pilots in their training, namely in the exploration of techniques and tactics, and, consequently, greater efficiency in real flight. One of the first examples of VR emerged in the 1950s by Morton Heilig. Sensorama, a booth equipment with stereoscopic 3D image reproduction and still reproduces sounds, vibrations, odors and even the feeling of the wind. Eighteen years later, in 1968, Ivan Sutherland created what would be considered the first VR display, the Head Mounted Display (HMD). In 1985 Thomas Zimmerman and Jaron Lanier created the company VPL Research, which launched several peripherals such as DataGlove, a glove that captures hand movement and also created EyeGloves, glasses that resemble those currently found on the market. Virtual reality was poorly accessible and undeveloped until then [4]. Currently, there are on the market some solutions of VR glasses among them the Oculus Quest[3], the glasses of PlayStation. In 2012, Palmer Luckey, Brendan Iribe and Michael Antonov created the Oculus Rift. The latest version of the Oculus Quest, innovative VR devices that have not need to be connected by wire or a computer, the advantages of Oculus Quest are that they can be used anywhere, by mapping the division where the user is in order to have a safe user experience and the incorporation of audio device without the use of external devices. In Oculus Quest the device detects the hands, which allows that in some games the user can use the hands.

[3] Available in: https://www.oculus.com/quest/.

3.2 Existing Simulator Analysis

Flight simulation is currently an asset for the Portuguese Air Force as it significantly increases the number of hours the pilot may be doing his training. On real flights there is a cost for planes to take off and the number of flight hours is also reduced.

There are currently several flight simulators in VR, the majority of which are non-military, and here we can consider aircraft/aircraft flight simulators and games for computers and video game consoles, some with the possibility of an immersive experience with the use of glasses, VR and commands.

The Glass cockpit is a military cockpit simulator where the pilot has all the controls and the image is displayed on three screens on the cabin. Over the years this was the simulator used for training, but it has become a simulator with some flaws mainly because it was not designed to give the information that the pilot needs in the helmets but rather on the simulator's screen (see Fig. 1).

Fig. 1. US military simulator, Glass cockpit. Source: U.S. Air Force photo by Javier Garcia

The Dismounted Soldier Training System (DSTS) is one of the simulators used in the training program of the American military [5]. It uses VR to give the military a simulation of a real scenario and for essential teamwork in missions. The gap of these simulators is that they are restricted to a flat room not allowing the military to have real tactical sensations (haptic sensation) such as running.

For Kirner and Siscoutto: "When working with virtual and augmented reality environments, manipulating virtual objects, you miss the feeling of touch (haptics) that imposes more realism on applications. In some cases, the haptic sensation, involving touch and strength, may even be dispensed with, but in others, it is essential, as occurs in training situations" [6].

The company Red6[4] owns an Airborne Tactical Augmented Reality (A-TARS) that fills all existing flaws in the simulators mentioned above. Its main advantage is to be able to give the pilot the cognitive load present in a real flight, the speed, the G-force among others that interfere with the tensions that the pilots suffer during the flight. With a field of view of 105° the pilot sees in the helmet all the information and can do the aerial combat in a team because it allows a network simulation. Although this project has not been completed it is expected to be a great asset.

3.3 Existent Helmets Analysis

Helmets are the main source of study as it is through them that data is generated and presented to pilots. As stated by Costa and Raposo (2011), "(…) draw to the eyes is draw to the brain, the most complete of all organs, that guides our behaviour and all activities" [7]. Helmets have, through the magnetic field, the pilot's position mapping and this feature allows information to appear on the helmet when the pilot is looking in one direction. Information such as speed, magnetic course, weaponry, targets, friends, enemies, altitude, warnings, among others, appear directly on the helmet's visor, allowing them to take more immediate action without having to look at the instrument panel and it also allows a greater viewing angle over the entire exterior of the aircraft. The use of color is a fundamental element in the visualization of the different helmet data. As stated by Gonçalves, Fonseca and Campos "color is (…) an aspect to carefully consider in the process of creating an interface" [8]. At the moment, the helmets used for F-16 flights are the JHMCS1 and JHMCS2. Joint Helmet-Mounted Cueing System 2 is a helmet that features colors such as green, red and yellow as opposed to the previous version JHMCS1, which featured only green. The second version of the helmet also features night symbols and night vision goggles, which allows it to continue to have the same efficiency of presenting data with different colors even in a night scene where the pilot sees everything green. There are other newer models with more advanced technology, such as Helmet Mounted Integrated Targeting (HMIT), used in F-35 fighters, or Scorpion Helmet Mounted Display (HMD), which make the helmet lighter, have an improvement when placing the gravitational center, more colors and symbols are verified and the layout of the data on the interface is improved.

Over the years there have been major technological advances, which has enabled VR today, as well as simulators and helmets, to have more efficient hardware, equipment to be more accessible.

4 Requirements

The requirements survey was important to understand the needs of the project with a survey of functional and non-functional requirements:

- Development a flight simulator with two views (Cockpit view and plane view);
- The flight should be accurate with the provided data;

---

[4] Available in https://www.red6ar.com/ 2020.

- Provide in real time some data like velocity, height, time, among others;
- The main requirement for the interface is that the simulation with the VR glasses is as close as possible with the visualization of a real flight;
- Use of more colors in addition to the green color used in JHMCS;

In the night view it is important that the data is contrasted in the night scene.

5 Final Remarks

This section considers two subsections, the Work in Progress Comments and Future Work suggestions.

5.1 Work in Progress Comments

This project aims to develop a VR simulator and interface, which allows F-16 pilots of the Portuguese Air Force to carry out highly effective training and debriefings.

The simulators that currently exist have some flaws, related to operation. The main requirement for the project is that a simulation using VR glasses is as close as possible to the visualization of a real flight.

In this phase of the project it was possible to identify the main requirements, to do a research of what already exists, identify the problems and also possible solutions. The development is already in progress and all data from a real flight file is being loaded to a software being built. It is expected that the use of simulation tools will be increased for training in various situations and different scenarios, which is not so plausible to happen in real flight, reducing the physical and monetary resources required. In conclusion this flight simulator and interface could be a powerful tool to the pilots training particularly in flight debriefings.

5.2 Future Work

The following phases of the project are the further development of the reading of the file with the data of a real flight made available from the Portuguese Air Force as well as to convert data flight coordinates to our simulator environment coordinates in order to reproduce the trajectory of the plane with precision. After that, during the simulation, we will need to display all important data to the pilots like, velocity, height, pitch and roll angles. The last phase in the simulator development is to make performance tests and improve what is possible in order to make it efficient as a debriefing tool.

References

1. Brown, T.: Change by Design: How Design Thinking Transforms Organizations and Inspires Innovation. Harper Business, New York (2009)
2. Martins, N., Martin-Sanroman, J., Suárez-Carballo, F.: The Design Process in the improvement of the experience between a brand and its target audience through a digital product: the Lexus Portugal's used car website case study. Adv. Sci. Technol. Eng. Systems J. 5(5), 620–629 (2020). https://doi.org/10.25046/aj050576

3. Tori, R., da Hounsell, M.S.: Introdução a Realidade Virtual e Aumentada. J. Chem. Inf. Model. SBC (2018). (in Portuguese)
4. Espinheira, N.R.: Arquitetura Digital a Realidade Virtual, Suas Aplicações E Possibilidades. Universidade Federal Do Rio de Janeiro, COPPE (2004). (in Portuguese)
5. Velichko, M.: Virtual reality in military training - Jasoren. https://jasoren.com/vr-military-training-the-next-step-of-combat-evolution/
6. Kirner, C., Siscoutto, R.: Realidade Aumentada: Conceitos, Projeto e Aplicações. In: Kirner, C., Siscoutto, R. (eds.) Realidade Virtual e Aumentada: Conceitos, Projeto e Aplicações Livro, vol. 1 (2007). (in Portuguese)
7. Costa, J., Raposo, D.: Design para os olhos: Marca, Cor, Identidade, Sinalética. Dina Livro, Lisboa, Portugal (2011). (in Portuguese)
8. Gonçalves, D., Fonseca, M.J., Campos, P.: Introdução ao Design de Interfaces (FCA (ed.) 3o edição) (2017). (in Portuguese)

Creativity for Good: How Advertising Can Impact Lives - Case Study on Binge Drinking

Sara Balonas(✉)

Communication and Society Research Centre, University of Minho, Braga, Portugal
sarabalonas@ics.uminho.pt

Abstract. The article discusses the impact of creativity in behaviour change seeking to improve individuals' and communities' lives. Focused on the binge drinking phenomena, quite common in university student parties, the article stresses the role of advertising and design in behavioural change, through a case study of an initiative launched by a portuguese beer leading brand and carried out with university students, based on co-creation. The challenge of promoting responsible behaviours was enormous: the brands' core business was to sell beer and, on top of that, it was the main sponsor of university parties. A smart drinking strategy was implemented and data allows to demonstrate the add value of creativity developed in a co-creation environment.

Keywords: Alcohol consumption · Behavioural change · Creativity · Design · Advertising

1 Creativity Beyond Consumerism

Creativity, expressed in advertising or design, is intrinsically associated to the consumer society as it creates objects and references that are beyond their utility and through which individuals seek the ideal of happiness and self-fulfillment. Advertising has evolved throughout the twentieth century as a creative industry at the disposal of capitalist societies. Establishes consensus, complicity and collusion to produce relation, cohesion and communication (Baudrillard) [1] being considered the cosmetic of communication (Lipovetsky) [2]. A long and successful journey, associated with the apology of material goods and consumption, might explain why this area can hardly be considered valid when it comes to finding innovative solutions beyond consumerism. However, advertising, and creativity in general, are becoming a determining factor in the search for new paths to the major societal challenges in a VUCA[1] world. Creativity is, as Brandt & Eagleman states, inherent to the human species and determines the collective future: "from our daily activities to our schools to our companies, we are all riding arm-in-arm into a future that compels a constant remodelling of the world" (2017) [3].

[1] Volatile, Uncertain, Complex and Ambiguous.

D. Raposo et al. (Eds.): AHFE 2021, LNNS 277, pp. 54–61, 2021.
https://doi.org/10.1007/978-3-030-80415-2_7

In fact, advertising for good, as well as design, are playing an increasing role on behavioural and social change (Balonas; Alvarado; Jones) [4–7]. This comes, first and foremost, from professionals in the field, to whom it is their duty to act as citizens: "the same design that fuels mass overconsumption also holds the power to repair the world.", says Bergman, designer (2009, p. 2) [8]. Also, advertisers feel that they can create beyond dispensable advertising because, now, what matters is the size of the idea (David Droga, cit. in Kolster) [9]. On the other hand, Kolster, creative advertiser, says: "advertising has got us up to our necks in the climate and humanitarian crisis, but that makes me even more confident that advertising can get us out of it. No one knows consumers, brands and the market better than those in the advertising industry and we have to take up the challenge" (2012, p. 6) [9]. In addition, there is growing pressure from citizens and consumers for companies to act responsibly (addressing the climate crisis and other pressing social challenges), stimulating the rise of new communication formulas - which implies a redoubled attention to what Breninger and Kaltenbacher refer to as "ethical creativity" (2020) [10].

2 Creativity and Behavioural Change

Advertising has extended its field of action to very different themes (promotion, territories, politics, public health, science or social causes, to name a few). There is a growing number of campaigns in the social sphere and their purpose is, above all, to change attitudes in order to facilitate the adoption of new behaviours. There has been much criticism about corporate social responsibility practices and campaigns, often accused of social or green washing. Indeed, an ethical code of conduct, based on authenticity, transparency and accountability are essential vectors of strategies to promote social change in social campaigns launched by private organisations. In the corporate world, displaying humanitarian concerns, and being perceived as authentic in 'doing good' has become increasingly important (Breninger and Kaltenbacher 2020).

To be really effective, this is not enough to be ethical. Creativity needs to be settled on the specific attitudes and beliefs of the community it wants to influence. Thagard [11] defends that all social change results from mental mechanisms in individuals and from social mechanisms for the interactions of thinking individuals, intriguingly weaves together a multilevel tapestry of social construction and individual cognition (2019). For this purpose, the authoritarian or shock tone of social campaigns have proved to be inefficient. Probably because they failed to see the problem from the affected audiences' eyes (French, Merritt & Reynolds) [12] and they miss the arguments that can led to adherence and behavioural change. Communication is not only about information but also about getting attention and to create affinity. Communication is persuasion.

People need to feel involved and engaged. Participatory involvement often creates behaviour change with greater effect (French et al. 2011, p. 22). It is what Hastings resumes as the "power of the ordinary people" [13], arguing for more individual and collective empowerment and a balance between experts and citizens. This can be achieved with an intervention framework that integrates elements of the community affected by a given social problem with the experts, through their participation in problem selection, goal setting, participation in research, strategic development and activity programming (Hastings).

The intention of the case presented in this article is to demonstrate how creativity can be articulated between professionals and a community affected by a problem, following the mantra of co-creation - with ethics and transparency - and what type of results can be achieved.

3 A Pilot Project on Smart Consumption Case Study

Super Bock, a leading sales beer company that sponsors university academic events, is often associated to negative behaviour, such as excessive alcohol consumption. In academic parties, binge drinking[2] episodes occur frequently. These are weeks known by the revelry and excesses of students, who deliberately search alcoholic states as a way to celebrate the end of the academic year and have fun.

Many young people gather for concerts, chats and drinks, with easy access to various alcohol outlets, without any restriction. Often, Super Bock brand is associated to negative behaviours once it is the official sponsor of those parties.

As a way of standing up to the problem, the brand launched a pilot project on smart consumption, aiming to promote changes in attitudes and behaviours of university students.

The behavioural objectives were to promote a smart alcohol consumption using evidences of the negative alcohol effects and rewarding a responsible consumption during the seven nights in all of the academic parties in Porto, Coimbra and Lisbon (the three bigger and most popular academic parties in Portugal). Target group were young people mainly between 17 and 22 years old, an age particularly vulnerable to new consumption patterns and at greater risk when combining the inexperience of alcohol consumption with inexperience on driving.

The Smart Consumption Strategy in Detail

The project began by a creative bootcamp to meet insights from the target group. Groups of students developed creative solutions on responsible alcohol consumption, oriented by mentors under the principle of design thinking and leading to ideas related to point of sale, events, campaigning and gaming. Projects were presented to brand managers. This method, based on customer orientation, allowed the development of a strategy in an ascending process – based on the target (Weinreich) [14].

On a second phase, a smart consumer awareness action was implemented in three Portuguese cities where festivities last for a week to celebrate the end of the academic year of 2018. Conceived by an advertising company, the action was based on the student's insights previously obtained. A physical space, designed in accordance with the brand's identity (Fig. 1 and 2), allowed students to measure their blood alcohol level.

They were rewarded with brand gifts if their consumption was within the legal BAC, following a nudge[3] strategy.

---

[2] Binge drinking usually refers to drinking lots of alcohol in a short space of time or drinking to get drunk.

[3] To influence the behaviour in a positive manner, suggesting rather than imposing.

Fig. 1. Physical space design project

Fig. 2. Smart alcohol consumption activation

The whole action was based on a light and humourous mood, combining fun design pieces with advertising phrases full of jokes related to students' parties. A structure inspired by a traffic light, designed for the purpose, showed the result: if they get the green light they received a gift; if the light was yellow, they were advised to drink wisely receiving popcorns to reduce alcohol effects; on the red level, they were advised to stop drinking and to avoid driving (Fig. 3).

Fig. 3. Breathalyser tests applied by students

In the same space, through creative mirrors, students could still foresee the drunken state. They also could take pictures on a wall with funny phrases about smart consumption and share them on social networks. Also, a funny car with a megaphone circulated around the parties to draw attention to the event. Finally, through free WIFI, students received cheerful SMS messages about smart drinking (Figs. 4 and 5).

Co-creation and Peer-to-Peer Intervention

The bootcamp provided important clues about how young people view the problem. Students are aware of the risks of binge drinking; therefore, a shock language would have no effect. For them, the challenge is how to enjoy the party by knowing when to stop drinking, allowing to have fun with friends and to keep good memories by the end of the night. Additionally, younger people want to avoid bad physical conditions or, worse, to increase the risk of accidents. In sum, the insight could be stated as "having fun with safety".

The same group of students was invited to participate in the awareness action in a peer-to-peer approach. They applied the breathalyser tests to the other students and explained to them the action goals. They were the promoters of an intelligent attitude towards beer consumption and, also, brand ambassadors.

Therefore, the bootcamp engaged the target by involving them in the problem on an early stage and also gave them the possibility to become endorsers of the action. The fact that students themselves explained the action to other students increased the credibility of the action.

Moreover, university academic associations (from Porto, Coimbra and Lisbon universities) who are responsible for organising the festivities, were involved in the action since the beginning.

Fig. 4. Interactive wall with funny phrases

Fig. 5. Funny car with a megaphone

Smart Drinking Strategy Evaluation

Direct observation showed that the queues for alcohol testing were constant, growing throughout the night and throughout the days of the action, probably due to word of mouth effect. Quantitative and qualitative methods were used to measure the impact of the smart drinking strategy during the implementation phase of the action. Quantitative data were obtained through: 1) number of breathalysers mouthpieces used and 2) number of gifts offered. In addition, questionnaires were applied on site, 67 of which were considered valid.

The data collected allowed to conclude that there was adherence of the young public. During the time the action was available – 4 h per night during 7 nights for each location - 721 alcohol tests were carried out. The last nights registered an average of 1 alcohol test per minute. The questionnaires led to the conclusion that students wanted to know if they could drive late at night (47%), others were motivated by the gifts (44%) and the animation around the stand as well as by the promoters (23%). Finally, all the respondents considered that the association of the smart consumption with the beer brand made sense.

Direct observation also led to the conclusion that, in future interventions, more physical spaces can be created to increase the impact because the queues were constant (Fig. 5). In addition, interventions can be tested in later hours because the action ended at 3 a.m. and the most critical alcohol states often occur later.

4 Conclusions

The present case study exposes the problematic between core business and the imperative to act in a responsible way without being contradictory and the role of creativity to provide effective solutions to that end. Co-creation and engagement, as parts of the creative strategy, prove to be a means to effective change.

The case presented also highlights the persuasive power of advertising, capable of building narratives that seduce by the lightness of its discourse, in contrast to the reprehensive or authoritarian tone. The emotional side of the brain is activated through a campaign in a humorous tone and that promoted moments of fun among friends. In fact, to induce a change in the attitude of young people towards alcohol consumption, emotive messages that explore the feeling of identification, belonging and status tend to be more effective. Social evidences show that when a behaviour is adopted by peers and when it is perceived as popular, people are more predisposed to adopt the same behaviour (Weinreich) [15]. Indeed, social relations, approval and social support have a strong and long influence on behaviour (Strategic Social Marketing, s/d) [15].

Finally, the case highlights the importance of being authentic about problems. A brand that sells beer can't say that drinking is bad but can advise to drink in a smart way. Even though it could be considered as a risky action, because it could go against the brand's core business, it ended up illustrating what Swann & Birke stated about creativity as something that everyone saw, and no one thought about (2005) [16].

Acknowledgments. The author would like to express her gratitude for Super Bock Group's consent to share the case study for academic purposes.

References

1. Baudrillard. J.: A Sociedade de Consumo. Edições 70, Lisboa (1981)

2. Lipovetsky G.: A Era do Vazio. Relógio d'Água, Lisboa (1989)
3. Brandt, A., Eagleman, D.: The Runaway Species - How Human Creativity Remakes the World. Catapult, Great Britain (2017)
4. Balonas, S.: Publicidade sem Código de Barras - contributos para o conhecimento da publicidade a favor de causas sociais em Portugal. Centro de Estudos Comunicação e Sociedade CECS e Ed. Húmus, Braga (2011)
5. Balonas, S.: A publicidade a favor de causas sociais: caracterização do fenómeno em Portugal, através da Televisão. Ph.D. thesis. University of Minho, Braga (2013)
6. Alvarado, M.: La Publicidad Social: Una Modalidad Emergente de Comunicación. Tesis de Doctorado, Universidad Complutense de Madrid, Madrid (2010)
7. Jones, C.W.: Advertising and the way forward. Westminster Papers Commun. Culture **15**(2), 1–5 (2020). https://doi.org/10.16997/wpcc.392
8. Bergman, D.: Do Good Design: How Designers Can Change the World. New Riders, Berkeley (2009)
9. Kolster, T.: Goodvertising - Creative Advertising That Cares, Thames & Hudson, London (2012). ISBN 978 0 500 51626 3
10. Breninger, B., Kaltenbacher, T.: Changing perceptions, changing lives – promoting intercultural competence and ethical creativity through advertising. Westminster Papers in Commun. Culture **15**(2), 129–150 (2020). https://doi.org/10.16997/wpcc.383
11. Thagard, P.: Mind-Society: From Brains to Social Sciences and Professions. Oxford University Press, New York (2019). https://doi.org/10.1093/oso/9780190678722.001.0001
12. French, J., Merritt, R., Reynolds, L.: Social Marketing Casebook. Sage Publications, London (2011) ISBN 978 0 85702 543 2
13. Hastings, G., Angus, K., Bryant, C. (eds.): The Sage Handbook of Social Marketing. Sage Publications, London (2011). ISBN 978 1 84920 188 9
14. Weinreich, N.: Hands-On Social Marketing: a Step-By-Step Guide to Designing Change For Good, 2nd edn. Sage, Los Angeles (2011)
15. Strategic Social Marketing (s/d): 30 Things we know about how to influence behaviour. https://strategic-social-marketing.vpweb.co.uk/free-tool-box
16. Swann, P., Birke, D.: How do Creativity and Design Enhance Business Performance? A Framework for Interpreting the Evidence. Nottingham University Business School (2005)

Design and Its Multiple Roles in Place Branding: The Case of Mississauga, Canada

Paula Malamud[1(✉)], Marco Neves[1], and Gabriel Patrocinio[2,3]

[1] Centro de Investigação em Arquitetura, Urbanismo e Design, Faculdade de Arquitetura, Universidade de Lisboa, 1349-063 Lisbon, Portugal
paulamalamud@campus.ul.pt
[2] ISMAT, Portimão, Portugal
[3] IFHT, UERJ, Rio de Janeiro, Brasil

Abstract. Place branding is a strategy to bring economic development to a territory. It is a complex, dynamic, and participatory process with a long-term vision that faces challenges such as the consensus between government, citizens and, other stakeholders around a common purpose. Its constructed with several stages and with the participation of interdisciplinary teams, including designers. This article aims to analyze how design can contribute to place branding from a systemic perspective and using the place branding case study in Mississauga, Canada, as methodology. By crossing the phases of the process with the respective design interventions, it was possible to observe the multiple roles that designers can play with different complexity levels.

Keywords: Place branding · Design · Complexity · Strategy · Brand experience

1 Introduction

In a oversimplified perspective, many practitioners and public managers consider place branding only as the creation of logos and visual identity [1, 2]. Indeed, the visual identity is part of place branding, but it alone will not solve the local problems [3].

According to the journal Place Branding and Public Diplomacy, "place branding applies brand strategy and related techniques to advance the economic, social, political and cultural development of cities, regions and countries [4]".

Hence, local brands are not logos: they are strategies. They are deep, dynamic, and participatory processes that face challenges such as consensus among diverse audiences and unfolding into long-term actions.

To build a local brand with purpose and consistency, it is necessary to align government, citizens and, other stakeholders around a central idea; bring the strategic plan to life by building an ecosystem of interactions between the brand and the public. In its execution, it involves interdisciplinary teams at different hierarchical levels, including designers.

In the same way that place branding should not be reduced to logos, design activity is not only about creating visual identity. Place branding is a complex process, and design

D. Raposo et al. (Eds.): AHFE 2021, LNNS 277, pp. 62–69, 2021.
https://doi.org/10.1007/978-3-030-80415-2_8

has evolved to deal with complex issues. This article aims to analyze how design can contribute to place branding from the literature review and the Mississauga's case study, in this intersection of disciplines.

2 Place Branding with Design Intervention

2.1 Defining Place Branding

Since 1998, when Simon Anholt made the first reference to the term nation-branding, to the present day, place branding has evolved both in practice and in academic circles. As presented by Lucarelli and Brorström [5], the discipline has affirmed its interdisciplinary nature when approached in publications specialized in marketing, urbanism, public diplomacy, geography, tourism, among others.

Even with so many studies and cases implemented, there is still a lack of understanding among public managers and practitioners of what place branding is and its potential. For many, it is just a logo, slogan, or promotional campaign [1, 2].

A territorial brand is much more than a logo. According to Eshuis and Edwards [6] it can be defined as a "governance strategy for managing perceptions about places". Also, according to Baker [7], "It sets guidelines for how the place should be communicated and how to deliver experiences for the target audiences", focusing on strengthening the competitive identity. It can be applied in nations, cities, and regions as a strategy to increase exports or leverage the local economy, attracting tourists, business, or residents [8], or yet, to promote civic pride, sense of belonging, and sense of place [9].

According to Baker, a place branding project is necessary when the territory needs a repositioning of its image; the communication is not consistent or relevant, or if there is a perception gap between promise and reality [7].

Initial studies associated place branding with corporate brands [10, 11], but with the evolution of its practice, experts concluded that to build authentic and true territorial brands, it was necessary to involve and engage residents and other stakeholders [12, 13]. Hence, place branding has come to be seen as a governance process [6], turning into a "complex, multifaceted, dynamic, and participatory" process [3].

A place brand is made up of tangible (functional) and intangible (experiential) aspects. For this reason, a critical factor for its success is the investment in actions and infrastructure to create brand experiences with the target audience, whether tourists, investors, or residents. It must be well planned since each touchpoint is an opportunity to translate in a physical, emotional, and sensorial way the intangible concepts of a place brand, creating memorable experiences [9, 14].

2.2 Design and Its Multiple Skills

Designers have a wide skill set to handle complex processes like place branding. For instance, Maffei and Villari [15] explain that designers can collaborate from a community-centered approach to building relationships, strategies, or artifacts from a territorial perspective.

According to Mozota [16], design is not only an activity; it is a creation and decision-making process, with problem-solving, creative solutions, systemic thinking, and coordination skills. Besides, designers can act at three different levels, according to their expertise: action (operational level), function (tactical level), and vision (strategic level). Mozota [17] also reinforces that "design is a core competency for a company but also for country, city, and institution." To conclude, Mozota [18] states that design activity brings competitive advantage and value.

If design has the power to conceive products that meet human beings' needs, the point is that the meaning of "product" has also been changing over the years. In this perspective, Buchanan [19] states design practice can encompass four orders: symbols, objects, actions, and thoughts, moving towards increasingly intangible and complex aspects.

The scope of design activity is becoming increasingly vast. Hill [18] affirms design can transcend the creation of products, services, and spaces for a context that involves civil society, creating relationships, contexts, and strategies.

According to Manzini [20], the designers' role is to make things visible and tangible, effective and meaningful. Designers are agents for solving problems and making sense of things.

Design activity is also related to innovation that, as described by Brown and Katz [21], is "no longer limited to the introduction of new physical products, but also new sorts of processes, services, interactions, entertainment forms, and ways of communicating and collaborating."

Design, therefore, is an activity and a process recognized for **solving problems** [20, 22], but it can also be applied to **adding value**, **generating innovation** [21, 23], **making sense** and **consensus** [20].

3 The Mississauga Case

In this research, we used the case study methodology, "that investigates a contemporary phenomenon in depth and within its real-world context" [24], to observe and analyze how the place branding project for Mississauga took place and how design intervention happened during the process. From information collected in interviews, reports, and other sources, it was possible to observe, describe and analyze the process, including the phases, the methods used, and the outcomes.

Mississauga, currently the sixth most populous city in Canada, was officially incorporated as a city from the merger with other neighborhoods in 1974. It is located 30 km away from Toronto, and it has consolidated itself as a multicultural municipality and a thriving financial center, made up of immigrants from diverse backgrounds.

Although it had positive attributes such as high quality of life and an inviting atmosphere, the external perceptions were outdated. "Many people continued to view Mississauga as simply a suburban bedroom community [25]".

In May 2012, the Communications Master Plan recommended the development of a strong reputation for Mississauga. Another issue was that visual communication was the same since 1974 and was evaluated as "industrial, conservative, and boring [26]". It was not expressing the soul of the new Mississauga.

Consequently, the place branding project started aiming to create a brand that would strengthen the reputation, nurture civic pride, and increase the key audiences' attractiveness [26]. This brand had stakeholders' engagement as a premise.

In May 2013, the city council hired an external brand agency to develop strategic stages of place branding. They were responsible for structuring the project, creating the engagement methodology, conducting the workshops, defining the brand positioning, and coordinating the visual identity creation.

After initial research and analysis stage, the brand strategy stage began to define the brand's key elements aligned with already existing strategic plan of the city. Four co-creation workshops were held with more than 100 stakeholders, including a brand advisory panel formed by city staff, residents, businesses, and community partners. To obtain dialogue and consensus around a central idea, the brand agency applied techniques such as scenario planning and building blocks.

As a result, three pillars of Mississauga brand were defined: welcoming world culture, naturally enriching and inspiring possibilities. Based on these concepts, the brand agency, together with the brand marketing manager, defined brand narrative. After this, visual identity was developed by the in-house team of six graphic designers under the coordination of the brand agency.

Then, from October to December 2013, the brand marketing manager developed an action plan for the implementation stage considering the key-touchpoints in four years.

Finally, in May 2014, city council officially launched the brand at a ceremony in Celebration Square, a venue for major events where residents could record videos of their Mississauga stories. Simultaneously, new visual identity was applied to the main touchpoints in the city. All communication narrative was aligned with the brand's pillars and positioning, sharing its vision of the future.

To create authentic and meaningful experiences for the community and stakeholders, the brand marketing team, with support of the design team, developed the "Mississauga Experience Program", based on the brand's pillars and considering the following attributes: open & engaging, vibrant, optimistic, collaborative, optimistic and effective [27].

The design team has also contributed to this stage by developing products, marketing campaigns, events, placemaking, and other forms of relationships for the brand. These actions have the role of improving the city's reputation and helping achieve the brand's strategic goals.

3.1 Mississauga's Place Branding Process with the Intervention of Design

Design intervention in place branding can occur at different levels of complexity, according to the professionals' expertise. These interventions are also influenced by the hierarchical structure of a public institution and by interdisciplinary relations.

An analysis matrix Table 1 of place branding for Mississauga was elaborated to understand this phenomenon, describing the process's stages, designers and other participant's involvement, the leadership roles, and the design outcomes. The classification was also carried out according to the four levels of complexity of the design proposed by Jones [28] Fig. 1.

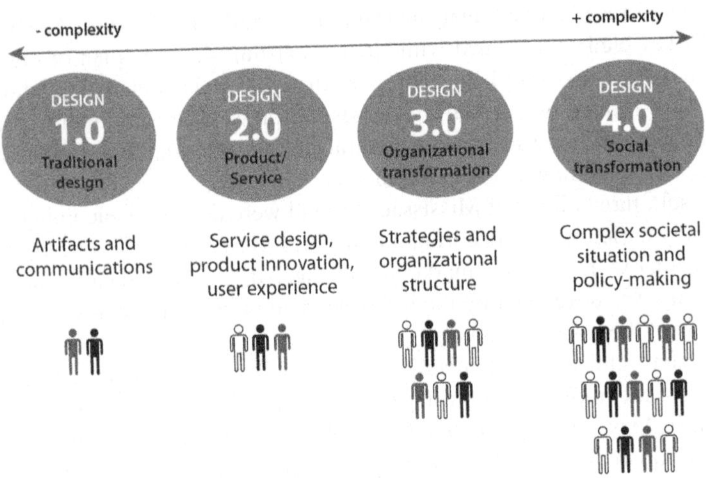

Fig. 1. Design domains to challenge complexity, adapted from Jones [28].

Design 1.0 refers to traditional design: "design as making" and involves communication activities. **Design 2.0** is about creating value, including service design, product innovation, and user experience. It's "design as integrating". **Design 3.0** refers to organizational transformation, where design is part of a complex context involving business or strategies. **Design 4.0** is related to social transformation and has methods and skills to deal with complex problems relating to stakeholders and community. According to Jones [28], "the four domains differ in their strategy, intention, and outcomes. Each domain requires skill and coordination of distinct methods, design practices, collaboration skills, and stakeholder participation." The greater is the complexity, more intangible are the design outcomes.

Table 1. Analysis of design intervention during the place branding process for Mississauga

Place branding steps	Designers involved	Other participants	Design outcomes	Level[a]
Strategic setup				
Place branding planning to define brand goals and processes, aligning with the strategic plan of the city	Branding agency as consultant (LEAD)	City staff	Strategy	3.0
Articulation				
Definition of the main stakeholders and how to engage with them	Branding agency as consultant (LEAD)	Brand manager	Methodology and tools for engagement	3.0
Research and analysis				
Evaluation of existing communication and marketing material (brand audit)	Branding agency as consultant (LEAD)	City staff	Methodology	3.0
Research about benchmarks including interview with experts	Branding agency as consultant (LEAD)	Research firm and city staff	Methodology	3.0
Stakeholder interviews	Branding Agency as consultant (LEAD)	Research firm and city staff	Methodology	3.0
Brand strategy				
Four workshops with stakeholders and residents to define the positioning and key-elements of the brand	Branding agency as facilitation and coordination (LEAD)	Brand Advisory Panel: city staff, residents, businesses, and community partners + Brand Manager	Dialogue and consensus between stakeholders and residents (sense-making)	4.0
Elaboration				
Definition of the brand components and brand history	Branding agency as consultant (LEAD)	Brand manager	Development of the brand narrative (making tangible)	1.0
Development of the logo and visual identity	Design team with the branding agency's support (LEAD)	Brand manager	Logo and visual identity (making tangible and innovation)	1.0
Implementation				
Elaboration of marketing and implementation plan	N/A	Brand manager	N/A	N/A
Brand launch on key touchpoints	Design team with the manager of creative services	Brand marketing team of the communication division of the city (LEAD)	Making tangible, transformation into action	1.0
Activation and management				
Development of "Experience Mississauga" program	Design team with the manager of creative services	Brand marketing team of the communication division of the city (LEAD)	Development of services and experiences	2.0
Day by day communication with target audiences in the city	Design team with the manager of creative services	Brand marketing team of the communication division of the city (LEAD)	Development of communication, products, marketing campaigns	1.0

[a]According to Jones' design complexity scale [28]

4 Conclusions

From literature review and Mississauga case study, it was possible to observe that designers can act in place branding in multiple ways - whether strategic, tactical, or operational, according to their expertise and the teams involved.

Initial stages are more complex, as designers need to deal with political (mayor, councilors, and city staff), economic (local business), and social (residents) spheres around common sense. In this phase, city council hired an external branding agency with expertise in strategy and stakeholder engagement. They contributed with tools and methodologies to generate strategy, consensus, shared vision, sense-making, and meaning.

Next steps, to implement and sustain strategy, are more tactical and operational. It involves creating communications, products, services, and experiences to bring the brand to life and it was carried out by creative services department's design team, subordinated to the city council's communication division.

Another point to highlight is that designers had to deal with interdisciplinary and hierarchical relationships that make up a public institution during all stages.

Due to the community-centered approach, its ability to solve problems and generate consensus, we can conclude that the design activity can contribute broadly to place branding, collaborating to **define, make tangible**, and **give sustentation** to the strategy, resulting in authentic brands with value, long-term purpose and consistency.

Acknowledgments. The authors would like to thank Mr. David Ferreira for providing helpful and constructive information about Mississauga's place branding project.

References

1. Govers, R.: Why place branding is not about logos and slogans. Place Brand. Public Dipl. **9**, 71–75 (2013). https://doi.org/10.1057/pb.2013.11
2. Ashworth, G., Kavaratzis, M.: Beyond the logo: brand management for cities. J. Brand Manag. **16**, 520–531 (2009)
3. Ntounis, N., Kavaratzis, M.: Re-branding the High Street: the place branding process and reflections from three UK towns. J. Place Manag. Dev. **10**, 392–403 (2017). https://doi.org/10.1108/JPMD-12-2015-0056
4. Place Branding and Public Diplomacy: Overview. https://doi.org/10.1057/pb.2009.1. https://www.palgrave.com/gp/journal/41254. Accessed 25 Feb 2021
5. Lucarelli, A., Brorström, S.: Problematising place branding research: a meta-theoretical analysis of the literature. Mark. Rev. **13**, 65–81 (2013)
6. Eshuis, J., Edwards, A.: Branding the city: the democratic legitimacy of a new mode of governance. Urban Stud. **50**, 1066–1082 (2013). https://doi.org/10.1177/0042098012459581
7. Baker, B.: Destination Branding for Small Cities - The Essentials for Successful Place Branding. Creative Leap Books, Portland (2012)
8. Gertner, D.: A (tentative) meta-analysis of the 'place marketing' and 'place branding' literature (2011)
9. Esteves, C.: Place branding. Editora Simonsen (2016)
10. Anholt, S.: Definitions of place branding-working towards a resolution. Place Brand. Public Dipl. **6**, 1 (2010). https://doi.org/10.1057/pb.2010.3

11. Kavaratzis, M.: Cities and their brands: lessons from corporate branding. Place Brand. Public Dipl. **5**, 26–37 (2009). https://doi.org/10.1057/pb.2008.3
12. Braun, E., Kavaratzis, M., Zenker, S.: My city - my brand: the different roles of residents in place branding. J. Place Manag. Dev. **6**, 18–28 (2013). https://doi.org/10.1108/17538331311306087
13. Kavaratzis, M.: From "necessary evil" to necessity: stakeholders' involvement in place branding. J. Place Manag. Dev. **5**, 7–19 (2012). https://doi.org/10.1108/17538331211209013
14. Florek, M., Insch, A.: Learning to co-create the city brand experience. J. Int. Stud. **13**, 163–177 (2020). https://doi.org/10.14254/2071-8330.2020/13-2/12
15. Maffei, S., Villari, B.: Design for local development. Building a design approach for the territorial capital resources based on a situated perspective (2006)
16. de Mozota, B.B.: Design Management - Using Design to Build Brand Value and Corporate Innovation. Allworth Press, New York (2003)
17. de Mozota, B.B.: Design economics – microeconomics and macroeconomics: exploring the value of designers' skills in our 21st century economy. In: 1st International Symposium for Design Education Researchers, pp. 1–23 (2011)
18. Borja de Mozota, B.: The four powers of design: a value model in design management. Des. Manag. Rev. **17**, 44–53 (2006). https://doi.org/10.1111/j.1948-7169.2006.tb00038.x
19. Buchanan, R.: Wicked problems in design thinking. Des. Issues **8**, 5–21 (1992)
20. Manzini, E.: Design, When Everybody Designs: An Introduction to Design for Social Innovation. The Mit Press, London (2015). https://doi.org/10.13128/Techne-21142
21. Brown, T., Katz, B.: Change by design. J. Prod. Innov. Manag. **28**, 381–383 (2011)
22. Cross, N.: Designerly Ways of Knowing. Springer, London (2006)
23. Liedtka, J., Ogilvie, T.: Designing for Growth: a Design Thinking Tool Kit for Managers. Columbia University Press, New York (2011). https://doi.org/10.1007/1-84628-301-9
24. Yin, R.K.: Case Study Research - Design and Methods. Sage, Thousand Oaks (2014)
25. The Place Brand Observer: How to Develop a City Brand Strategy – Example Mississauga in Canada. https://placebrandobserver.com/how-to-develop-city-brand-strategy-example-mississauga/. Accessed 21 Sept 2020
26. City of Mississauga: Mississauga's new brand – FAQ's (2014). http://mississaugabrand.ca/assets/mississauga_brandfaqs.pdf
27. City of Mississauga: Shaping Our Brand Story, Mississauga, Canadá (2014)
28. Metcalf, G.S. (ed.): Social Systems and Design. TSS, vol. 1. Springer, Tokyo (2014). https://doi.org/10.1007/978-4-431-54478-4

Additive Manufacturing Re-designs the Industry

Ciro Scognamiglio[1](✉), Rosario Borrelli[2], Assunta Capece[1], Francesco Caputo[1], Stefania Franchitti[2], and Mario Buono[1]

[1] Engineering Department, University of Campania Luigi Vanvitelli, Via Roma 29, 81031 Aversa, CE, Italy
{ciro.scognamiglio,assunta.capece,francesco.caputo, mario.buono}@unicampania.it

[2] CIRA, Italian Aerospace Research Centre, Via Maiorise, 81043 Capua, CE, Italy
{r.borrelli,s.franchitti}@cira.it

Abstract. The initial spread of Additive Manufacturing (AM) technologies, within the manufacturing processes, is attributed to the expiration of some of the key patents on additive printing technology, including the Stratasys' FDM (Fused Deposition Modeling) one. In a short time, researchers, through open-source projects such as RepRap [1], have reduced the critical issues of additive processes, making 3D printing more accessible and defining new ways to use it beyond its traditional use for rapid prototyping. Moving through the early applications of additive technology in industry, which involved visualization and rapid development of prototypes, within a decade the use of AM processes for the fabrication of a wide range of functional components in a variety of industrial fields has grown exponentially.

There are many benefits from introducing AM techniques into design processes, such as high level of customization and reduced waste material. The most significant benefit that researchers are investigating is the capability to produce lattice structures that would otherwise be impossible to obtain with other processes. Primarily through biomimetics, they are investigating how to mimic biological structures that are constantly evolving to optimize both weight and strength. The aerospace sector was one of the first to adopt cutting-edge AM technologies combined with topological optimization methods, that allow to redesign components by removing geometry constraints related to the traditional production methods, while ensuring the reduction of the overall weight and therefore bringing beneficial effects on fuel consumption and environmental impact. In fact, through AM technologies there is a significant improvement in the "buy-to-fly ratio", which is the ratio between the weight of the raw material and the weight of the finished product, which in additive manufacturing tends to 1 and brings significant reductions in material waste [2]. The article illustrates the main methods of Design for Additive Manufacturing (DfAM) oriented to the aerospace sector in order to explore the possible fields of application and to suggest guidelines for the design process. Through DfAM it will be possible to explore new configurations, by diversifying existing products and creating new forms of design "materialization". AM technologies in particular provide efficient manufacturing solutions for small production volumes, improving supply chain responsiveness through manufacturing strategies and enabling the reduction of additional logistics costs. In addition, with the implementation of the Rapid Tooling approach, AM will contribute to improving the performance of traditional mass production systems by

D. Raposo et al. (Eds.): AHFE 2021, LNNS 277, pp. 70–77, 2021.
https://doi.org/10.1007/978-3-030-80415-2_9

enhancing the production speed of injection molding machines. Finally, the introduction of new tools for additive design will allow the definition of new scenarios for manufacturing oriented to produce lightweight solutions, with high levels of performance and efficiency, reducing the time between design and production, in order to reduce the time to market.

Keywords: Additive manufacturing · Design · Product sustainability · Biomimetic

1 Technologies and Application Areas of Additive Processes

The spread of Additive Manufacturing (AM), more commonly known as "3D printing", is increasing more and more and in recent years there have been more manufacturers of devices; the main reason for this growth was the expiration of some patents of the main additive printing technologies, especially the key patent of Stratasys related to FDM (Fused Deposition Modeling) technology in 2009. Since then, companies have begun to proliferate and recognize the potential, driven by researchers and open-source projects like RepRap, that have quickly decreased the complexity and made 3D printers accessible outside the rapid prototyping environment of companies. Bre Pettis first in 2009 saw the opportunity and founded Makerbot which was the first to produce open-source 3D printers, and at the same time was created an accessory site with a repository of projects uploaded by users, to print independently without having the skills in 3D design software [3]. Also, in 2009 Josef Prusa, a student at the University of Prague joins the RepRap community and develops his own low-cost printer starting from the RepRap Mendel model, which are assembled with the use of parts easily available on the market. The Prusa printer is an improved version with the addition of a heated "bed" obtained with a simple printed circuit board. The Prusa Mendel as defined by the RepRap community is also simpler by requiring fewer components and especially halving assembly time and has been called the Ford Model T of the 3d printer world. The "third iteration" of the Prusa Mendel, which goes by the name Prusa i3, has become the standard for most FDM printers manufactured in the world. The simplification and cost reduction of these machines have allowed a widespread and exponential diffusion of 3D printers worldwide. The proliferation of AM technologies has made them one of the pillars of Industry 4.0. AM methods and technologies have been developed to produce complex structures at precise resolutions. The triggers for the rush toward these new technologies have been rapid prototyping, the ability to print large structures, reduced printing defects, and improved mechanical properties. AM refers to many types of technologies, the main ones of which can be divided into seven different categories, which include other subcategories. Photopolymerization was the first 3D printing technique developed, and it dates back to the early 1980s. The first to patent and industrialize the technology was in 1984 Chuck Hull, who then founded the world's first 3D printing company, 3D Systems Inc. SLA (Stereolithography) technology provides ultra-high precision rapid prototyping and is used by doctors, dentists and other industries that need ultra-high-definition prototypes. The extrusion of plastic material, FDM (Fused Deposition Modeling) or FFF (Fused Filament Fabrication), is the most popular because it is cheaper and therefore widely used by hobbyists and makers. The use of FDM printers is not limited only to private use. In fact, the FDM is the most diffused also as concerns the rapid prototyping for companies thanks to the reduced times and costs. Instead jetting technologies are often compared to standard inkjet printing. There are two categories of jetting; material jetting and binder jetting. In material jetting, photopolymers, metals or wax are used that solidify when exposed to light or heat. The material jet is done simultaneously by hundreds of small nozzles in a print head and this allows material to be deposited and polymerized much faster than other technologies. The main application is rapid prototyping, in particular, thanks to the possibility of printing materials with textures it lends itself very well to aesthetic prototyping, with the aim of faithfully producing the final part. It is also used in jewelry to produce molds for lost wax technology and in optics for the production of eyeglass frames. Binder jetting involves the deposition of an adhesive binder onto thin layers of powdered material ceramic-based, such as glass or plaster, or metal-based, such as stainless steel. After printing, the parts are in an incomplete state and require further post-processing before they are ready for use. The purposes of use are also similar to Matirial jetting. Technologies using metal powders, are among the most widely used in the automotive, aerospace and medical industries. With these 3D printing technologies called Powder Bed Fusion (PBF), geometrically complex products can be generated through an energy source, mainly laser beams (SLS-SLM) or electron beams (EBM), to fuse the powder particles layer by layer, thus forming a solid part. The main materials used in the SLS 3D printing process include polyamide (nylon), aluminum (a mixture of gray aluminum powder and polyamide) and rubber-like materials. Nylon is a durable material and also offers some flexibility, which makes it widely used for clips and spring functions. Designers using these technologies must take into account the susceptibility to shrinkage and deformation of the parts during the design phase, as there is a change in the final dimensions as the molded parts cool. While SLM (Selective Laser Melting) technology uses the same technical principle, it is used exclusively to produce metal parts. Electron Beam Melting (EBM) is also part of the powder bed melting category. EBM achieves melting using a high-energy electron beam and produces less residual stress resulting in less distortion. Compared to SLM technology, less energy is used during this process and stacked parts can be produced with supports that do not need to start from the printing plate and layers can be produced faster. Another PBF technology is Multi Jet Fusion (MJF), which differs from the previous methods in that it uses an inkjet die to apply fusing and detailing agents, which are then fused by heating the elements. Directed Energy Deposition (DED) 3D printing technology is the one that conceptually comes closest to FDM, but instead of having Cartesian or delta axes of motion, it uses 5-axis robotic arms so it has more freedom of movement. DED creates parts by directly melting materials and depositing them on the part, layer by layer. This AM technique uses metal powders that are deposited at the desired location and fused through a laser or electron beam. In addition to the ability to build parts from scratch (often with the hybridization of a CNC milling/rotating tool), DED is also capable of repairing complex damaged parts, such as turbine blades or propellers. The 3D printing technique of sheet lamination (SL), also known as LOM (Laminated Object Manufacturing) involves layering several layers of material composed of a sheet to produce an object. Each sheet represents a printing layer and can be colored by "normal inkjet" and then cut to the defined shape with a blade or laser, stacked and glued to the previous layer. The prevailing use is mainly the production of non-functional prototypes to be obtained in a very short time at very low cost.

2 Additive Manufacturing in the Aerospace Industry

In industry, new AM technologies were initially seen as the solution to all needs and, in some cases, this intuition has proven to be valid by meeting the needs of each individual end user. The implementation of AM techniques brings benefits to the design processes in terms of creativity and product customization, in addition to the reduction of raw materials needed and waste materials produced and consequently the reduction of product manufacturing costs (Fig. 1). Through AM techniques there is a significant increase in the so-called "buy-to-fly ratio", which represents the ratio between the weight of raw material used for a product and the weight of the product itself, which in the case of AM tends to 1, significantly reducing the waste of materials. On the other hand, some still consider AM as a supplement to traditional manufacturing, to be used for non-functional, but purely aesthetic components and prototypes; this might be true if we refer to the previous performance of 3D printers, but today this view is overcome thanks to the development of printing techniques and technologies [4]. With the advent of 3D printing technologies, it is possible to rethink traditional design methods to propose new ones. Especially in the field of engineering, there is a need to rethink Design for Manufacturability (DFM) from the potential expressed by AM. Some of the methods that can be used for "Additive Design" can provide the product to be printed with features that were previously unthinkable with other manufacturing processes. Typical DfAM methods primarily include topological optimization, design for multi-scale structures, multi-material design, mass customization, part consolidation, and the use of lattice structures. Often, DfAM-related methods can be used in conjunction with classical DFM methods, such as for Electron Beam Melting (EBM) molded parts. In fact, objects molded with EBM technology have a very rough surface and are often post-processed with a CNC machine to make them smoother and specially to create holes where needed. Starting from these requirements, it is necessary to carefully rethink the whole process of designing an object, so that it is possible to make it light by exploiting the potential granted in the freedom of shapes and considering that it is possible to simplify a system of components by reducing their number. AM has also made the production of die-casting and material injection molds more efficient and immediate in small batch production where conventional tools such as CNC milled molds and EDM molds are expensive. Integrated Rapid Tooling enables rapid mold development, optimizing the product in a short period of time and at a low cost, while being able to incorporate cooling channels to increase the overall speed of the production process. However, even these molds are usually designed as a solid leading to a major waste of resources.

"AM is well suited for lightweight design because of the layering process. The core of the mold can be emptied completely or in a timely manner without increasing the production effort. As a result, material consumption can be minimized. However, the molds in this process con-temporarily lose stiffness, which means that the required production accuracy cannot be achieved. This represents an optimization problem between low material consumption and low build time while maintaining sufficient mold stiffness." [5] AM, especially in aerospace, has become essential as components are redesigned for significant weight reduction, which translates into immediate effects on fuel consumption and environmental impact. There are many examples in the literature of the potential of AM in this area, such as the consolidation of General Electric parts in the Cessna Denali aircraft where 12 AM components replace 855 components made by traditional manufacturing methods with a 5% weight reduction, reduced fuel consumption and increased power. Another significant example comes from Asco Industries with The Gooseneck Bracket that acts as a hinge between the Krüger flap and the wing structure. The buy-to-fly ratio of the conventionally made components is about 17, meaning they started with a block weighing about 34 kg to have a final product that weighs only 2 kg. While the buy-to-fly ratio of the AM version is reduced to 1.5 including the support material. The optimized weight of the new com-ponent is 1.4 kg, which corresponds to a 31% weight reduction. In addition, two more components have been integrated, reducing overall assembly time. The possibility of reducing the weight of the components of a vehicle, is optimal to reduce emissions while maintaining performance. For the moment, this feature is mainly used in motor sports, but as seen for other technologies, the step is short to bring to market new products with these features that will be very important in the future sustainable mobility. DfAM, therefore, can help to rethink and redesign an object in a more efficient way and improve the whole production system. The main goal of such an approach is to rethink the design from the roots in order to abandon the old production approaches and have a product conceived and designed to be made with additive technologies. Over the years, designers have absorbed DFM methods as an approach to abandon old design approaches.

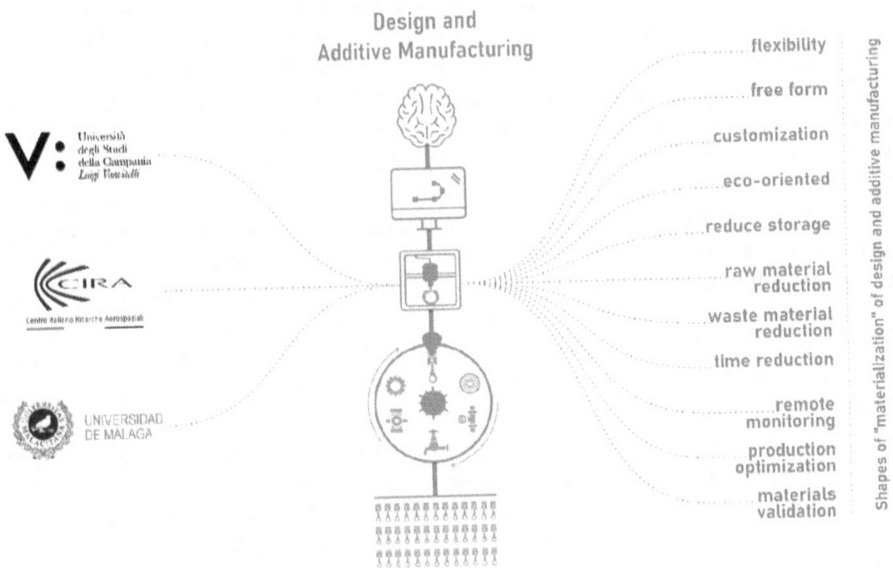

Fig. 1. Shapes of "materialization" of design and additive manufacturing

3 Shapes of "Materialization" of Design and Additive Manufacturing

The DfAM approach enables the extension of the range and configuration of manufactured goods, not only through the diversification of existing products but also by giving rise to new shapes of "materialization" of design and production [6]. This approach removes the constraints of traditional design and production methods by using new tools, it is a production-oriented approach to solution configuration to create lightweight, customized and high-performance solutions, reducing the distances between the design and production phases in order to reduce the time to market [7]. The designer approaching DfAM must consider that it can include functional improvements through a multi-scale approach. These design methods are divided into three groups based on the design scales: mesoscale if they deal with dimensions between 0.1 and 10 mm [8]; macroscale for features larger than the time scale and microscale for smaller features. These three methods can be integrated into different parts of the same project without having to go through different manufacturing processes. On a macroscale, structural optimization is the commonly used method for structural parts that are intended to support loads. In general, these structural optimization methods are characterized by size optimization; shape optimization; and topology optimization. Therefore, on a mesoscale, "Lattice" structures are used to achieve features and performance to reduce weight as well [9] To facilitate the reading of these structures we will divide them into two types. The disordered cellular structure i.e. cellular units with different sizes and shapes are randomly distributed within the design space. Lattice structure, on the other hand, is identified by a periodic cellular structure that can be considered as a three-dimensional structure created by a regular repetition of a unitary object with a predefined shape. Unlike the disordered cell structure, only a unit cell that is a small portion of the periodic cell structure is required to determine its physical properties. Currently, the DfAM methods used lead the designer to rely on algorithms for shape optimization based on the constraints and rules established in order to fit the Lattice structures into the body of the object to be designed. Topological optimization is a technique used to make objects lightweight without losing their structural characteristics. This optimization is done by subtracting material where it is not needed. But the use of software for topological optimization must be a targeted tool for redesigning structures, often, the use of these tools is relegated to only replacing a solid solid with Lattice structures, which allow the reduction of weight and material [10]. This is not an optimal way to exploit AM and topological optimization because it is too closely tied to design directed at other manufacturing methods. From this consideration, designers' tools and approaches must be reconfigured to govern the process of form design and optimization using additive technologies. The new shapes of "materialization" are designed as purely dynamic and flexible with a systemic design approach of interdependencies between components allowing for adaptation and evolution, to manage complexity by analyzing the overall context and not the individual parts.

4 Conclusions

Design and AM allow to transfer and accelerate innovative processes in local areas where technological and digital practices are not present and to increase productivity and competitiveness in the international market through a systemic and eco-sustainable approach to respond properly to change in the manufacturing industry. Therefore, the adoption of new design methods and techniques to support AM ensures the strengthening of the industrial framework, according to the integration approach of knowledge and applied research in processes, through sustainable production and consumption models, reduction of capital needed to achieve an economy of scale and reduction of capital needed to achieve an economy of purpose, in other words, the diversification of production in the same production facility. As mentioned previously, mobility is one of the application areas that will benefit most from these technologies. The possibility of reducing the weight of the components of a vehicle is optimal for reducing emissions while maintaining performance. Today, the first critical issue for designers to address is to acquire the necessary skills and know-how to design the additive in a focused way. On the one hand, training closely with companies using the technology will be important for 3d printing machine manufacturers, establishing a two-way flow of information and protocols to improve the performance of products and printing tools.

References

1. Horn, T.J., Harrysson, O.L.A.: Overview of current additive manufacturing technologies and selected applications. Sci. Prog. **95**(3), 255–282 (2012). https://doi.org/10.3184/003685012X13420984463047
2. Yigit, I.E., Isa, M., Lazoglu, I.: Additive manufacturing with modular support structures. In: Solid Freeform Fabrication 2018: Proceedings of the 29th Annual International Solid Freeform Fabrication Symposium – An Additive Manufacturing Conference (2018)
3. Rimmer, M.: 3D printing, the maker movement, IP litigation and legal reform. WIPO Mag. (5), 40–45 (2019). https://ssrn.com/abstract=3628122
4. Junk, S., Tränkle, M.: Design for Additive Manufacturing technologies: new applications of 3d-printing for rapid prototyping and rapid tooling. In: International Conference on Engineering Design, ICED 2011. The Design Society (2011)
5. Lušić, M., Barabanov, A., Morina, D., Feuerstein, F., Hornfeck, R.: Towards zero waste in additive manufacturing: a case study investigating one pressurised rapid tooling mould to ensure resource efficiency. Procedia CIRP **37**, 54–58 (2015). https://doi.org/10.1016/j.procir.2015.08.022. ISSN 2212-8271
6. Pradel, P., Zhu, Z., Bibb, R., Moultrie, J.: Investigation of design for additive manufacturing in professional design practice. J. Eng. Des. **29**(4–5), 165–200 (2018). https://doi.org/10.1080/09544828.2018.1454589
7. Bitonti. F.: 3D Printing Design: Additive Manufacturing and the Materials Revolution. Bloomsbury Visual Arts (2019)
8. Michopoulos, J.G., Iliopoulos, A.P., Steuben, J.C., Birnbaum, A.J., Lambrakos, S.G.: On the multiphysics modeling challenges for metal additive manufacturing processes. Add. Manuf. **22**, 784–799 (2018). https://doi.org/10.1016/j.addma.2018.06.019. ISSN 2214-8604

9. Tang, Y.: A multiscale and multifunctional design method for mesoscale lattice structures fabricated by additive manufacturing processes (Doctoral dissertation, McGill University Libraries) (2018)
10. Ferro, C.G., Mazza, A., Belmonte, D., Seclì, C., Maggiore, P.: A comparison between 3d printing and milling process for a spar cap fitting (Wing-fuselage) of UAV aircraft. Procedia CIRP **62**, 487–493 (2017). https://doi.org/10.1016/j.procir.2016.06.028. ISSN 2212-8271

Human-Centered-Design for Definition of New Collaborative Scenarios

Fabrizio Formati(✉), Elena Laudante, and Mario Buono

Department of Engineering, University of Campania Luigi Vanvitelli, 81031 Aversa, Italy
{fabrizio.formati,elena.laudante,mario.buono}@unicampania.it

Abstract. Recent technological advances have changed user-centered design criteria in industrial work contexts. The growing potential of technologies is changing industrial activity, in particular the use of collaborative robots able to involve the production operator.

Starting from the study of the regulatory framework of the Robotics and the state of the art, the paper provides an overview of the different categorizations in the literature related to human-robot collaboration through the identification of illustrative industrial application associated with these categories.

From a Human-Centered perspective and through the methods and approaches of the design discipline, the contribution proposes new evolutionary scenarios for the identification of "implementations" to be introduced in collaborative robotics, where human-robot interaction methods optimize the production process in terms of predictability, reliability and usability.

It will be possible to focus on regulatory aspects and on the hypothesis of new regulatory tools and protocols needed to clearly and effectively define human-robot interactions.

Keywords: Manufacturing industry · Human-oriented · Collaborative categories · Intelligent systems · Robotic standards

1 Introduction

From the analysis of industrial contexts, the collaboration between production operator and robotic system allows the increase of productivity and the improvement of working conditions through the reduction of health risks and the definition of innovative technological paths for the improvement of the production performance, product quality and safety of production operators. The evolution of the industry is therefore characterized by the synergy between robotic capabilities and human skills [1] for the definition of efficient and human-centered production systems [2].

The increase in production speed – supported by the use of technologies – makes it possible to raise the level of efficiency and productivity and therefore it is necessary to pay special attention to the human factor, safety and well-being of the user who interfaces with the robot. In fact, the massive use of robotic solutions in industrial environments leads to the optimization of production processes and the identification

D. Raposo et al. (Eds.): AHFE 2021, LNNS 277, pp. 78–85, 2021.
https://doi.org/10.1007/978-3-030-80415-2_10

of new solutions and "smart" workstations based on physical, cognitive, sensory, social and emotional interaction between man and robot for the enhancement of human capital. Industrial workspace management imposes new requirements to satisfy such as the reliability and safety of the users who generally use robots and work in spaces dedicated to collaborative robotics [3]. Current collaborative robots have limitations in "interactions" and insufficient safety protocols exist suggesting the need to rethink factors related to human-robot interaction and adaptability of robotic systems through the correct safety assessment of the system to be deployed. Previously, no user was allowed to cross the robotic cell, but thanks to technological and regulatory advances – albeit slow ones – human-robot interaction is now allowed.

However, without concrete safety guarantees, users are not allowed to work with robots in the immediate vicinity. In fact, collaborative tasks require a shared location, simultaneous efforts, less rigid physical barriers, or only in some cases absent [4]. The implementation of collaborative systems defines the paradigm shift from traditional methods of ensuring the safety of production operators without the use of fences or light barriers [5]. The issue of safety assessment for the user in the performance of collaborative tasks is an essential component in the evaluation of human-robot systems. The paper, in this sense, investigates the collaborative workspace and the activity of the robotic system in relation to the user-operator. In particular, industrial interaction environments are identified through the analysis of collaboration that meets regulatory requirements and safety standards that affect the user during the performance of operations.

2 Human Robot Collaboration in Production Processes

The transition of manufacturing towards the adoption of collaborative systems projects, manufacturing systems towards the development of the factory that proactively responds to changing market demands. The inclusion of robotic systems in the industrial fields, aims to implement "smart" workstations by optimizing human-robot interactions. This approach changes the concept of work and invests in new skills aimed at smart, sustainable, and inclusive growth by improving autonomy in automation processes. The Human-Robot Collaboration methodology changes the design criteria of collaborative workstations and foreshadows innovative ways of future production, aiming to identify the cells that benefit most from the application of collaborative robotics. Human Robot Collaboration refers to ISO Technical Specification TS/15066[1] which integrates the provisions and information on the operation of collaborative industrial robots given in ISO 10218-1[2] and ISO 10218-2[3] and provides guidance for the operation of collaborative systems that share the same workspace as people, where process parameters such as speed and force are controlled.

1 ISO/TS 15066. Robots and Robotic Devices: Collaborative Robots; International Organization for Standardization: Geneva, Switzerland, 2016.

2 ISO 10218-1. Robots and Robotic Devices—Safety Requirements for Industrial Robots—Part 1: Robots; International Organization for Standardization: Geneva, Switzerland, 2011.

3 ISO 10218-2. Robots and Robotic Devices—Safety Requirements for Industrial Robots—Part 1: Robot Systems and Integration; International Organization for Standardization: Geneva, Switzerland, 2011.

It is mainly based on the collection of data of the performance parameters deriving from the analysis of the ergonomic factors and of the position of the user-operator with respect to the robotic system in the production line as well as from the analysis of the times and of the logistic system in order to improve the performance in carrying out the tasks in a collaborative perspective.

In particular, the ISO/TS 15066 technical specification responds to the new needs that have emerged from the implementation of collaborative robotic systems within industrial production contexts and the need to provide concrete answers in terms of safety, defined as a tool in favor of collaboration between robots and human operators [6]. ISO/TS 15066 regulates robotic operating cells, according to different applications without the inclusion of protective perimeter cages. Through the application of safety measures on various levels and the definition of invisible barriers with boundaries not to be crossed, the robotic system slows down to a standstill in case of unsafe contact with the operator.

3 Categorizations of Human-Robot Collaborations

The prospect of configuring a robot as a human "collaborator" currently represents one of the most encouraging frontiers of the industrial world able to meet the needs of fields and to ensure precision, efficiency, and flexibility. The Human-Robot Collaboration is able to effectively perform collaborative actions, reducing costs, safely, and preserving the specific skills and abilities of operators in interactions by enabling ergonomic reconfiguration of production processes.

Different modes of classifying human-robot collaboration can be found in the literature in the context of industrial scenarios, starting from the classification realized to describe the three levels of collaboration identified by Shi et al. [7] based on the possibility of sharing the workspace and the way the robot operates and moves. In detail, low level collaborations are considered when the user does not enter the robot's field of work; medium level when the robot's servo systems are disengaged while the human is present; high level when the robot has the possibility to be close to the human to perform simultaneous actions.

In the same year, Someshwar et al. [8] introduced time and synchronization in relation to cooperative task performance. They then describe how the robotic system can be activated in three different ways: time-dependent based on previously established fixed intervals; sensor-dependent on the system where the robot adapts its actions to those of the user; and finally the environmental parameters that take into account buffering and the presence of single and multiple robots, exclusive or shared tasks, and repetitive or single processes. A further categorization is offered to us by Michalos et al. [9] who describe task sharing through various levels of interaction to optimize the synergy between user and system. In detail, they classify: the shared task and workspace, the shared task in separate workspaces, and finally the shared task and workspace with the inactive state of one component at a time. Subsequently, Cesta et al. [3] realize a categorization based on the degree of spatial and temporal interdependence of the tasks of each agent. The different categories identified are shown below: independent in which for individual production processes the robot and the operator work on separate parts independently (Fig. 1).

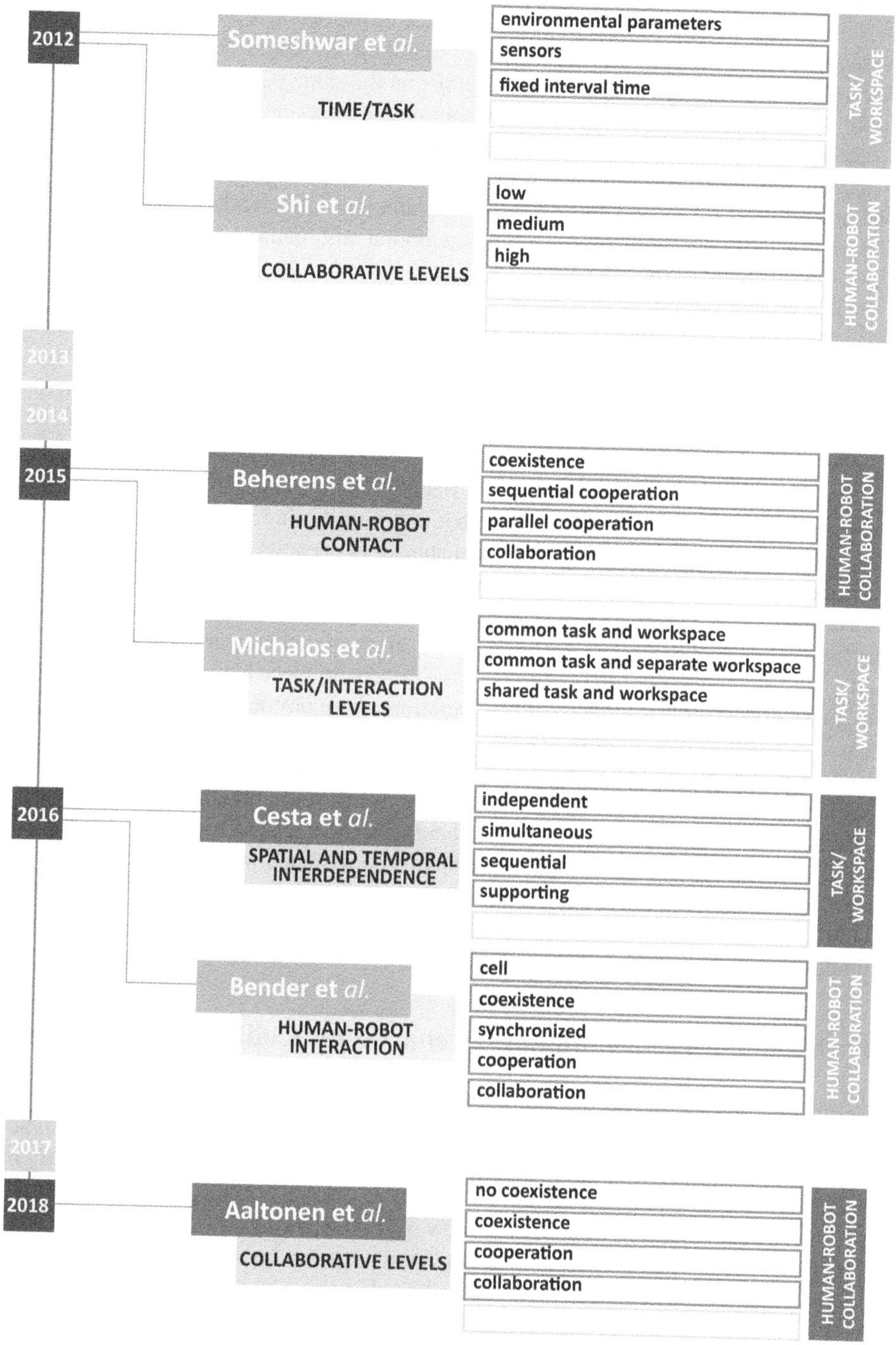

Fig. 1. Evolution of human-robot collaborative characterization typologies.

Collaboration occurs through the co-presence of the operator and robot in the same workspace without protection and enclosure; simultaneous where the cobot and operator work simultaneously but on separate processes on the same part; sequential where the cobot and operator perform sequential machining processes on the same part.

In this situation there are time dependencies between the robot and the operator and a machining process performed by the cobot represents an input needed to support the operator in the next task; support where the operator and cobot work in the same process and on the same part interactively, defining temporal and spatial dependencies between the actions of both.

The five levels of interaction described by Bender et al. [10] are interesting to investigate the relationship between robots and operators after analyzing several industrial applications such as coexistence, assembly, and interaction. The identified levels are cell without cooperation, coexistence with non-shared workspace, synchrony involving the presence of the robot or the user, cooperation with shared spaces and non-simultaneous tasks, and finally collaboration with simultaneous work on the same product.

Further classification was defined by Behrens et al. [11] taking into account the presence of physical contact between cobot and human, and in detail, the categories identified are coexistence where adequate distances or separation structures are present, without physical overlap between the work areas of the two agents; sequential cooperation during which physical contact can occur and where on the same workpiece in order, the human and the cobot perform successive tasks; parallel cooperation where human and robot simultaneously perform tasks on the same workpiece in the shared workspace, but physical contact is excluded; and cooperation where physical contact is essential in joint and simultaneous actions.

As reported by Aaltonen et al. [12], collaboration must be expressed through the use of multiple factors to obtain the satisfactory and clear classification, proposing a classification model based on four levels of collaboration: no coexistence where there is physical separation between humans and robots; coexistence where humans work with robots in shared space but without shared goals; cooperation where humans and robots work for a common goal in a shared space; collaboration where humans and robots work simultaneously on a shared object in a shared space (Fig. 1).

4 Defining New Evolutionary Scenarios for Collaborative Robotics

Starting from the categorization realized by Aaltonen et al. [12], the different "interpretations" of human-robot interactions of the authors have been individually analyzed, implementing the work done through representative illustrations of collaborative applications found in industrial contexts (Fig. 2).

Subsequently, starting from the overview of the different categorizations in the literature and the identification of reference applications, it was possible to propose a further classification that takes into account the technical specification ISO/TS 15066 of 2016 "Robot and robotic devices - Collaborative robots" and refers to the criteria for assessing the risks generated by the use of collaborative robots and the levels of safety such as to be able to work next to operators without danger (Fig. 2).

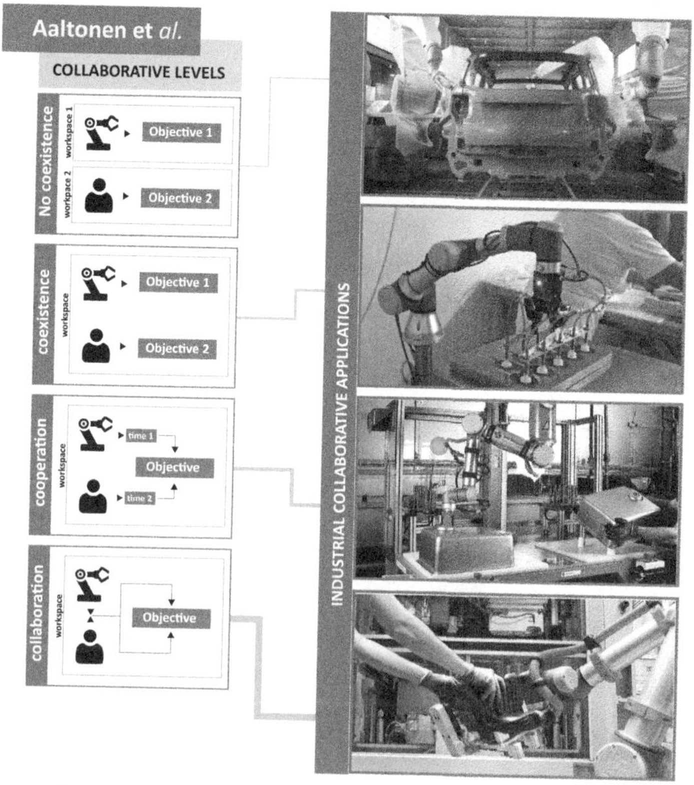

Fig. 2. Correspondence between characterizations identified by Aaltonen et al. and industrial applications.

The proposed categorization is in line with the operations foreseen by the above-mentioned regulation in particular:

- safety monitored stop that links robotic systems with workspaces where the robot acts alone and interacts occasionally with the user-operator;
- speed and separation monitoring that considers the minimum safety distance detected that the user-operator must respect through the use of scanners and vision systems and if not, the robot reduces its speed of action until it stops;
- hand guiding where the operator comes into contact with the cobot to guide the robotic arm and plan the desired trajectory through kinaesthetic learning modes;
- power and force limiting where the cobot is able to sense abnormal force levels by detecting excessive loads so as to stop and dissipate forces in case of impact [6]. In addition, the new classification considers the design criteria in EN ISO 13849-1[4] "Safety of machinery - Safety-related parts of the control system - General principles for design", which provides instructions for implementing safe systems (Fig. 3).

[4] ISO 13849-1. Safety of Machinery—Safety-related parts of control systems—Part 1: General principles for design; International Organization for Standardization: Geneva, Switzerland, 2015.

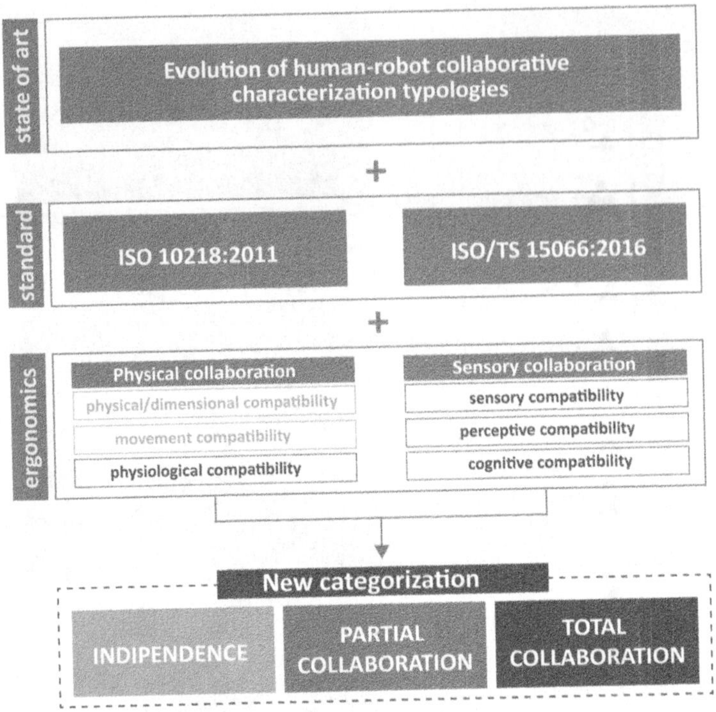

Fig. 3. Levels of construction of new collaborative categorization.

The classification implements the previously outlined levels of collaboration and focuses on the previous cases introduced by Behrens et al. [11], Cesta et al. [3], and Aaltonen et al. [12], while making a simplification of the subcategories into Independence, Partial Collaboration, and Total Collaboration. The Independence category includes examples of non-direct human-robot interaction, where no physical contact occurs but they can coexist even in the same workspace. Partial collaboration includes cases in which there is contact between humans and robots, but only from a physical point of view. Finally, in the Total Collaboration category, factors related to the sensory-cognitive sphere are evaluated in addition to physical interactions. Effectively, in the previous categorizations, all the factors analyzed were always found to be strictly physical in nature. Instead, the proposed implementation considers the possibility of making humans and robots interact also from a sensory and cognitive point of view through the analysis of sensory, perceptual, and cognitive compatibilities (Fig. 3). This process will allow the analysis and design of possible interactions between humans and robots for the implementation of safety levels in the use of new collaborative systems.

5 Conclusions

Actually, the use of collaborative robotic systems favors the study of human-robot interaction, opening new scenarios and new fields of research. The collaborative robot together with the tools of Industry 4.0 and digital manufacturing, represent valid solutions with which to meet the needs of product customization.

We are now talking about Industry 5.0, which will strengthen robot-human collaboration in an inclusive, human-centric manufacturing future that will define collaborative systems no longer as innovative tools but as concrete options applied in the industrial world.

The research has provided a framework within the categorizations of human-robot collaboration present in the literature until the definition of new collaborative modes, implementing the previous approaches characterized by the analysis of physical factors through the inclusion of additional factors of sensory-cognitive type while maintaining in the foreground the safety of human-robot interactions, defined by current standards of reference.

References

1. Krüger, J., Lien, T.K., Verl, A.: Cooperation of human and machines in assembly lines. CIRP Ann. **58**, 628–646 (2009)
2. Gualtieri, L., Monizza, G.P., Rauch, E., Vidoni, R., Matt, D.T.: From design for assembly to design for collaborative assembly - product design principles for enhancing safety, ergonomics and efficiency in human-robot collaboration. Procedia CIRP **91**, 546–552 (2020)
3. Cesta, A., Orlandini, A., Bernardi, G., Umbrico, A.: Towards a Planning-based Framework for Symbiotic Human-Robot Collaboration. IEEE 21st International Conference on Emerging Technologies and Factory Automation (ETFA), pp. 1–8. (2016)
4. Pervez, A., Ryu, J.: Safe physical human robot interaction-past, present and future. J. Mech. Sci. Technol. **22**(3), 469 (2008)
5. Franklin, C.S., Dominguez, E.G., Fryman, J.D., Lewandowski, M.L.: Collaborative robotics: New era of human–robot cooperation in the workplace. J. Safety Res. **74**, 153–160 (2020)
6. Vicentini, F.: La robotica collaborativa. Sicurezza e flessibilità delle nuove forme di collaborazione uomo-robot. Tecniche Nuove, p. 25 (2017)
7. Shi, J., Jimmerson, G., Pearson, T., Menassa, R.: Levels of human and robot collaboration for automotive manufacturing. In: Performance Metrics for Intelligent Systems (PerMIS) Workshop, December, pp. 95–100 (2012)
8. Someshwar, R., Meyer, J., Edan, Y.: Models and methods for H-R synchronization. IFAC Proc. Vol. **45**(6), 829–834 (2012)
9. Michalos, G., Makris, S., Tsarouchi, P., Guasch, T., Kontovrakis, D., Chryssolouris, G.: Design considerations for safe human-robot collaborative workplaces. Procedia CIRP **37**(2), 48–53 (2015)
10. Bender, M., Braun, M., Rally, P., Scholtz, O.: Lightweight robots in manual assembly – best to start simply. Examining companies' initial experiences with lightweight robots. In: Bauer, W. (ed.) Report. Fraunhofer Institute for Industrial Engineering IAO (2016)
11. Behrens, R., Saenz, J., Vogel, C., Elkmann, N.: Upcoming technologies and fundamentals for safeguarding all forms of human-robot collaboration. In: Proceedings of the 8th International Conference on the Safety of Industrial Automated Systems (SIAS), Königswinter, Germany, pp. 18–23 (2015)
12. Aaltonen, I., Salmi, T., Marstio, I.: Refining levels of collaboration to support the design and evaluation of human-robot interaction in the manufacturing industry. Procedia CIRP **72**, 93–98 (2018)

Information Design and the Hermeneutic Process of Knowledge

Maria Luísa Costa[1,2](✉) and Sílvia Rala[1,2]

1 CIAUD, Faculdade de Arquitetura da Universidade de Lisboa, Rua Sá Nogueira, Polo Universitário da Ajuda, 1349-063 Lisbon, Portugal

2 Instituto Superior Miguel Torga, Largo da Cruz de Celas nº1, Coimbra, Portugal

Abstract. In this article, we start from a literature review on the concept of Information Design and analyze how and why the hermeneutic process of knowledge construction can be applied to visual information systems. We present several typological approaches associated with Information Design, such as Diagrammatic Design, Schematic Design, Infographic Design, and Wayfinding Design, sometimes with common or different graphic characteristics, the greater or lesser complexity associated with it and how the elements that constitute the language and visual grammar contribute to the organization, systematization, and understanding of the information produced in this context.

Keywords: Information Design · Diagrams · Infographics · Wayfinding systems · Hermeneutic process

1 Introduction

The field of Information Design covers various formal applications and different graphic approaches. Examples of this are graphics, pictograms, diagrams, illustrations, maps, signage, technical, educational, or scientific drawings, in which we can use various representation resources and even the combination of several such as photography, drawing, illustration, color, and text, to convey information. The understanding of this information is not immediate, and it derives from an interpretation process based on the interaction between the whole and the parts that constitute the design object and the context in which it is presented. This comprehension process is referential since everything we understand derives from a knowledge we have a priori and from the connections we thus manage to establish.

According to Bonsiepe [1], information design is a way to communicate complex data, articulating several visual communication elements that aim to transform primary data into information. That communication is structured based on a visual grammar composed of expressive and symbolic elements. Which constitute a visual language and, considering that, like any language, this one is likely to be interpreted and understood, we analyzed which media are recurrently used in the context of Information Design, the designations, and functionalities assigned to them by different authors regarding diagrams, infographics, wayfinding systems, and maps, as well as how they enable the transmission of information and what are the underlying objectives.

D. Raposo et al. (Eds.): AHFE 2021, LNNS 277, pp. 86–92, 2021.
https://doi.org/10.1007/978-3-030-80415-2_11

2 Design as a Visual Language and the Hermeneutic Process of Knowledge

A language is a communicational resource that takes various forms but, in order for it to be effective, it implies that all members of a given group share the meaning associated with a standard body of information [2], know its grammar, which in the case of visual communication is as Leborg [3] states the same as that of any other language, it defines the basic elements, the relationship processes existing between them and the way in which through these elements communication systems are created.

Line, point, plan, shape, size, color, but also structures and the relationships that are established between all the elements, create systems that are sources of information and need to be interpreted and understood so that this information is transformed into knowledge, i.e., we reach the knowledge through a hermeneutic process of understanding that results from the interaction between the whole and the parts that compose it. In this sense, we consider the information design as a visual language, liable to be understood through the hermeneutic process of knowledge.

From literature to medicine, different areas proceed to hermeneutic analyses as processes of data interpretation and translation, aiming at a comprehensive understanding.

Thus, hermeneutics can be understood as the science that seeks to understand and interpret the meanings inherent in a given discourse to achieve comprehension [4].

Palmer [5] refers that Dilthey saw in hermeneutics the central discipline that would serve as a basis to all the disciplines centered on understanding art, behavior, and writing. Ricoeur [6] understands hermeneutics as a set of rules that enable interpretation of a text or set of signs that can be considered as texts and, as such, interpreted.

According to Palmer [5], signification has to do with context, the explanatory process being the space of understanding; that is, a narrative or event only has meaning within a specific context.

Still, for the same author, understanding happens via a dialectical interaction between the parts and the whole, where each one will give meaning to the other, in what is called a hermeneutic circle, since understanding consists of a referential procedure, that is, we only understand something by comparison with something we know. "What we understand is grouped into systematic units or circles composed of parts. The circle as a whole defines the individual part, and the parts together form the circle." [5].

In this interaction and dialogue between the whole and the parts resides the understanding and knowledge in the systems' scope generated in the information design context.

3 Information Design

Information Design is the representation of information in a visual format that can include visualizing data, processes, hierarchy, anatomy, chronology, and other facts [7]. The visualization of information has different sources: images, signs, symbols, schemes, and texts, perceived at different hierarchical levels with iconic, schematic, and symbolic decoding, transformed into information with the conceptual purpose [8].

Wildbur e Burke [9] define Information Design as the selection, organization, and presentation of an idea to a particular audience. According to the authors, the areas of information design can originate from almost any source, such as weather map, timetable listing flight departures, statistical data, orientation on a map or signage system, and can represent a vast content, where the user needs to extract what is needed for a particular purpose.

Tufte [10] states that the principles of Information Design are universal and independent of a particular language or culture; they result from the intersection between image, text, numbers, and art, which we can articulate in charts, diagrams, graphs, tables, guides, instructions, directories and maps.

Concerning terminology, we find that theorists and designers sometimes title information Design as Diagrammatic Design, Schematic Design, Infographic Design and Wayfinding Design.

Holmes [11], a graphic designer and theorist of the graphic information area, titles Information Design as Diagrammatic Design and divides it into categories: diagrams, maps, architecture, and other designs. Similarly, Perderson [12] divides the area of diagrams into: statistical and comparative, flow and organization, technical and functional, maps and plans, architectural, and finally, scientific and medical.

On the other hand, Costa [8] calls Schematic Design the Information Design, and considers it the graphic design area that operates with a didactic, informative, professional, and dissemination function. According to the author, the world of schematic visualization is characterized by its utility, is defined by the motivations of the target audience, and is expressed by different types of graphic language in three fields of action: that of scientific research, that of the technique and that of everyday practice, divided into families, characterized by schemes: of reality, of structures, of relationships, of history, of the analysis of results and the presentation of textual data (not phenomena or demonstrative), with more significant predominance in cartographies, organigrams, diagrams, histograms, and semantograms.

Another term also commonly used in the medium is Infographic Design. The word "infographics" results from the contraction of "information" and "graphics" [13]. Sancho [14] defines infographics as an informative narrative, prepared with iconic and typographic elements, enabling or making it possible to understand significant events, actions, or facts. It is considered to have eight essential characteristics: 1) to give meaning to information, 2) to guarantee conformity with current events, 3) to enable the understanding of the message, 4) to contain written information with textual elements, 5) to contain perceptible iconic elements, 6) to include relevant content or to have a synthesis or complementary function, 7) to have an aesthetic concern, 8) to have no errata or lack of concordance.

For Kanno and Brandão [15], infographics enrich the text with visual elements and embellish the composition making it more attractive.

According to Meirelles [16], in graphic design, two terms are mainly used for information visualization: infographics and information design. He defines infographics as visual compositions, encompassing text illustrations, symbols, maps, diagrams, from complex illustrations of the human body to maps of train or metro routes. On the other hand, he considers that the term 'Information Design' is used to describe communication design practices, where the main objective is to inform and not to advertise, to persuade. He also states that infographics are one of the possible applications and others, such as the design of information systems, wayfinding, and visualization of statistical data.

Concerning the operational purpose of Information Design, it can be seen that the different approaches and classifications are similar by function/field of action (research, dissemination, learning, organizational/orientation), graphic expression/graphic language (iconography, schematic design, technical design, illustration) and applicability to a given target audience (specialists from the various areas or general public). However, we may have different levels of complexity of graphic representation, recourse to various visual elements, and different information analysis phases.

In this framework, Information Design, regarding the graphic representation of geographical territory or dedicated to the projectual development of wayfinding systems flows, different forms of design and levels of complexity may be included, from the schematic/diagrammatic representation, through illustration, to the relation between orientation signs in an area, where drawing, image, pictograms, signage, and text combine to transmit certain cartographic information.

4 Visual Information Systems and Wayfinding

Within the scope of Design, visual information systems are sets formed by interrelated visual and textual components of greater or lesser complexity, whose existence and operation derive from the interaction between the whole and the parts that compose it.

The visualization of information allows an adequate understanding and better management of the vast amount of data that we are recurrently called to process.

Tufte [10] states that it is necessary to work with intersections between images, words, numbers, and art to visualize information.

In this sense, we can identify as part of this group the information produced through diagrams, since these are abstract, structured, and simplified representations of a particular event, process, system, space, or micro or macrostructure, materialized with the line, color, and typography, such as a plan of underground lines and stations.

Infographics are the abbreviation for "information graphics", a term that has become popular with online marketing in recent years. In short, an infographic makes use of visual signals to convey information [7], for these authors, infographics can be as simple as a traffic sign or as complex as an analysis of the global economy.

Infographics are two or three-dimensional diagrams that describe a step-by-step process with the help of iconic, chromatic, and typographic elements, allowing the understanding of complex information, such as the representation of a geographical surface, and may privilege narrative, instructive, exploratory, or simulation aspects.

A wayfinding system consists of a set of visual, textual, and physical information that appeals to the user's sensorial and cognitive interpretation to facilitate access to highly complex spaces.

According to Costa and Amaral [17], wayfinding systems are sets of information elements that facilitate accessibility and enhance citizens' experiences, using, according to Gybson [18], explicit signs and information, as well as implicit signs and landmarks.

Wayfinding systems, which have been studied for decades, are at the core of the development of multiple cognitive science specialties, namely in-depth studies on legibility, color perception, and typographic legibility [19]. We can state that a wayfinding system comprises multiple elements that integrate the information systems mentioned above, namely maps, whose representation can be simplified and diagrammatic or complex and with a three-dimensional expression. "In addition to maps, wayfinding systems integrate a set of signs to inform, identify, guide, functions inherent to signage" [20]. These signs integrate what we call signposting. We can consider it a system inside the other system - the wayfinding - for having visual components, that despite being integrated into the broader system, has particular specificities, both relational and formal or chromatic.

The development of any of these forms of Design is based on multiple primary data, ranging from numerical and statistical to more subjective data, such as physical and identity characteristics and particularities of a space or individuals. The process of collecting, analyzing, and systematizing this data is essential to produce this information. The knowledge of the signs' formal and chromatic characteristics (pictograms, arrows, typography), in their symbolic, denotative, and connotative aspects, to construct information that articulates image and text fulfills the objective of informing.

Thus, the hermeneutic process of knowledge, previously mentioned, should enhance understanding, through 1) expressive aspects (how to say); 2) explain (meaning), relates to the symbolic, historical and connotative aspects of the graphic elements; 3) translate (make accessible), lies in safeguarding the principle of universality and the good understanding of what is graphically represented.

5 Schemes, Maps and Diagrams

As we have seen, the Information Design area can acquire various formal approaches and different graphic languages. Examples of this are maps, diagrams, illustrations, pictograms, and signage. Which may be organized by types with their particularities, contain graphic design features ranging from the simplest to the most complex representation, and may use various representation resources and even the combination of several such as photography, drawing, illustration, color, and text.

The pictorial representations of a schematic nature precede writing in the era of cave paintings [14].

The drawing characteristics of prehistoric art, established through abstraction, transparency, and superimposition, are attributes of the schematic universe's representation. Likewise, the Fatimid era Egyptians needed to deform the drawing of maps or route schemes expressing more the economic and cultural reality than the geographical one [21].

The use of aerial photography in the mid-nineteenth century made it possible to reproduce cartographic or street maps with the representation of scale and precise drawing; however, according to Valero, the cartographic representation of a terrestrial surface requires the reproduction of a faithful drawing; on the other hand, when drawing a map for information purposes, we can ignore the rules of cartography in favor of information [14].

For example, early underground map designs had the basic conception of the place's geographical representation with the underground lines and sometimes drawings of the streets superimposed. In 1931, Harry Beck changed this paradigm by designing the London Underground map, where he organized the "routes into a system of lines all drawn at consistent angles. He structured the typography over a grid and noted the station interchanges symbolically" [18].

Holmes [11] establishes the difference between geographical maps, orienteering maps, and statistical and pictorial maps. When constructing geographic maps, the author fixes a set of lines, coastlines, borders, and places in the territory that cannot be tampered with; if they infringe, the cartographic representations become erroneous. Creating an orienteering map, the designer can disregard, exclude details, and adapt the map to specific needs. On the other hand, there are statistical and pictorial maps, where the designer combines images on a geographical basis for illustration purposes.

The structured and simplified visual representation of a given place, space, system, macro-structure, or micro-structure, according to Haslam [22], can be configured by tree diagrams, linear diagrams, three-dimensional diagrams in two dimensions, and sequence diagrams. The tree diagram representing a system's data relationships with abstract graphical language depicts relationship models as in a family tree. It understands by the linear diagram, representation of relations between points or the crossings without connection with the geographical position, where the use of the color can allow a better hierarchic reading of the linear ways independent of the sequence of intersections, as in the representation of a map of the underground lines. On the other hand, a three-dimensional diagram in two dimensions represents three-dimensional relations, or elements in two dimensions, through the linear drawing of view, perspective, or axonometric projection, as the configuration of a route or geographical area in infographic map with two-dimensional or three-dimensional representation. A sequential diagram represents an action through sequences of abstract or iconic representation, where we can represent a unidirectional route where it is necessary to accomplish a sequence of tasks.

Therefore, the universe of Information Design in the scope of the presentation of routes in places or geographical and spatial areas, diagrams, maps, and wayfinding systems presents different typologies, each with its own potentialities as graphic expression.

In any of these representation domains, the sense of information and meaning must be considered to facilitate the search and discovery and improve the perception and recognition of accurate or theoretical data [16].

6 Conclusions

Graphic representations in the universe of Information Design may result in a synthetic drawing to represent an idea that one wants to be easily recognized by what it intends to represent, which is elucidative and easy to understand, accessible to the user whom it is addressed. Since an abstract idea or notion may be expressed literally, concretely, iconically, or abstractly, a schematic/diagrammatic design may be a leveled or accentuated design, reduced to an expressive synthesis situated between the literal and the abstract. However, within a leveled logic, it may also be a very complex composition.

Information Design encompasses different information systems ranging from schemes, diagrams, infographics, and maps to complex systems like wayfinding that may include all the previously mentioned systems to make complex information accessible by making it as universal as possible.

For that, Information Design makes use of the visual language, the basic elements, and the existing relations between them, searching for the most appropriate register and expressiveness to make its results - the efficient communication, considering the graphic efficacy and the complexity of the visible and invisible world, in the construction of a precise and impartial narrative. The choice of visual language, or what we refer to as its expressive aspects, where the symbolic, historical and connotative aspects of the graphic elements are crucial to make the information accessible, safeguarding the principle of universality and a good understanding of what is graphically represented, facilitating the process of dialectical interaction between the parts and the whole, in a hermeneutic process of understanding and knowledge.

References

1. Bonsiepe, G.: Design Cultura e Sociedade. Blucher, S. Paulo (2011)
2. Donis, D.A.: La Sintaxis de la Imagen: Introducción al alfabeto visual. Gustavo Gili, SL, Barcelona (2011)
3. Legorg, C.: Gramática Visual. Gustavo Gili, SL, Barcelona (2014)
4. Figueira, L. Sampaio, D. Afonso, P.: Manual de Psiquiatria Clínica. Ed Lidel, Lisboa (2014)
5. Palmer, R.E.: Hermenêutica. Edições 70, Lisboa, p. 93 (1969)
6. Ricoeur P. de L'interpretation, essai sur Freud. Ed du Seuil, Paris (1965)
7. Lankow, J., Ritchie, J., Ross, C.R.: The Power of Visual Storytelling Infographics. Wiley, Canada (2012)
8. Costa, J.: La Esquemática: Visualizar la información. Paidós, Barcelona (1998)
9. Wildbur, P., Burke, M.: Information Graphics: Innovative in Contemporary Design. Thames and Hudson, London (1998)
10. Tufte, E.R.: Envisioning Information. Connecticut. Graphic Press, Cheschire (2013)
11. Holmes, N.: Best in Diagrammatic Graphics. Rotovision, USA (1996)
12. Perderson, B.: Graphis Diagrams 2: The International Showcase of Diagram Design and Technical Illustration. Graphis Inc., New York (1997)
13. Smiciklas, M.: The Power of Infographics: Using Pictures to Communicate and Connect with Your Audiences. Que Publishing, Indianapolis (2012)
14. Sancho, J.: La infografía: técnicas, análisis y usos periodísticos. Universitat de València, Barcelona (2001)
15. Kanno, M., Brandão, R.: Manual de infografia. Folha, São Paulo (1998)
16. Meirelles, I.: Design for Information. Rockport Publishers, USA (2013)
17. Costa, M.L., Amaral, I.: Cidades e Sistemas Wayfinding. Convergências - Revista de Investigação e Ensino das Artes, vol XI (21) (2018). http://convergencias.ipcb.pt
18. Gibson, D.: The Wayfinding Handbook: Information Design for Public Places, p. 40. Princeton Architectural Press, New York (2009)
19. Berger, C.: Wayfinding: Designing and Implementing Graphic Navigational Systems. Rotovision, Mies (2005)
20. Costa, M.L: Rotas culturais: Património e Sistemas Wayfinding. Convergências - Revista de Investigação e Ensino das Artes , vol XIII (26), p.s/p (2020). http://convergencias.ipcb.pt
21. Moles, A.: La imagen. comunicacion funcional. Trillas, Medellín (1991)
22. Haslam, A.: O livro e designer II. Edições Rosari, São Paulo (2007)

Human Dynamics for Social Cohesion

bYou: A Research Proposal About and with Children and Youngsters as Creative Agents of Change Through the Use of the Media

Sara Pereira, Daniel Brandão(✉), and Manuel Pinto

University of Minho/CECS, Braga, Portugal
{sarapereira,danielbrandao,mpinto}@ics.uminho.pt

Abstract. This article presents the relevance, objectives, methodologies and expected results of a funded research project started in March 2021 in Portugal, seeking to provide children and young people with an opportunity to express and discuss their own views on the effect of media in their lives. The project will cross traditional research methods (questionnaires and focus groups) with participatory methodologies, implemented within formal and informal learning contexts. Participants' production will be organized and shared in the project's website for further interpretation and discussion. Simultaneously, the project will engage with teachers and students in order to revitalize media production in a set of schools. By encouraging, listening and sharing young people's voices as potential forces of the present time we aim to raise awareness and inspire public projects and policies addressed at them. These are the ideas that give the project its name: bYou – *be you* and *by you.*

Keywords: Children and young people · Media · Expression and participation · Media literacy · Social change

1 Introduction

In December 2019, when the American magazine Time named 16-year-old Swede Greta Thunberg as Person of the Year for her environmental activism, adult society was showing signs of acknowledging and listening to the voices of youth. Although youth activism is not a recent phenomenon, the fact is that the worldwide movement to raise awareness for climate change led by Thunberg, the media coverage it has been given, its dissemination on social networks and the impact it has had on political leaders and institutions such as the UN has illustrated what Childhood Sociology has sought to emphasise and acknowledge children and young people as social actors and agents of change. Young people themselves have clearly shown and communicated their role at a global level through their activism and by taking the lead in this social cause.

At the Convention on the Rights of the Child (CRC) [1] participation appears enshrined, along with protection and provision, as a category of rights for all children from birth to 18 years of age. Providing children with opportunities to participate and to

D. Raposo et al. (Eds.): AHFE 2021, LNNS 277, pp. 95–103, 2021.
https://doi.org/10.1007/978-3-030-80415-2_12

express themselves on the most diverse subjects that concern their lives is, therefore, a responsibility of all agents and structures of society, in particular those that most directly deal with children. In order to apply this set of rights to the digital environment, the UN Committee on the Rights of Children approved on February 4, 2021 the General Comment 25. The Committee intends with this General Comment to propose to the States measures to fulfill its obligations to promote and protect children's rights in the digital environment and ensure that other actors, including companies, fulfill their responsibilities. This measure will make it possible to support and promote the safety of children online, but also to create online spaces for them, to express themselves about their media practices and experiences.

Based on the potential of this intended participatory culture, this study seeks precisely to provide children and young people between the ages of 11 and 18 with an opportunity to express their views on their relationship with the media and thereby get to know and discuss one of their daily experiences which is most shared globally [2].

In the following sections we will briefly present the main theoretical and methodological assumptions that sustain this three year research project and reflect on its potential impact.

2 Theoretical Assumptions

This study acknowledges that childhood and adolescence are dynamic processes and that children and young people are not to be regarded as future-adult projects but rather as subjects of and in the present time [3, 4]. Following the perspectives of Spyrou [5, 6] on children's voices and joining the discussion of other authors on this subject [7], it starts by theorizing voice in research with children. By doing that, we follow Couldry's conceptualization of voice, considering voice as a process and as a value [8]. As stated by Couldry, "treating voice as a value means discriminating in favour of ways of organizing human life and resources that, through their choices, put the value of voice into practice, by respecting the multiple interlinked processes of voice and sustaining them, not undermining or denying them" [8, p. 2]. Under the frameworks of valuing voice we consider, as suggested by Spyrou, the "multi-layered and non-normative character" of children's voices [5, p. 151] and "one of its more problematic features, namely, silence" [6, p. 8].

Children and young people will be heard and will express themselves about their experiences with the media and online communication technologies as an important part of their everyday lives. Internet and social networks, videogames, television, cinema, mobile phones, music and a huge number of applications are well-established in the majority's daily lives, as building elements of socialization, culture and identity. Their engagement with these media have reconfigured their play, friendship, sociability, self-expression and learning, drawing the attention of researchers around the world. This reconfiguration became stronger and more evident during the COVID-19 outbreak in which media and digital technologies became even more present in their daily lives and essential for the teaching-learning process. This situation makes it even more necessary and relevant to study the relationship of children with digital media and the internet. In addition, although the Committee on the Rights of the Child has underlined that children's right to participation "does not cease in situations of crisis or in the aftermath" [1, p. 28], Bennouna et al. [9] and Cuevas-Parra [10] refer that there is a body of evidence from other humanitarian crises and disasters that children's right to participate is limited and affected.

Meanwhile, in the last years, studies on children and the Internet have had a significant growth. In Europe, the EU Kids Online project [11] is one of the examples of research in this area involving more than 30 countries in some of its phases and making important contributions to understand the risks and opportunities that children face online [12]. Another European project – Transmedia Literacy - which involved researchers from the current team, analysed the transmedia consumption of adolescents between 12 and 18 years old in eight countries. The project contributed to a better understanding of how teens are consuming, producing, sharing, creating and learning in digital environments and provided a map of transmedia skills and informal learning strategies used by teenagers to be explored in the formal education system [13]. The Portuguese team found out there was a digital divide between in-school and out-of-school media uses [14] and concluded, from the analysis of teenagers' media practices, that they are large media consumers but much more restrained producers [15, 16]. The same conclusion was emphasized by a study carried out in Portugal focused on Media Literacy competences of young people aged 17–18 [17]. The sample surveyed (N = 679) was a group strongly connected to the media, revealing a good level of functional literacy but low competences of critical reading, analysis and production.

Despite the awareness developed by these and other studies on the importance of the context of the lived experiences of children and on cultural differences, there is a need to go further in studying children and youth's media practices as part of a broader media ecology, and in understanding how they are experiencing the convergent media culture [18]. These are important assumptions for this study. On the one hand, it aims to deepen the holistic approach of media uses [19] and develop the notion of media ecologies [20]. On the other hand, it seeks to value the production and expression of young people of and through the media, withdrawing the adult-centric perspective that sometimes stood out in research projects involving the youngest. It also aims to empower children and young people on issues related to production, sharing and dissemination of personal and public data and content.

For studying children and young people's media ecologies in their everyday lives, the study follows the concept of media repertoires proposed by Hasebrink and Domeyer [21]. According to the authors, "the media repertoire of a person consists of the entirety of media he or she regularly uses" [21, p. 758]. Media repertoires, as stated previously by Hasebrink and Popp "can be understood as integral part of lifestyles and they have to be interpreted with regard to their practical meaning" [22, p. 374], being conceived as "comprehensive patterns of media use" [22, p. 374]. Therefore, taking into account that "in a time of deep mediatization, cross-media approaches to investigating media practices are becoming increasingly relevant", as stated by Hasebrink and Hepp [23, p. 362], the repertoire-oriented approach is considered a relevant model for this study. Its focus on the patterns of media use composed of different media interrelated with users' everyday practices is an important approach angle as it allows to analyse the ever more mediated children's daily lives. In addition, the research methodological triangulation to be followed is in line with the authors' methodological proposal to address the repertoire approach [23].

Media-related experiences, which are interwoven with other social practices, will be studied recurring to innovative methods that give a voice to children and young people, value it and call for their active participation. Participation of children and young people appears today in an extensive literature of many academic fields, suggesting potential benefits of a participation culture [24–26]. This is why we argue for the innovative potential of this project. Recurring to participatory methods, it values the voice and creative expression of children, based on what they choose for narrating and documenting their everyday lives and the media instead of following a script created and imposed by researchers. Although the studies we developed previously have shown that young people are more consumers than producers, they also demonstrated a centrality of informal media creation in the everyday communication of youth and in the peer-based exchanges and culture. A growing body of work on Media Literacy and production [27–30] shows how engaging youngsters in media production should lead to their empowerment, being a cornerstone for Media Literacy. As stated by Lange and Ito, "shifting youth identity from that of a media consumer to a media producer is an important vehicle for developing youth voice, creativity, agency, and new forms of literacy in a media-saturated era" [31, p. 247]. And these are crucial skills for engaging with a digital world [32], which we believe should encourage active rather than passive participation.

In the current context of children and media studies, the commitment of this project is to produce academic knowledge that matters, bearing in mind that "at a time, when neoliberalism has infiltrated all aspects of daily life and has limited our ability to imagine how things could be otherwise, children are showing us the way" [33, p. 6].

3 Main Objectives

Through the children and young people's voices, this study seeks to understand their worlds in the light of technological developments, which enable but do not ensure that these voices are let out, heard, reproduced and shared. The societal challenges we are facing make it all the more crucial that these voices have a say to enrich and distinguish public projects and policies aimed at them. Therefore, the main objectives of this study are:

- Understand how the daily lives of young people are interwoven with the media ecosystem;
- Listen to young people about the presence, role and importance of the media in their daily lives;
- Analyze their media uses and practices in a close perspective;
- Explore their comprehension of the media;
- Promote an active and creative expression of their media experiences;
- Identify and analyze the main areas in which children express themselves on the media;
- Provide for the expression and participation of children and young people through school media;

- Contribute to enhance school media as means of communication and participation in the community;
- To make proposals to integrate these practices in formal learning and to inform public policies.

4 Methodological Design

Despite the abundance of studies on children, young people and media, there are few which focus on media ecology in children and young people's daily lives. In recent years several studies have focused mostly on the Internet's risks and opportunities, whereas previously it was children's relationship with television that occupied the central place of research. The European project Transmedia Literacy[1] made a significant contribution at this level by studying transmedia practices of teenagers between 11 and 18 years old. This study sought to understand their production practices and to make proposals to integrate these practices in formal learning.

Inspired by the results of that project and looking to go further, this study intends not only to analyze media production practices, but to promote children and young people's participation, encouraging them to express themselves on and through the media. We seek to gain a broad picture of their everyday life media uses and experiences in different contexts, what aspects of the media are more problematic to them, and what they know about crucial media issues for citizenship, such as disinformation and fake news, online privacy and data protection, online safety, social networks and algorithms, ethical principles in media production and participation. The team will collect data and encourage discussion on these topics, but children will also take a leading role in choosing which aspects of their relationship with the media they wish to explore. This will give us information about how media helps shaping their identities and cultures, taking into account their social and geographical environment, gender and age range.

The study applies three main forms of children's participation in research, identified by Holland et al. [34].

In the first form, children are invited to participate in research methods designed and directed by the team. In the project, this step includes a questionnaire that will be applied to a national non-probabilistic sample of approximately 1380 students aged between 11 and 18 years old. The constitution of this sample involves 23 schools located in mainland Portugal and a total of 69 classes from 6th and 9th grades (basic education) and from 12th grade (secondary education). Quantitative data provided by the questionnaire will be discussed and further explored in focus groups with a subsample of students. A total of 15 classes of 6th, 9th and 12th grade, that is, approximately 300 students will be invited to participate in this second step. We intend to discuss media-related topics mentioned by the young people in the questionnaires and to be proposed by researchers (eg. misinformation and false news, data, social networks, digital media and algorithms, privacy and data protection). It is up to them to decide and it is up to researchers to identify and register the topics they want to discuss and how to do it. Authorizations and informed consents for holding questionnaires and focus groups will be requested.

---

[1] https://transmedialiteracy.org/.

In the second form, the team prepares methods that enable children's views to be expressed through 'child-centered' forms of communication and creation (such as videos, media arts, photography, drawings, dance, drama, games, etc.).

In the third form, through the previously proposed methods, children are involved in research about aspects of their own lives and are encouraged to discuss and reflect on the research process and contribute to the dissemination [34, p. 361].

As also considered by Holland et al. [34], we assume that there is an overlap between the last two forms. To put them into practice, the research project adopts participatory and reflexive methodologies, which will involve active participation of children and young people in the production of media content and in the process of interpreting and discussing the different media outputs. Firstly, audiovisual methods will be used, considering, as pointed out by Pawels and Mannay, that "contemporary visual methods involve scrutinizing visually observable aspects of society as a gateway to the deeper traits of culture; they also include using visual means to visualize the material, immaterial and conceptual, generating a more nuanced understanding of social worlds" [35, p. 1]. Besides, visual methods are relevant because they "are not confined to the visible world, as they intimately relate to visualising the invisible and the (in)conceivable" [35, p. 1]. That is, audiovisual and textual data generated by young people will give us rich insights into their everyday media routines, their media worlds, their concerns, what they value, what they want to highlight in their relationship with the media. It is our aim to promote the creative expression of children and young people on and through the media. By involving formal and informal learning contexts at a national level, we intend to encourage this audience to use different media – video, podcast, drawing, photography, text, memes, cartoons, etc. – to creatively narrate their experiences with the media. Children and young people will be able to participate, individually or in groups, following the privacy and data protection recommendations to be provided by the team. This will be encouraged through a campaign to be launched at schools, cinema clubs, dance schools, theatre schools, among other institutions that work with children.

The material to be collected will be subject to categorization and analysis, aiming to identify the areas and themes on which children and young people manifest themselves the most, the type of content and messages they elaborate, the way their worlds and visions are communicated and the means they use most for this purpose. Based on these expressions, the team intends to encourage reflexive and critical practices, in a Media Literacy perspective. At the same time, a 'mural of expression' for online sharing of experiences will be created at the project's website in coordination with MILObs - Observatory on Media, Information and Literacy[2].

At another level, we will study the role of students in school media—newspapers, radio, TV, blogs—with the aim of promoting their participation in those school projects. We will work with 10 schools already producing their own media. Workshops will be organized with the team—teachers and students—responsible for the school media. Based on what they already do, we will work together to give school media the strength of students' expressions, exploring different media languages and contributing to enhance school media. In order to get other teams inspired by the result of this work, a video will be produced, briefly reporting its process and the results.

[2] http://milobs.pt.

This participative approach will be conducted within a strong ethical framework that aims to protect children's data and respect their privacy and image. This will be strictly followed by the team but participants will also be encouraged to be self-reflexive and careful in what they will produce and share. It will be an opportunity to empower children on ethical issues arising from accessing, using, interacting and producing contents through media, and also issues related to private and public space.

5 Conclusions: Expected Results

The innovative contribution of this project is partly in the research methods and the type of data they are going to provide and, of course, in the analysis that will follow. The project follows a step-by-step methodology, starting with listening to children's voices, opinions and visions, to learn more about their social, cultural and media worlds, and extending to the application of methods that involve their active participation and creative expression as creative agents of change through the use of the media. Teachman and Gladstone [36], in the Introduction to a special issue of the International Journal of Qualitative Methods dedicate to "Construction of 'Children's Voices' in Qualitative Research", mention that in research with children "there is potential for children's "voices" to be represented in ways that serve adult researchers' aims, but fail to account for the situated, relational contexts wherein meanings are co-produced and intergenerational" [36, p. 1]. According to Teachman and Gladstone the understandings of children's voices have been internationally criticized by scholars who "called for more critically reflexive methodological approaches to research with children and youth" [36, p. 1], being also necessary to define and theorize the term 'voice'.

The methodological design of this project takes into account that "when children are permitted in those rare cases to become active participants telling their own story in their own way, the research experience is often personally moving and meaningful and the data provided rich and complex" [37, p. 84]. It also considers, as noted by Holland et al. [34, p. 362], that "locating children as active social agents via participatory methods to facilitate children's 'voice', 'agency' and 'empowerment' have been highly influential in the early wave of childhood research". Rather than conducting research defined solely by adults' interests and agendas, this study offers children the opportunity to express themselves through participatory methods. We expect this research design to be particularly fruitful with young people. There are several studies [24, 38] based on child-centred forms of expression and communication (such as photos, video, drawings, drama and dance) with the aim to enable children's views on certain topics that proved to be particularly rewarding in terms of results.

Acknowledgments. This project is being conducted by researchers of the Communication and Society Research Centre at the University of Minho, Portugal, and it is funded by the Portuguese Foundation for Science and Technology under the reference PTDC/COM-OUT/3004/2020.

References

1. Committee on the Rights of the Child (CRC): Convention on the rights of the child. General comment no. 12: The right of the child to be heard (2009)

2. Lemish, D.: Children and Media: A Global Perspective. Wiley, Oxford (2015)
3. Lee, N.: Childhood and Society. Growing up in an Age of Uncertainty. Open University Press, Maidenhead (2001)
4. Pereira, S.: More technology, better childhoods? The case of the Portuguese 'One Laptop per Child' programme. Child. Cult. Media Cult. Special Issue Commun. Manage. Quart. **29**, 171–198 (2013). https://doi.org/10.5937/comman1329171P
5. Spyrou, S.: The limits of children's voices: From authenticity to critical, reflexive representation. Childhood **18**(2), 151–165 (2011)
6. Spyrou, S.: Researching children's silences: exploring the fullness of voice in childhood research. Childhood **23**(1), 7–21 (2016)
7. Facca, D., Gladstone, B., Teachman, G.: Working the limits of "Giving Voice" to children: a critical conceptual review. Int. J. Qual. Methods **19**, 1–10 (2020). https://doi.org/10.1177/1609406920933391
8. Couldry, N.: Why Voice Matters. Culture and Politics After Neoliberalism. Sage Publications, London (2010)
9. Bennouna, C., Mansourian, H., Stark, L.: Ethical considerations for children's participation in data collection activities during humanitarian emergencies: a Delphi review. Conflict Health **11**(1), 5–15 (2017). https://doi.org/10.1186/s13031-017-0108-y
10. Cuevas-Parra, P.: Co-researching with children in the time of COVID-19: shifting the narrative on methodologies to generate knowledge. Int. J. Qual. Methods **19**, 1–12 (2020). https://doi.org/10.1177/1609406920982135
11. EU Kids Online: EU Kids Online: findings, methods, recommendations (deliverable D1.6). EU Kids Online, LSE, London, UK (2014). http://eprints.lse.ac.uk/60512/
12. Livingstone, S., Haddon, L., Görzig, A. (eds.): Children, Risk and Safety Online: Research and Policy Challenges in Comparative Perspective. Polity Press, Bristol (2012)
13. Scolari, C.: The transmedia literacy research project. In: Scolari, C. (ed.) Teens, Media and Collaborative Cultures. Exploiting Teens' Transmedia Skills in the Classroom, pp. 8--10. Barcelona, Ce.Ge (2018). http://transmedialiteracy.upf.edu/sites/default/files/files/TL_Teens_en.pdf
14. Pereira, S., Fillol, J., Moura, P.: Young people learning from digital media outside of school: the informal meets the formal, Comunicar **58**(XXVII), 41–50 (2019). https://doi.org/10.3916/C58-2019-04
15. Pereira, S., Moura, P.: Production skills. In: Scolari, C. (ed.) Teens, Media and Collaborative Cultures. Exploiting Teens' Transmedia Skills in the Classroom, pp. 22–25. Ce.Ge, Barcelona (2018). http://transmedialiteracy.upf.edu/sites/default/files/files/TL_Teens_en.pdf
16. Pereira, S., Moura, P., Masanet, M.-J., Taddeo, G., Tirocchi, S.: Media uses and production practices: case study with teens from Portugal, Spain and Italy. Comunicación y Sociedad **33**, 89–114 (2018). https://doi.org/10.32870/cys.v0i33.7091
17. Pereira, S., Pinto, M., Moura, P.: Níveis de Literacia Mediática: Estudo Exploratório com Jovens do 12.º ano. Braga, Centro de Estudos de Comunicação e Sociedade (2015). http://hdl.handle.net/1822/40488
18. Jenkins, H.: Convergence Culture. Where Old and New Media Collide. New York University Press, New York (2006)
19. Haddon, L.: Research question for the evolving communications landscape. In: Ling, R., Pedersen, P.E. (eds.) Mobile Communications. Re-negotiation of the Social Sphere, pp. 7–22. Springer, London (2003). https://doi.org/10.1007/1-84628-248-9_2
20. Horst, H.A., Herr-Stephenson, B., Robinson, L.: Media ecologies. In: Ito, M., et al. (eds.) Hanging Out, Messing Around, and Geeking Out. Kids Living and Learning with New Media, pp. 29–78. MIT Press, Cambridge (2009)

21. Hasebrink, U., Domeyer, H.: Media repertoires as patterns of behaviour and as meaningful practices: a multimethod approach to media use in converging media environments. Participations J. Audience Reception Stud. **9**(2), 757–779 (2012). https://www.participations.org/Volume%209/Issue%202/40%20Hasebrink%20Domeyer.pdf
22. Hasebrink, U., Popp, J.: Media repertoires as a result of selective media use. A conceptual approach to the analysis of patterns of exposure. Communications **31**(3), 369–387 (2006). https://doi.org/10.1515/COMMUN.2006.023
23. Hasebrink, U., Hepp, A.: How to research cross-media practices? Investigating media repertoires and media ensembles. Convergence **23**(4), 362–377 (2017). https://journals.sagepub.com/doi/abs/10.1177/1354856517700384
24. Clark, A.: How to listen to very young children: the mosaic approach. Child Care Pract. **7**(4), 333–341 (2001). https://doi.org/10.1080/13575270108415344
25. Jenkins, H., Purushotma, R., Weigel, M., Clinton, K., Robison A.J.: Confronting the challenges of participatory culture. MacArthur Foundation, Chicago, IL (2009). https://mitpress.mit.edu/books/confronting-challenges-participatory-culture
26. Jenkins, H.: Youth voice, media, and political engagement. Introducing the core concepts. In: Jenkins, H., Shresthova, S., Gamber-Thompson, L., Kligler-Vilenchik, N., Zimmerman, A.M. (eds.) By Any Media Necessary. The New Youth Activism, pp. 1–60. New York University Press, New York (2016)
27. Goodman, S.: Teaching Youth Media: A Critical Guide to Literacy, Video Production and Social Change. Teacher's College Press, New York (2003)
28. Buckingham, D., Fraser, P., Sefton-Green, J.: Making the grade: evaluating student production in media studies. In: Sefton-Green, J., Sinker, R. (eds.) Evaluating Creativity: Making and Learning by Young People, pp. 129–153. Routledge, London (2000)
29. Eleá, I., Mikos, L. (eds.): Young & Creative. Digital Technologies Empowering Children in Everyday Life. Göteborg, Nordicom (2017)
30. Hobbs, R.: Create to Learn. Introduction to Digital Literacy. Wiley, Hoboken (2017)
31. Lange, P., Ito, M.: Creative production. In: Ito, M., et al. (eds.) Hanging Out, Messing Around, and Geeking Out. Kids Living and Learning with New Media, pp. 243–291. MIT Press, Cambridge (2009)
32. Cortesi, S., Hasse, A., Lombana-Bermudez, A., Kim, S., Gasser, U.: Youth and digital citizenship+ (plus): understanding skills for a digital world. Youth and Media, Berkman Klein Center for Internet & Society (2020). https://papers.ssrn.com/sol3/papers.cfm?abstract_id=3557518
33. Spyrou, S.: Children as future-makers. Childhood **27**(1), 3–7 (2020). https://doi.org/10.1177/0907568219884142
34. Holland, S., Renold, E., Ross, N.J., Hillman, A.: Power, agency and participatory agendas: a critical exploration of young people's engagement in participative qualitative research. Childhood **17**(3), 360–375 (2010). https://doi.org/10.1177/0907568210369310
35. Pawels, L., Mannay, D.: Visual dialogues across different schools of thought. In: Pawels, L., Mannay, D. (eds.) The Sage Handbook of Visual Research Methods, pp. 1–11. Sage Publications, London (2020)
36. Teachman G, Gladstone B.: Guest editors' introduction: special issue: constructions of "children's voices" in qualitative research. Int. J. Qual. Methods **19**, 1–5 (2020). https://doi.org/10.1177/1609406920980654
37. Grover, S.: Why won't they listen to us? On giving power and voice to children participating in social research. Childhood **11**(1), 81–93 (2004). https://doi.org/10.1177/0907568204040186
38. Solé, L., Torrent, S.: Youth Media Visions. Exploring the pedagogic potentialities of learning with and from media produced by young people. Teachers College-Columbia University in partnership with United Nations Alliance of Civilizations (2013)

Brand Models: A Comparative Study on Brand Creation and Management

Emílio Santos[1(✉)] and Daniel Raposo[1,2]

[1] CIAUD, Lisbon School of Architecture, Universidade de Lisboa, Rua Sá Nogueira, 1349-063 Lisbon, Portugal

[2] RETHINK, Research Group On Design for the Territory and Polytechnic Institute of Castelo Branco, Av. Pedro Álvares Cabral, nº 12, 6000-084 Castelo Branco, Portugal

Abstract. It has been observed, since the 2014s, the emergence of brand creation and management models that contribute to the sustainability of entities, organizations, territories and businesses. Each brand model proposal results from the knowledge, perspective and vision of the respective authors, in the search for answers to complex problems, not always similar. Brand sustainability depends on the experience it represents for stakeholders. Both from the perspective of commercial brands and for Place Branding, the models seem to have common visions, with their advantages and limitations. Brand models are compared from the perspective of their definition, creation, design and management. The non-interventionist methodology based on the descriptive case study, allowed the identification of the essential vectors to be considered in a brand model or in a brand creation process, specifically in Place Branding.

Keywords: Brand model · Brand creation · Brand management · Place branding

1 Introduction

The brand, as a contemporary phenomenon, seems to us to be necessary for anything in which we want to establish connections. From eggs to fruits, from people to countries, the brand has expanded its domains and adapted to the representations of the desires of each individual in accordance with their cultural context [1]. The brand, during the course of its evolution, has already been limited to a mere association with the producer and his products and services, serving as a link to identify them, according to Raposo [2]. However, today, the brand arises from a branding process that aims to record and keep it alive in the minds [3] and hearts of people.

It is observed, that since the decade of 2014, the territories have advanced in the proposition of brands that reveal their identity. Concomitant to brands, models for the creation and management of those brands, have been proposed with the aim of contributing to the sustainability of entities, organizations, territory and businesses. For Anholt [4], Places are brands and, therefore, are an integral and important part of the economy. Globalization has led territory managers to insert place branding in their agendas and, consequently, these territory managers have resorted to brand designers to visually

D. Raposo et al. (Eds.): AHFE 2021, LNNS 277, pp. 104–110, 2021.
https://doi.org/10.1007/978-3-030-80415-2_13

materialize their identity and their singularities. This phenomenon appears, at first, as a field of opportunities for Design, however, the complexity of the task requires the application of a model that can support this complexity. Therefore, I reiterate that there is a complexity peculiar to place branding and in that sense, we intend to compare some brand models in the perspective of its definition, creation, design and management.

2 Brands: The Representation of Authenticity

Brands strengthen bonds. They connect people to products and services through the meanings it emanates. The brand carries meanings that are subdivided between graphic meaning and emotional meaning. According to Gobé [5], in the intersection between those meanings, there is the symbol, a representative element configured by the brand mark (symbol and/or logotype).

In the current context, brands are not only the identification of products and services, but they have also become complex signs of origin and social positioning, according to Perez [6]. The brand is a symbolic manifestation that must transmit a clear message to its audience. According to Perez [6], without a brand, a product is a thing without meaning, significance and value. The brand is an important con-temporary phenomenon that today communicates about products, services and places, including.

A widely known brand is visually recognized by its design. As it is composed of a verbal sign and a visual sign, it is a double sign, according to Costa [7]. It arises from a name that will be visually configured by graphic elements that will be an integral part of its visual identity system. These elements can be defined by a logotype that represents the verbal sign (the name), the symbol and the colour which represent the brand name or its core concept, in Costa's view [7].

A sign is intended for someone capable of interpreting its message. The sign is not, in itself, the represented object. It assumes the character of representation of the object and, therefore, is part of a system composed of various elements that make up the functional whole [7]. The mark, likewise, aims to represent an object that is beyond it and, in this sense, the mark is not limited to a mere representation of the product [6]. It expresses much more. As a sign, the brand is associated with the satisfaction of a need supported by the product's function. For Costa [7], it refers to brand/function. On the other hand, when it refers to the emotional aspects attributed to a brand, the symbol emerges as a representation of values associated to those attributes. Therefore, we have the brand/emotion [7]. The brand, in its genesis, does not emerge as a brand but as a product [7]. Its autonomy arises when the meanings and attributes of products and services are incorporated by it. It is in the vision of the receiver that the messages emanated about a brand make sense and, consequently, an image about it is formed. Therefore, according to Raposo [8], the process for the identity design starts with knowledge about the corporate image and this starts from the image perceived by people.

Authenticity is another aspect to be considered. The visual representation of identity, especially of a territory, must be authentic and in tune with the temporal dimensions linked to the history of the place through its past, the conditions of the present that signalize the vision of future about the territory. It is important to point out that identity provides sustainability and, consequently, considers people's quality of life [9].

The image of the place must reflect an authentic identity about itself. The positive image of the territory adds value to its products and services [10]. This favours competitiveness. This requires control. This requires management. This is called branding.

3 Branding: The Brand in People's Minds and Hearts

Branding is a continuous process that aims - to present, activate and gradually crystallize the brand in the minds of consumers. The purpose is to keep the brand active in people's minds [3]. It is the management of the intangible assets of a corporation or entity. In branding, one aims to increase brand equity which, in Keller's perspective [11], is possible through brand awareness through the components - brand notoriety and brand image. The notoriety can be distributed in two levels: assisted, which refers to the consumer's ability to admit that he has already been exposed to the brand and, the spontaneous, where the consumer recognizes the brand when some product is exposed [11].

According to Tybout and Calkins [12], branding is based on three conceptual pillars: positioning, brand design and brand meaning. Positioning is how the company establishes its differences in the consumer's mind [13]. It is also understood as a platform on which the planning of a company establishes the forms of relationship with its clients [14]. The positioning helps in the definition of the alternative means to implement the strategies [12]. In the conceptual pillar brand design is understood as the challenge of bringing the brand concept to consumers through perception, form and components of the brand system [12]. Brand design is an important part of branding.

4 Place Branding: A Brand to Represent the Reputation of the Place

The territory, according to Haesbaert [15], can be defined on 3 conceptual aspects: 1) legal-political, where the territory is the space for the exercise of power and social control relations; 2) cultural, where the symbolic relations, appropriation of the imaginary coexist with a socio-spatial identity and, 3) economic, where the capital-labor relations are materialized. The material and immaterial resources of the territory define the nature of its heritage and, in this sense, there is something relevant to place branding - the feeling of belonging. The city dwellers should have an affective relationship with the place and with the things of the place. The image of the territory is the reflection of an identity that reveals the attributes contained therein. There are products that are peculiar to the territory as well as the geographical indications that designate the agricultural and food products so linked and imbricated to the place and that designate a certain production zone [16]. Parma ham/Italy, coffee from the Cerrado/Brazil, pastéis de Belém/Portugal, lavender/Provance/France, among others. The territory's products can obtain relevance and visibility from place branding, which aligns the necessary channels to communicate the development strategy of the city, country or region [4]. Place branding is the equivalent to the concept of living the brand in the sense of corporate branding. It is a process in favour of a coherent communication about the territory considering intellect, income, talent and voice [4].

The models for place branding are mostly recent and have different perspectives: brand communication, brand identity formation, brand image construction, branding process, among others [17]. Among the pretensions and concerns of public authorities is the search for results in terms of attractiveness, competitiveness and economic performance [18]. However, a model that focuses on brand communication, for example, expresses, through the message, the identity, but does not mean that it guarantees economic performance. On the other hand, places must be sustainable in several aspects and, consequently, be interesting both to live in and to visit.

The territory, to have future perspectives, must involve creativity, innovation and sustainable ways of life [19]. Therefore, it can be observed that among the components of a model an important element to consider is the people, or rather the citizen. The sense of belonging of the people of the place is fundamental for place branding. The people of the place have relationships with the territory beyond the affections built there in the course of their lives. They are an integral and important part of the place and have their own ways of appropriation and vision of the place and its things. At the level of the process of managing a brand for the territory, one observes, from Gaio's perspective [20], the following elements: diagnosis of the situation, territorial claims, strategic formulation, communicational engineering, control and implementation. The relationship between these elements seeks the creation of a favorable environment to attract investments and visitors, motivate entrepreneurship and create a virtuous circle for the construction of the brand. Therefore, it was decided to analyse models that consider a dynamic and constant action for the creation of a brand design for a place branding.

5 Methodology

The study followed a non-interventionist methodology based on a descriptive case study, for the identification of the essential vectors to be considered in a brand model or in a brand creation process, specifically in Place Branding. Representative and reliable sources of information were sought to build a database pertinent to the case study, and finally, to arrange the evidence in sequence. This sequence presents the following phases: a) exploratory for the survey of the cases for study; b) selection of the cases for study; c) data organization; d) data analysis; e) review of the bibliography and, f) results. It is expected to understand how to think the territory from the design of a brand that uses design tools in the re-flection of a complex problem called territory.

6 Results and Discussion

The models that are the object of this research present a dynamic and interactive form between their components. To present the models, the following identification was defined: model A (Fig. 1) and model B (Fig. 2). In model A, its main components are: place, place-identity, place-brand, place-image, place-culture and citizens. This model has been used by the Planning and Economic Development Commission of Pomfret in the city of Connecticut/USA. In the place component, an arc is observed which continues to the temporal dimensions: history, current conditions and vision of the future. These dimensions dialogue with the place-identity which is intertwined with the place-brand.

In this dynamic, the place-brand expands to two arcs. The first, for the impressions that reveal the place-image that is the mirror for the place-identity. The second, is a reflection of the place-culture that expresses the place-identity. The citizen opens to two arcs which define the collective production about the things of the place, on the other hand, about the place brand, in the citizen axis, that defines the users and participants who interact with the constant process of understanding of the brand by the impressions emanated from its identity.

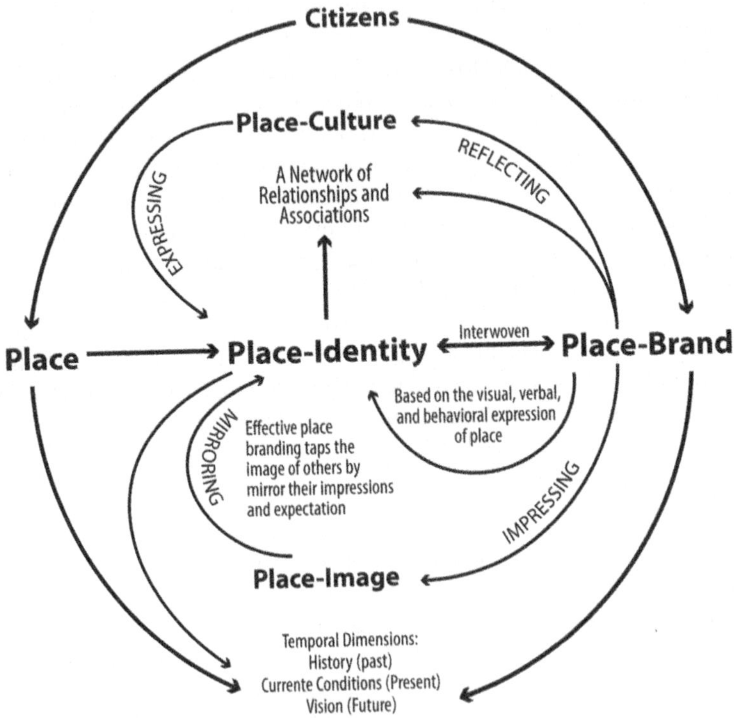

Fig. 1. Model A – Pomfret brand model. Source: adapted from Pomfret/NECCOG [21]

In model B, the outer, dotted circle highlights two elements: the brand image and the brand identity. surrounded by the infinity shape, the purple highlight presents the following elements: local people, investors, economic development and regeneration. In the area in grey, informing, consulting, engaging, glue-bearing and empowerment wrap the elements in the left part of the arc. These elements are described as adding value. The design tools present the diversity of means by which information is collected to support the actions described in the infinite element.

The approximations between model A and B are in the interaction between the elements. Both present a dynamic and constant action between the elements of the model. The expression of the brand reveals the brand identity and consequent brand image that moves suggesting a process that is constantly renewed. The models arise as an object of reflection on how places can think their brands involving and engaging people. The citizen must be included in this process, where public managers cannot limit themselves to a vision of the territory. In model A, in the temporal dimensions, it is observed that citizens are part of the process of construction of the place and in this sense, they can contribute to the process of building the brand design for the territory.

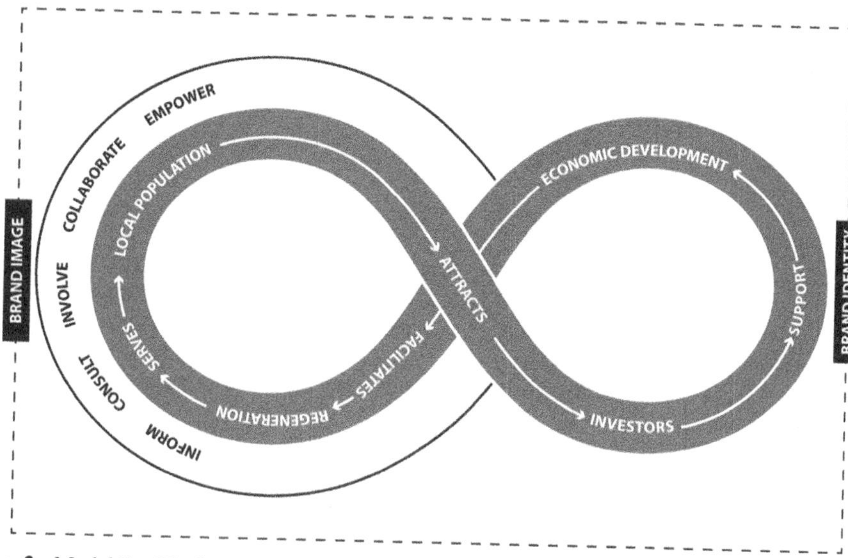

Fig. 2. Model B – The brand community ecosystem. Source: diagram adaptation from Neumeier [22]

7 Final Considerations

The design of a brand for a territory should emerge from a reflection on the history of the place, its present and its prospects for the future. In this sense, the people of the place should be involved as an integral and important part of these decisions. Models A and B show a dynamic and constant relationship between their components. This dynamic process has a tenuous relationship with the essence of branding - being a continuous process. Models A and B reveal this. We can also see the involvement of people, citizens, in the process of thinking about the territory, and this is important. Economic development is an evident factor in model B and this opens up space for investments and promotes sustainability, including economic sustainability. The place, its identity and its brand, should be the object of a management process that does not end with the visual configuration of its identity by a graphic brand. This requires a broader look at branding as an important pillar for sustaining the competitiveness of the place in the face of fierce competition and, to do so, one must extract its singularities that define it in a special way. On the other hand, it is necessary to look to the future with responsibility so that the territory can guarantee its future today. A place branding model to meet today's demands should consider the temporal dimensions of the territory associated to an economic development that considers the people of the place, to make room for a sustainable future.

References

1. Perez, C.: Signos da marca: expressividade e sensorialidade. Cengage Learning, São Paulo (2016)
2. Raposo, D.: Design de identidade e imagem corporativa: branding, história da marca, gestão de marca, identidade corporative. Edições IPCB, Castelo Branco (2008)
3. Consolo, C.: Marcas: design estratégico, do símbolo à gestão da identidade corporativa. Blucher, São Paulo (2015)
4. Anholt, S.: Branding de locai e de países. In: Clifton, R., Simmpns, J. (eds.) The Economist, pp. 241–254. Atual Editora, Lisboa (2015)
5. Gobé, M.: Emotional Branding: The New Paradigm for Connecting Brands to People. Allworth Press, New York (2001)
6. Perez, C.: The Grid: Signos da marca: expressividade e sensorialidade. Cengage Learning, São Paulo (2016)
7. Costa, J.: Imagem da marca: um fenômeno social. Rosari, São Paulo (2011)
8. Raposo, D.; Martín-Sanroman; J. Neves; J. Silva, J.: Visual Identity Design in the New Economy. Convergências - Revista de Investigação e Ensino das Artes, vol. X (19) (2017). http://convergencias.ipcb.pt
9. Raposo, D., et al.: Visual identity design as a cultural interface of a territory. In: Rebelo, F., Soares, M. (eds.) AHFE 2020. AISC, vol. 1203, pp. 65–72. Springer, Cham (2020). https://doi.org/10.1007/978-3-030-51038-1_10
10. Ruschel, R.: O valor global do produto local. Senac, São Paulo (2019)
11. Keller, K.L.: Strategic Brand Management: Building, Measuring, and Managing Brand Equity. Pearson/Prentice Hall, Hoboken (2008)
12. Tybout, A.M., Calkins, T.: Branding: gestão de marcas. Saraiva, São Paulo (2006)
13. Trout, J., Rvkin, S.: Reposicionamento: marketing para a era de competição, mudança e crise. M. Books, São Paulo (2011)
14. Ries, A. Trout, J.: Posicionamento: a batalha por sua mente. Pioneira, São Paulo (1986)
15. Haesbaert, R.: Identidades territoriais. In ROSENDAHL, Z.; CORRÊA, R. L. (Org.). Manifestações da cultura no espaço. Editora UERJ, Rio de Janeiro (1999)
16. Santos, E.R.M.; Raposo, D.: Entre o sentir e o tocar: a (i)materialidade da marca de São Luís do Maranhão, estudo de caso em place branding. In: 5.o ENCONTRO DE DOUTORAMENTOS EM DESIGN, 5., 2016, Aveiro/PT. Anais eletrônicos. Aveiro: Universidade de Aveiro, 2017. Disponível em:http://ud16.web.ua.pt/Atas_UD16.pdf. Acesso em 21 Jan 2020
17. Hanna, S., Rowley, J.: Towards a strategic place brand-management model. J. Mark. Manag. **27**(5–6), 458–476 (2011)
18. Berrada, M.: Towards a holistic place branding model: a conceptual model proposal. Chin. Bus. Rev. 17 (2018). https://doi.org/10.17265/1537-1506/2018.05.002
19. Morgan, N., Pritchard, A., Pride, R.: Destination branding: Managing Place Reputation. Elsevier, Butterworth-Heinemann, London (2011)
20. Gaio, S.; Gouveia, L.: O branding territorial: uma abordagem merca-dológica à Cidade. Revista a Obra Nasce. Edições UFP (2007)
21. Pomfret Branding Strategy Committee; NECCOG. (2019). Pomfret Branding Study - Provide Your Input with the Citizen Survey, 01 2021. https://www.pomfretct.gov/home/news/pomfret-branding-study-provide-your-input-with-the-citizen-survey
22. Neumeier, M.: ZAG. A Estratégia Número 1 das Marcas de Sucesso. Bookman (2009)

Co-creating Places: Human Participatory Dynamics Through Territorial Communication

Ana Duarte Melo(✉)

Communication and Society Research Centre, University of Minho, Braga, Portugal
anamelo@ics.uminho.pt

Abstract. Co-creation and participatory experiences of place branding as expressions of more resilient, inclusive and more human societies are at the core of this paper. Based on state-of-the art co-creative territorial communication review, and using a methodological approach of interpretative hermeneutics and case studies, we critically reflect on the implications of these phenomena and their contribution to placemaking. If the benefits of stakeholders' involvement and co-creative practices in different stages of placemaking may add value to territories and coherence to place brands not offering substantial dispute, the implementation of participatory practices expose pragmatic and ethical issues, enhancing the steering role of the facilitator and the vulnerability of deliberative participatory processes. Nevertheless, co-creative contexts powered by human dynamics seem to provide a fruitful ground to achieve territorial consonance, authentic experiences, sense of belonging and a shared vision of a place essence, central to more involved, more sustainable, and more resilient communities.

Keywords: Placemaking · Co-creation · Territorial communication · Participation · Place branding

1 Introduction: Placemaking as Co-creation

Placemaking is an overarching idea of how to relate with territories that involves urban design, management and planning but also embeds the representation and communication of places as a central dimension. It is intrinsically a co-creative process with a co-created outcome, powered by the dynamization of human interaction, focused on making places more liveable and sustainable.

In 2008, the Project for Public Places and the Chicago Metropolitan Planning Council established 11 hands-on approach principles and stated that placemaking "put simply, it involves looking at, listening to, and asking questions of the people who live, work and play in a particular space, to discover their needs and aspirations. This information is then used to create a common vision for that place (…) capitalizes on a local community's assets, inspiration and potential, creating good public spaces that promote people's health, happiness, and economic well-being" [1] (p. 5).

Co-creation definition tackles multiple dimensions but for the purpose of this paper we would focus on its empowering and performative use—"Co-creation puts tools for

D. Raposo et al. (Eds.): AHFE 2021, LNNS 277, pp. 111–117, 2021.
https://doi.org/10.1007/978-3-030-80415-2_14

communication and creativity in the hands of the people who will benefit directly from the results" [2].

The added social value attributed to the introduction of co-creation in innovative and constructive processes is consistently and commonly accepted on a range of fields, from politics to design, to industrial innovation and development systems, to marketing and branding, to urban planning and community building processes [3].

In line with this, co-creation and participatory phenomena related with the management, planning and communication of places have been emerging and increasingly valued in recent years both by academics [4–7] and practitioners [8].

2 The Role of Territorial Evaluation Systems and Place Branding Models

The evolution of territorial evaluation tools and place management and communication models through the perspective of participatory and co-creation valuation offer an interesting ground to assess how human dynamics (should) play a decisive role on place-making processes. Previous observations indicated a shift from quantitative-centred to more qualitative criteria in territorial valuation systems such as place rankings [9], the introduction of non-tangible and symbolic variables and an evolution from unidirectional paradigms to collaborative communication and branding models [10–13].

The smart city paradigm focused on improving citizens quality of life is based on the intensive use of technology and citizen behaviour monitoring to provide real-time intelligent information for the management of cities, namely regarding resources management or mobility, in a high efficiency and complex approach [14]. Notwithstanding the focus on indicators provided by non-human sources result in fine-tuned accurate numbers and valuable data, their use—besides general questioning regarding access, privacy and the return of benefits to the citizens—might lack the human approach and insights that are central to assess how a city is actually lived and perceived. That is why the smart city has been also evolving to incorporate, more than technological and digital infrastructure and performance criteria, a more holistic territorial intelligence [15, co-creation [16] as innovation driver [17] an idea of collective creativity, a continuum between urban and human ecology, the inclusion of collaborative citizen platforms and crowd economy inputs to become a "socially constructed space-territory for the exercise of full citizenship, if you will, a crucible of humanity in permanent reconstruction" [18].

As comparative territorial evaluation systems, city rankings are a parallel mirror of the lack of the human insight peril. Although they might be built on sound methodologies and indicators and that they have been evolving to more and more intangible and emotional insights, such as happiness, they still might contribute to biased assessments. That is relevant because it influences cities competition for attracting visitors and investors and the self-esteem of its residents. For good and for bad, this value-adding (or subtracting) dynamics influences places′ reputation and therefore their value.

A metaphor for the incorporation of human dynamics in territorial evaluation systems is the assessment of the weather. One might know important and extremely accurate indicators such as temperature, humidity, wind speed and chance of rain, but from the user perspective what matters is the "real feel" and that is why it has been included in weather forecast apps (and been established as an iconic ice breaker topic in conversations) due to its common ground and interest.

Moreover, management and communication models have to be considered when addressing placemaking.

Contemporary territorial management models include place branding, city marketing and territorial communication [19]. And communication models take into account not only what a place is, what it offers, the infrastructures and amenities it provides, but also the perceptions of the "lived" territory, the potential of experience and network it holds [20].

Central to this rationale is the idea of territorial brand and how it is formed. Territorial brands have, like other brands, two main purposes: to identify and to differentiate. That is, to create, manage and promote a competitive identity [11].

Going beyond simplistic emission-reception approaches to communication, contemporary models assume a holistic perspective to brand building, reflecting contemporary trends of strategic communication and the inclusion of participatory dynamics and its implications for brand identity and governance [21–23].

Robert Aitken and Adriana Campelo [10] conceptualized a participatory approach to place brands. Drawing from the challenge of providing a basis for developing a place brand for the Chatham Islands archipelago, in New Zealand, they highlighted the importance of cultural context and elected the four Rs – rights, roles, responsibilities, and relationships - as central concepts to understand the essence of the place and its social ontology.

Moreover, the authors defend that brands are formed as sums of mental associations that are interactive and evolve in time as further interaction takes place, therefore, a social construct, that is in a continuous ongoing co-creative process. "Assuming that brands are artefacts to aggregate meanings, infuse and diffuse values, influence culture, and provoke and create cultural change (…) co-creation does not work to provide brand meanings in one direction or another but is open-ended so that meaning is achieved through the interplay between social relationships and communal experience" [10] (p. 916).

Furthermore, co-created meanings reflect the experiences of different stakeholders, the result of complex and dynamic human interaction with the territory and its representation. This is an empowerment process as "this co-creation changes the control and ownership of the brand (…) consumers are moving to own the brand in a very tangible and immediate sense" [10] (p. 916) and the development of "a brand strategy based on a co-created experience empowers the community with decisions around brand positioning, representation, brand governance, and brand ownership" [10] (p. 926) which will influence the brand's sustainability and authenticity.

Concurrently, all the place related interactions and associations develop in multilayer and dynamic dimensions, co-creating value added synergies: "territory actively participates in value co-creation through interactions with other actors (e.g. firms, inhabitants and tourists). The territory is not only an output of human actions but also a process through which its essence and traits emerge over time. It can infinitely inspire firms with ideas, provided they are able to listen to it and recognise its value co-creator nature" [24] (p. 926).

An approach to systematic value co-creation in place branding has been developed, taking into account the participatory and relational nature of stakeholder involvement and establishing five co-creation types that proved the positive impact of co-creation, both considering: 1) "The inclusion and participation of stakeholders in the place branding process as co-creators is critical." [25] (p. 1) and that 2) "A co-creation approach can leverage unique opportunities for the place brand, enhancing brand equity, and representing a more authentic and coherent place identity and image" [25] (p. 76). Furthermore, the study proposes a shift from place brand management to place brand facilitation as it was observed "that 'facilitating' co-creation is more effective than 'managing' co-creation in place brands (…) implying a more flexible and dynamic structure that can encourage and promote participation in value-creating processes" [25] (p. 76).

Communicating a place through place branding recurrently entails an exercise of identity definition and that process proves to be a crucial placemaking step—and frequently a participatory one—as it implies a negotiated and shared meaning of what a territory is and a shared vision of what it wants to become [26], thus a co-created operational strategic dimension. Recent research indicates a nexus between co-creation and place attachment [27] and between this and attitudes and behaviours towards the territory [10, 28], summoning ownership and legitimacy issues [29], therefore recentring the human dimension of a co-construction, a co-creation of an idea of territory, place, community and its practices.

Furthermore, the recurring emergence of topics such as territorial co-intelligence [15], place attachment [27, 28, 30] and sense of place [31], stakeholders-based branding [32, 33] or co-creative storytelling [34] with their structuring endeavour search for territorial consonance, authentic experiences and the essence of a place seems to indicate the direction of a co-creative participatory paradigm as an essential condition for the effectiveness of territorial development and of a consistent, involved and resilient sense of community central to contemporary sustainable societies.

3 Assessing Co-creative Participatory Practices

If the benefits of stakeholders' involvement in different stages of placemaking may not offer substantial dispute, the implementation of participatory practices expose pragmatic challenges and ethical issues.

Participatory budgeting, for instance, has been promoted as common practice to strengthen democracy and give voice to citizens about their own territory. It has implications in place attachment and social identity [35] but it might be exposed as a legitimation strategy for pressure groups in deliberative processes frequently lacking accountability and governance.

Designing place brands increasingly incorporate citizen views through co-creative practices in some innovative experiences [36] such as "O que marca Porto Alegre?" [37] "Pacto Alegre" [38], in Brazil, but often implementation challenges arise, highlighting the crucial role of the designer both as facilitator of co-creation and as interpreter of a shared vision insight.

This leads to the already mentioned issue of territorial brand ownership. Co-creative participatory processes may be led by strategic and design teams that intend to understand the stakeholders' vision of the territory, but they can be also triggered organically by citizens and grassroot movements motivated to express their place attachment and sense of belonging against the misuse of territorial capital they feel they are entitled to as their own [39].

Furthermore, the effective outcome of the co-creative process of territorial brands and communication strategies might be eventually cannibalized. Final decisions on which narrative will prevail might be heavily sensitive to strategic interests on the territory and vulnerable to the balance of powers at stake.

Considering participation as intrinsically political [40], this entails the assumption that in placemaking not all co-creative processes are participatory, as they do not result in significant transformations for the people involved or an effective transfer of power does not occur in the deliberation process. That is, not all territorial engaged co-creation derives in a significant participatory outcome.

4 Final Notes

Placemaking is an intrinsically co-creative process based on human participatory dynamics. It is a continuous ongoing social movement of interaction, construction and reconstruction of a territory by its stakeholders that gives a place meaning and value.

The search for territorial consonance is the placemaking touchstone and can only be achieved by the deep understanding and the collective formulation of a shared vision of the essence of a place. Because it deals with identity, culture and strategic communication, place branding is a central part of placemaking. This process is in itself essentially transforming as it emerges from grassroots and authentic experiences and drives the development of a sense of place, place attachment and authenticity adding value to the territory.

But no matter how well intended co-creative and territorial communication processes are, sensitive issues emerge in their implementation. Ownership and governance of territorial brands, reducing territories to marketing logics, the instrumentalization of public participation to legitimize political decisions and strategies, the appropriation of communal symbolic capital by private initiatives are some of the questions that need to be approached with critical thinking. The role of the facilitator of co-creating actions must be oriented with an ethical filter, respecting participants and providing a truly flow to channel their views, transmitting them into the chain of decisions that will make their deliberative intentions transform into real achievements, thus being transformative, empowering and effectively participatory.

References

1. PPP: A Guide to Neighbourhood Placemaking in Chicago, Project for Public Places and the Chicago Metropolitan Planning Council (2008). http://www.placemakingchicago.com/cms files/placemaking_guide.pdf
2. Sanders, L., Simons, G.: A social vision for value co-creation in design. Open Source Business Resource, December 2009. http://timreview.ca/article/310
3. Frow, P., McColl-Kennedy, J.R., Payne, A.: Co-creation practices: their role in shaping a health care ecosystem. Ind. Mark. Manage. **56**, 24–39 (2016)

4. Hanna, S., Rowley, J.A.: Practitioner-led strategic place brand management model. J. Mark. Manag. **29**(15/16), 1782–1815 (2013)
5. Kavaratzis, M., Kalandides, A.: Rethinking the place brand: the interactive formation of place brands and the role of participatory place branding. Environ. Plan. A **47**(6), 1368–1382 (2015)
6. Pamment, J., Cassinger, C.: Nation branding and the social imaginary of participation: an exploratory study of the Swedish Number campaign. Eur. J. Cult. Stud. **21**(5), 561–574 (2018)
7. Zenker, S., Erfgen, C.: Let them do the work: a participatory place branding approach. J. Place Manag. Dev. **7**(3), 225–234 (2014)
8. Hankinson, G.: Place branding research: a cross-disciplinary agenda and the views of practitioners. Place Brand. Public Dipl. **6**(4), 300–315 (2010)
9. Duarte Melo, A.: City rankings and the citizens: exposing representational and participatory gaps. In: Pereira, P., Ribeiro, R., Oliveira, I., Novais, P. (eds.) SC4Life 2019. LNICSSITE, vol. 318, pp. 154–169. Springer, Cham (2020). https://doi.org/10.1007/978-3-030-45293-3_12
10. Aitken, R., Campelo, A.: The four Rs of place branding. J. Mark. Manag. **27**(9–10), 913–933 (2011)
11. Anholt, S.: Competitive Identity – The New Brand Management for Nations, Cities and Regions. Palgrave Macmillan, London (2007)
12. Anholt, S.: Places: Identity, Image and Reputation. Palgrave Macmillan, Basingstoke (2010)
13. Ashworth, G., Kavaratzis, M. (eds.): Towards Effective Place Brand Management: Branding European Cities and Regions, pp. 173–190. Edward Elgar Publishing, Massachusetts (2010)
14. Eremia, M., Toma, L., Sanduleac, M.: The smart city concept in the 21st century. Procedia Eng. **181**, 12–19 (2017)
15. Atlee, T.: Participatory Sustainability: notes for an emerging field of civilizational engagement. CreateSpace, Co-Inteligence Institute, Oregon (2017)
16. Zandbergen, D.: We are sensemakers": the (anti-)politics of smart city co-creation. Public Cult. **29**(3 (83)), 539–562 (2017)
17. Hambleton, R.: The New civic leadership: place and the co-creation of public innovation. Public Money Manag. **39**(4), 271–279 (2019). https://doi.org/10.1080/09540962.2019.1592908
18. Covas, A.: Smart City: O decálogo da cidade inteligente e criativa, Observador, 15 February 2020
19. Hankinson, G.: Relational network brands: towards a conceptual model of place brands. J. Vacat. Mark. **10**(2), 109–121 (2004)
20. Govers, R.: Rethinking virtual and online place branding. In: Kavaratzis, M., Warnaby, G., Ashworth, G. (eds.) Rethinking place branding, pp. 73–83. Springer, Berlin (2015)
21. Kavaratzis, M., Warnaby, G., Ashworth, G. (eds.), Rethinking Place Branding, pp. 73–83. Springer, Heidelberg (2015). https://doi.org/10.1007/978-3-319-12424-7
22. Hatch, M.J., Schultz, M.: Toward a theory of brand co-creation with implications for brand governance. J. Brand Manag. **17**(8), 590–604 (2010)
23. Iglesias, O., Ind, N., Alfaro, M.: The organic view of the brand: a brand value co-creation model. In: Advances in Corporate Branding, pp. 148–174. Palgrave Macmillan, London (2017)
24. Baccarani, C., Cassia, F., Rossato, C., Cavallo, D.: Territory, firms and value co-creation synergies. J. Place Manag. Dev. **12**(2), 197–208 (2019)
25. Tavlian, S.: A Co-creation Approach to Place Branding: How Participatory Marketing Processes Can Leverage Opportunities of Value Co-creation in Place Branding. Copenhagen Business School, Copenhagen (2016)
26. Giovannella, C.: Smart territory analytics: toward a shared vision. Paper presented at SIS - Scientific Meeting 2014, Italy (2014)

27. Suntikul, W., Jachna, T.: The co-creation/place attachment nexus. Tour. Manage. **52**, 276–286 (2016)
28. Daryanto, A., Song, Z.: A meta-analysis of the relationship between place attachment and pro-environmental behaviour. J. Bus. Res. **123**, 208–219 (2021)
29. Martin, E., Capelli, S.: Region brand legitimacy: towards a participatory approach involving residents of a place. Public Manag. Rev. **19**(6), 820–844 (2017)
30. Zhang, C.X., Fong, L.H.N., Li, S.: Co-creation experience and place attachment: festival evaluation. Int. J. Hosp. Manag. **81**, 193–204 (2019)
31. Trelohan, M., Gentric. M., Manuelle Aquilina, M.: Putting sense of place at the centre of place brand development. Journal of Marketing Management33:5–6, pages 400–420 (2017)
32. Burmann, C.: A call for 'user-generated branding.' J. Brand Manag. **18**(1), 1–4 (2010)
33. García, J.A., Gómez, M., Molina, A.: A destination-branding model: an empirical analysis based on stakeholders. Tour. Manage. **33**(3), 646–661 (2012)
34. Bassano, C., Barile, S., Piciocchi, P., Spohrer, J.C., Iandolo, F., Fisk, R.: Storytelling about places: tourism marketing in the digital age. Cities **87**, 10–20 (2019)
35. Anders-Morawska, J., Hereźniak, M.: Beyond Figures and Numbers. Participatory Budgeting as a Leverage for Citizen Identity and Attachment to Place, International Studies, Stakeholder Engagement, Partnership and Collaboration in Public Policies, 24, 2/2019 (2019)
36. Silva, D.L., et al.: Designers em experiências de cocriação associadas ao place branding. In: Nunez, G., Zani, J., Oliveira, G.G. (eds.) Design em pesquisa, vol. 3, pp. 733–750. Marcavisual, Porto Alegre (2020)
37. ABEDESIGN: O que marca Porto Alegre? (2019). http://abedesign.org.br/lorem-ipsum-dolor-sit-amet/
38. Pacto Alegre. https://pactoalegre.poa.br/o-que-e
39. Duarte-Melo, A., Balonas, S.: Stickers on politics. The power of a brand is its weakness – a case of activism and subvertising. In: Ruiz-Mora, I., Gonçalves, G., Somerville, I. (eds.) Organizational and Strategic Communication Research: Global Trends, pp. 173–197. LabCom. IFP, Covilhã (2019)
40. Ribeiro, F., Melo, A.D.; Carpentier, N.: Introductory note. In: Comunicação e Sociedade 36: Rescuing participation, pp. 9–14 (2019)

Collaborative Pedagogy for Co-creation and Community Outreach: An Experience from Architectural Education in Social Inclusion Using the Miro Tool

Emilio Brandao(✉), Marco Adelfio, Shea Hagy, and Liane Thuvander

Department of Architecture and Civil Engineering, Chalmers University of Technology, Sven Hultins gata 6, 412 96 Gothenburg, Sweden
{brandao,adelfio,shea.hagy,liane.thuvander}@chalmers.se

Abstract. The Covid-19 pandemic has hugely affected our lives, including the daily work of university students and teachers, although such difficulties can emerge as drivers for change to discover new pedagogical possibilities. This paper explores this challenge in the context of the Design and Planning for Social Inclusion master's course within architecture, at Chalmers University of Technology (Sweden). It examines the pedagogical and societal contribution arising from a systematic use of a digital whiteboard as a collaborative tool, following an interlinked process of co-creation in which stakeholders and students interact continuously to co-create architectural and urban design proposals. Results of such an innovative process can be used to revisit the impact of Covid-19 on students' work and highlight positive and unexpected discoveries, and at the same time integrate feedback from local community and stakeholders, contributing to societal outreach and architectural practice.

Keywords: Architecture pedagogy · Co-creation methodology · COVID-19 · Digital tools · Miro · Online collaboration whiteboard

1 Introduction

The Covid-19 pandemic has heavily impinged on university education, with a significant amount of teaching being converted into a distance or online format. As noted by Rapanta et al. [1: 923] such a situation has required an "urgent and unexpected" change impacting on "social, cognitive and facilitatory" aspects of teaching. These challenges have become even more evident when the teaching/learning activity has been focused on community outreach and stakeholder engagement, as it has occurred with the Design and Planning for Social Inclusion architectural master's course, at Chalmers University of Technology (Sweden). The focus of this course is on stigmatized areas in suburban Gothenburg, belonging to the so-called Million Homes Programme, built from the mid-1960s to the mid-1970s, and usually connected to a negative imagery of socioeconomic

D. Raposo et al. (Eds.): AHFE 2021, LNNS 277, pp. 118–126, 2021.
https://doi.org/10.1007/978-3-030-80415-2_15

problems and decay of the built environment. The critical issues of these areas are tackled, within the course, by means of a collaborative learning and critical pedagogical approach, through which local stakeholders engage with students working on existing challenges and design projects. Under normal circumstances (the last 12 years), the course would consist of intense weeks combining lectures and workshops with interaction with citizens, organisations and local employees, often out in the field, but the contingencies of the pandemic have converted almost all activities into an online format [2]. Taking difficulties as drivers for change to discover new pedagogical possibilities, the teaching team has explored the use of new digital tools for supporting students' interaction and engagement with local stakeholders, including a systematic use of a digital whiteboard. Given this context, a research question is posed in this paper: What is the contribution of a digital whiteboard in terms of collaborative pedagogy and societal outreach for architectural students?

2 Collaboration and Co-creation

This work calls upon theories associated with the concepts of collaboration and co-creation, both from a pedagogical (architectural students' learning) and a societal outreach perspective (stakeholders in a local suburban context). The first theory; collaborative pedagogy, was adopted to provide "a set of teaching and learning strategies" [3: 103] that "recognize collaboration as an aid" [4: 54], engaging with both students and stakeholders as "collaborating learners" [5: 3]. The societal contribution of collaborative pedagogy that emerges when engaging with communities, is also interlinked with the realm of critical and radical pedagogies [6–8]. The second theoretical concept is related to co-creation, through which the interactions between students and stakeholders can be forged, aiming at "integrative strategies" [9] towards a common shared vision and goals. Following Adler [10, translated], "co-creation can be derived from the concept of participation and means that citizens are involved and create from the beginning to the end of a decision-making process. A co-creative dialogue approach is both a dialogue method for and an approach to participation and democracy".

3 Local Context: The Swedish Million Home Programme Suburbs in Gothenburg

The Swedish Million Home Programme suburban areas were built in the 1960s and 1970s as a result of an initiative driven by the Swedish government to provide affordable, accessible homes as well as to improve the housing standards in Sweden. In spite of the good intentions to promote housing for people independently from their income or social class, "the majority of the housing that was built took the form of large, rapidly developed areas in peripheral locations" [11: 303] and the Programme "has become almost synonymous in people's general consciousness with uniform, large-scale housing estates with buildings of grey pre-cast concrete slabs" [11: 304]. The geographical context for the course is composed of the districts of Angered and Bergsjön, in the northeastern part of Gothenburg, characterized by a series of "socially exposed and stigmatised neighbourhoods" with high levels of unemployment and large shares of first and second generation immigrant inhabitants [12: 140].

4 Academic Context: An Architectural Master's Course for Social Inclusion

The course Design and Planning for Social Inclusion (Social Inclusion) is part of the master's programme Architecture and Planning Beyond Sustainability at the Department of Architecture and Civil Engineering, Chalmers University of Technology, in Gothenburg, Sweden. The course runs each year full time (22,5 ects) between September to January and is open for postgraduate students with a background in architecture, urban design and planning, landscape architecture, interior architecture, environmental engineering, human geography, and conservation of build environments. The course provides knowledge and practice about challenges and opportunities for development in the Swedish Million Programme suburban areas of Gothenburg [13]. Social aspects of sustainable development and co-creation methodologies for citizen participation are specific focus areas.

The students' work is embedded with a norm-critical perspective [14], permeated by reflexive methodologies [15] and reflective practice [16, 17]. Such an approach, on the one hand, rediscusses (the decolonization of) the professional and societal role of architects (and their inherent power) in the shaping of the built environment (and the direct and indirect consequences that the profession's actions have on local communities and livelihoods) and, on the other, disentangles the multi-faceted and often challenging aspects of co-creation and participatory processes in architectural and urban design projects and practices.

The physical course facilities are located in the suburban housing area of Hammarkullen, part of the district of Angered, a typical area of the Million Programme in the sense of housing structures and socio-economic profile. Due to the Covid-19 situation, in the Autumn of 2020, the students had to work in hybrid settings, carrying out most of the collaborations digitally and online.

5 Methodology

5.1 Co-creation as Methodological Framework

Since 2017, the course applies a co-creation methodological framework, an extended version of Adler [10], with 5 stages of co-creation: co-initiate, co-analyze, co-design, co-implement, and co-evaluate. Additionally, the students write a critical reflection. In the course, each stage has a pedagogical purpose with goals and assignments. A collaborative data library supports knowledge transfer over time [18]. A summary of the pedagogical purpose for the different co-creation stages is provided in Table 1.

Table 1. Co-creation process in the course Social Inclusion, stages and pedagogical purposes.

Stages	Pedagogical purpose of the module, students…
Co-initiation (why?) 2 weeks	Learn about the course's main topics and theory and the local context; connect students with local stakeholders; collaboratively initiate projects together with stakeholders; map and analyse project stakeholders
Co-analysis (what?) 2 weeks	Collaboratively analyse and understand the project's (socio-cultural, physical, etc.) context and main topics/challenges through qualitative and quantitative analysis, the use of specific digital tools, and production of audio-visual narratives
Co-design (how?) 6 weeks	Develop and report own participatory design processes (including workshops and other activities) always involving respective project stakeholders, and supported by teachers with orientation and thematic workshops and supervision of design proposals
Co-implementation (who?)	Finalization of design process, synthesization of project work and production of and interactive online exhibition in the style of a common co-design workshop, to be shared with and collect feedback from peers, the public, local citizens and all the stakeholders involved in the course
Co-evaluation (follow-up!) 1 week	Connect back to main project stakeholders for collaborative evaluation and formal hand-over of the project material to stakeholders, reception of feedback on the entire collaborative process and outcome; students give something back to the community
Critical reflection 1 week	Individual toolbox and written critical reflection about the context, the collaborative learning and the view on the professional role

5.2 Using the Miro Tool in the Co-creation Process

The use of online digital whiteboards in academic teaching "facilitates far-flung users to communicate and interact with each other collaboratively" [19: 121]. The Miro tool (miro.com/about), an online collaborative whiteboard platform, is easy to learn, simple to use, with versatile and dynamic navigation, integration of multimedia possibilities. Miro has been tested in Social Inclusion in the academic year 2020–2021 to follow and implement the above described 5 interlinked stages of co-creation in which stakeholders and students interact continuously to co-create design proposals.

5.3 Data Collection

Data on the use of Miro have been collected through teachers' observations during all stages in the co-creation process, from the students' critical reflections assignment regarding the learning experience, the collaborative learning process and the view on the professional role formulated throughout the course. Takeaways are also extracted from the compulsory anonymous course evaluation (a survey where 20 out of 28 students answered) filled in by the students after finalisation of the course.

6 Results

Details about the results from using Miro in the different co-creation stages, how Miro supported the methodology and pedagogies, and reflections based on teachers observations are presented in Table 2. Figure 1 illustrates how Miro has been used in the workshops and interactive exhibition.

Overall, from the teachers' observations, the use of Miro can be deemed as extremely positive with clear benefits for enhancing students' reflective processes and interaction with stakeholders. Among the responses from the course evaluation, the students highlighted relevant aspects of using Miro such as; interactivity, collaborative value (especially in the context of an online exhibition), potential for use in future professional work, user-friendliness, no need for previous training (but recognizing that the quality of work improves with use), and contribution in adapting and reorganizing courses towards an online format. The individual critical reflections provided further input on the contribution of Miro. The students appreciated the possibility to take notes and sketch together on ideas as a way to document discussions in the project teams, this was seen as a huge help in the students' digital work process. Miro has also been perceived as an effective way to mixed-media-co-work, exemplified by the game board development where it sparked interesting discussion between all stakeholders, including the students. Generally, working with online platforms like Miro from home also entails some conveniences and students indicated that they will continue to use those platforms even after the pandemic due to the abilities to instantly provide a structure for collaboration and meetings not depending on travel and meeting in person. The pandemic forced the students (and teachers) to get better in digital participation methods and working with tools like Miro helped to understand the digital divide and find ways to bridge it. Also, some challenges emerged, for example, students mentioned difficulties to conduct proper online workshops with private persons as some of them were unfamiliar with digital platforms. To overcome this, it is important to spend some time on introducing the digital online platform in order to make all workshop participants comfortable in using the tool. Thus, to make digital co-creation workshops more accessible and efficient careful planning and organization is needed.

Table 2. The use of Miro, reflections and challenges at the different stages of co-creation.

Stages	How Miro support the methodology	Reflections and challenges using Miro (own observations)
co-initiation	• intro to Miro in 2 short exercises; • co-initiation workshop on Miro: stakeholders bring project ideas & together with students transform them into projects	+ students learned fast to use Miro; - stakeholders may have different learning curves, but quickly adapted to the new workshop format and tool.
co-analysis	• workshops on collaborative mapping and collection of quant. & qual. data related to the context and stakeholders; • sharing of audio-visual workshop material within the whole class	+ effective for the organisation of methods workshops with students; - challenging to understand settings for internal-only accessibility to boards, but the logic behind was eventually found.
co-design	• workshop on how to run online participatory workshops; • game design workshop by guest teachers; • students own use of Miro to run several of their own workshops, group work and even individual work; • teachers supervision of design projects through direct interactive sketching over students' work on Miro	+ Miro is effective in design, development and implementation/use for basic online board games; - stakeholders experience challenges in accessing Miro in co-design workshop as it requires a computer/tablet to easily access boards. Adequate prep and adaptation to the participants is crucial; + students use Miro for their design process, supporting internal group interactions & iterative processes; + the use for design supervision is effective, with students able to follow live the teacher feedback (text & sketch).
co-implementation	• structuring, collaborative design, mounting and navigation of a fully online and interactive exhibition, with	+ the public has full access to a versatile multimedia exhibition;
	versatility of approaches in the application and use of Miro.	+ students creative process and design skills are fully applied and assessed; + interactivity is easy to conduct through comments and sketches; + exhibitions can be open for a much longer time than physical versions.

(continued)

Table 2. (*continued*)

co-evaluation	• co-evaluation workshop on Miro with project stakeholders and handover of project material.	+after following the projects during the semester, stakeholders have easier access & interaction to the tool and project.
critical reflection	• sharing of the graphical manifestos on a common/whole class board; • short class mood-exercise evaluating the course by the timeline of events (usually done physically on a whiteboard).	+Miro is good in supporting students integrated reflective processes while being fun to use and discover at the same time.

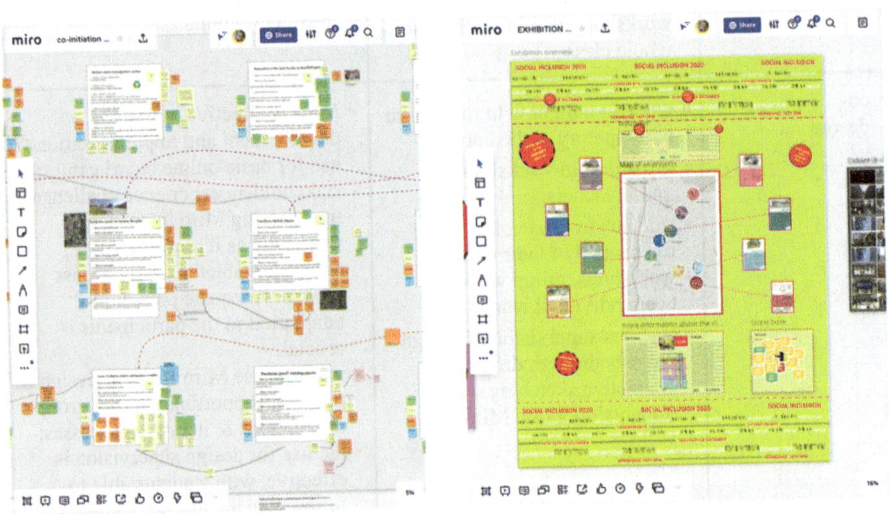

Fig. 1. Screen dumps from Miro sessions. Left: Results of the co-initiation workshop (Sept 29th 2020). Right: Interactive Online Exhibition of all the projects on Miro (opened Dec 16th 2020), https://miro.com/app/board/o9J_lcU-aSI/

7 Discussion and Conclusion

This paper has explored the use of digital tools for students' interaction and for engaging with local stakeholders, more specifically the systematic use of the digital whiteboard tool Miro. Miro supported the pedagogy and the constructive alignment of a course, as well as helped the students in aspects of project management, organization, and communication of the work, through effective and synthesized presentations.

Miro, used in the online exhibition both facilitated and catalyzed the spread of the intended collaborative pedagogy and co-creation embedded within the course. Through the use of the digital tool the students and teachers became both learners and designers of collaborative strategies, experimenting and discovering new ways of presenting, designing and engaging with one another and the other stakeholders. While the digital tool was inaccessible to some and could have been a barrier, a large increase in engagement from all stakeholder groups was observed in comparison to previous years when the exhibitions were in a physical space. There were actually two student projects dealing directly with the digital divide in these communities and through the online exhibition tested their methods, designs and approaches. The temporal and versatile nature of the digital tool also allowed for an interaction at many different levels, from emojis, to comments and surveys and most interesting the ability for all to co-creatively re-align or reset the goals of the projects. This happened not only at the shorter afternoon opening of the exhibition where all students and 100+ invitees were interacting on a pre planned schedule but there was so much interest and engagement that the teachers kept the exhibition open for weeks after to allow for continued interactions, comments and feedback.

The innovative use of this tool supported the students' design iterations, interactions and creative processes, culminating in a final artistic and interactive exhibition, which was open to the online public. Results from this process have included feedback from local community and stakeholders which contributed both to societal outreach and architectural practice, as well as highlighted positive and unexpected discoveries on and of students' work during the Covid-19 pandemic.

References

1. Rapanta, C., Botturi, L., Goodyear, P., Guàrdia, L., Koole, M.: Online university teaching during and after the Covid-19 crisis: refocusing teacher presence and learning activity. Postdigital Sci. Educ. **2**(3), 923–945 (2020). https://doi.org/10.1007/s42438-020-00155-y
2. Chalmers: Course PM: Design and Planning for Social Inclusion. https://chalmers.instructure.com/courses/10588/assignments/syllabus (2020)
3. Le, H., Janssen, J., Wubbels, T.: Collaborative learning practices: teacher and student perceived obstacles to effective student collaboration. Camb. J. Educ. **48**(1), 103–122 (2018)
4. Howard, R. M.: Collaborative pedagogy. A guide to composition pedagogies, pp. 54–70 (2001)
5. Zhou, X., Chen, L.-H., Chen, C.-L.: Collaborative learning by teaching: a pedagogy between learner-centered and learner-driven. Sustainability **11**(4), 1174 (2019)
6. Freire, P.: Pedagogy of the Oppressed. Penguin Books, London (1970)
7. Hooks, B.: Teaching to Transgress. Education as the Practice of Freedom. Routledge (1994)
8. Hooks, B.: Teaching Community. A Pedagogy of Hope. Routledge (2003)
9. Savage, G., Bunn, M., Gray, B., Xiao, Q., et al.: Stakeholder collaboration: implications for stakeholder theory and practice. J. Bus. Ethics **96**, 21–26 (2008)
10. Adler, I.-L.: Medskapardemokrati. Interaktiva styrningsprocesser och medskapande dialogarbetssätt. Göteborgs universitet, Förvaltningshögskolans rapporter, vol. 134 (2015)
11. Hall, T., Vidén, S.: The million homes programme: a review of the great Swedish planning project. Plan Perspect **20**(3), 301–328 (2005)
12. Stenberg, J.: Citizens as knowledge producers in urban change: participation changing procedures and systems. Footprint - Participatory Turn Urbanism **7**(2), 131–142 (2013)
13. Roussou, E., Da Cruz Brandao, E., Adelfio, M., Thuvander, L.: Social Inclusion: When community outreach becomes the core of architectural education. Report ACE, Chalmers University of Technology, Sweden (2019).

14. Petrescu, D., Trogal, K.: The Social (Re)Production of Architecture. Routledge, London (2017)
15. Alvesson, M., Sköldberg, K.: Reflexive Methodology: New Vistas for Qualitative Research. SAGE Publications, Thousand Oaks (2009)
16. Dewey: How we think. Prometheus Books, New York (1991)
17. Schön, D.A.: The Reflective Practitioner. How Professionals Think in Action. Basic Books Inc., New York (1983)
18. Thuvander, L., Green, C., Adelfio, M., Brandao, E., et al.: Piloting a collaborative data library of fine-grained data to support knowledge facilitation in architectural courses. In: IOP Conference Series: Earth and Environmental Science, vol. 588, no. 052042, pp. 1.15–1.19 (2020)
19. Prasetya, D., Ashar M.: Design of interactive whiteboard to support E-learning. In: 1st International Conference on Vocational Education and Training (2017)

Design Infrastructures: Proposing Alternative Strategies for Countries with a Lower Maturation of Design Culture

Nina Costa[1,2(✉)], Vasco Branco[1,2], Rui Costa[1,2], Afonso Borges[1,2], Raul Cunca[1,3], António Modesto[1,4], and Ana Vieira Silva[1,5]

[1] Research Institute for Design, Media and Culture (ID+), Aveiro, Portugal
ndc@ua.pt
[2] University of Aveiro, Aveiro, Portugal
[3] Faculty of Fine Arts, Lisbon University, Lisbon, Portugal
[4] Faculty of Fine Arts, Porto University, Porto, Portugal
[5] Polytechnique Institute of Cávado e do Ave, Barcelos, Portugal

Abstract. In Europe, Design Centers and Associations are considered as key infrastructures to efficiently promote and represent the discipline. However, in some countries with a lower maturation of Design culture – such as the case of Portugal - there are no official actors fully dedicated to these activities. Previous research indicated Design schools as a potential alternative infrastructure to promote and represent Design, but further research is needed to understand what they can learn/adapt from the activities currently undertaken by Centers and Associations. This paper maps the European landscape looking in particular at BEDA (Bureaux of European Design Association) members. Based on these insights and recent infrastructuring literature, it develops adapted strategies for observation activities to test with Design schools in the Portuguese territory. The results obtained are a first step to bring countries with lower maturation of design culture under the EU Design Ecosystem radar.

Keywords: Design observation · Design networks · Infrastructuring · Design schools

1 Introduction

Design is recognized as a key factor of innovation [1], as well as a cultural mediator and decisive agent in increasing the quality of life. To better capture its multiple realities and develop more adequate national design policies, several models and indicators have emerged [2]. According to Terence Love [3, 4], Design Centers such as the UK design council or the Danish Design Center, are considered as key infrastructures to guide and apply these models in Europe. Also characterized as gatekeepers, they adopt a central role in Design networks, providing access to, and connecting various elements in the Design ecosystem, giving them visibility [3, 4]. However, in some European countries, where there are no official entities dedicated to the representation and promotion of Design

D. Raposo et al. (Eds.): AHFE 2021, LNNS 277, pp. 127–134, 2021.
https://doi.org/10.1007/978-3-030-80415-2_16

(e.g. Bulgari, Cyprus), information tends to be scattered and, as such, difficult to use. This can hamper the development of more performing Design systems in geographical areas where no central actor exists to perform this role.

The Portuguese case falls into this latter category. After the closure of the Portuguese Design Center (2013) and the loss of representativeness of the national design associations, there have been few alternatives to represent and promote Design – and consequently for systematic data collection about the ecosystem. Moreover, the funding to undertake such operations is becoming thinner because of the socio-economic crisis installed. A previous study undertaken within the project "Towards a Design Observatory in Portugal" [5] proposed Design Schools network as a potential alternative design infrastructure to apply a distributed design observation approach. Built with a territorial reach and proximity to local communities, schools seem to be a fundamental national infrastructure which can contribute to the co-creation of more resilient Design observation systems. However, additional research is needed to confirm and explore this hypothesis.

Design Infrastructures. Early notions of design infrastructures indicate Design Centers and associations as key components of wider design systems [3, 4]. Their presence or absence already acts as an indicator that differentiates between economies led by design; and economies whose knowledge and culture about the discipline is still developing. According to Love [3, 4] Design centers are made of complex connections, each with its own objectives, vision, mission and strategies and identifies four archetypes in particular: (i) Promotion: demonstrates how companies benefit from the use of design through case studies, products, storyboards, photographs and others; promotes government programs that support the use of design and activity improvement services; (ii) Consulting: usually offers skills and advice for product design, processes; patents, rights, design and development of new businesses; it can offer access to specific software for small and medium businesses; (iii) Services: has advanced resources and facilities to design, prototype, test various types of products and services; (iv) Investigation: focuses on research on multiple aspects of the discipline, provides access to data and research results on design. Studying these keystone structures is important to a better and more detailed understanding of the activities they develop, their main beneficiaries, operation mechanisms and resources allocated, as well as their role within design ecosystems. However, replicating such structures as-is might be ineffective given that - as mentioned by Love - having a mature design culture is a pillar for their continuance in the ecosystem. This condition has yet to be achieved in multiple countries across the globe.

More recent literature interprets infrastructuring as "continually renewing, complex socio-material relationships, in which embedded politics, voice and authorship are articulated components of the system" [6]; complex objects of design which need to account for emergent components of the ecosystem, plural views and need for intentional, long-term engagement/change [7]. Participatory infrastructuring refers to activities that focus on how we do and create capacity to do infrastructuring work, locally, with people and groups, with shared goals or interests, affected by and working in relation to the systems we seek to engage [7]. It is the work of creating resources that both socially and technically, enable adoption and appropriation beyond the initial design; and creates fertile ground to sustain a community of participants [6, 7], in an iterative loop of reflection-action [8]. Although this approach is increasingly relevant, there are still few empirical examples informing practitioners, researchers and other actors, on how to navigate within such complexity [8].

2 Methodology

Based on the challenges detailed in the previous chapter, this study's objectives are two folded: (1) to explore the current activities undertaken by key design infrastructures in Europe and understand the limitations and advantages of adopting/adapting their activities in geographical areas where there are no formal Design infrastructure; and (2) to develop adapted strategies for infrastructuring activities focused - in a first instance - on developing new design observation practices, like we are trying to do in Portugal. To achieve these objectives, we follow a two-stage research process. First, the paper characterizes the Centers and associations, members of BEDA (Bureau of European Design Associations). It collects the mission, activities and main beneficiaries of these Centers/Associations. It maps their emergence chronologically, and classifies their activities according to the archetypes proposed by Love [3] i.e. promotion, consulting, services and investigation. Based on the pillars of the Design Ecosystem Model proposed by Whicher [9] we also categorize the mains stakeholders/beneficiaries of these Centers. The model's main pillars are offer, demand, demand-offer - which we adapt, in this study, to designers, users and policy makers (government), respectively. Next, it looks more closely at the centers which have more prominent research/investigation activities. These steps rely on desktop research and qualitative data analysis [10], iteratively coding the available digital information about the Centers/associations' websites. It also uses an interview with the current program director of the Danish Design Center to complement the research findings. Second, it reflects on the limitations and advantages of adapting and applying existing observation practices in countries such as Portugal, which does not have a formal representative Design infrastructure. Within the DesignOBS project, it debates and develops an infrastructuring work with the community in an attempt to infuse systematic design observation mechanisms.

3 Results

BEDA Members Characterization. BEDA has in total, 47 members from 25 different European countries. Bulgari, Czech Republic, Cyprus and Portugal - countries from the European Union - are not part of this list. The map (Fig. 1) shows the year of foundation of these centers: half emerged before the 2000's, 20% were created between 2000–2009, and 26% between 2010–2018. About half of the countries members of BEDA have more than one representative. France is the leading (and only) country, with 5 different centers/associations, followed by Germany with 4. England, Slovenia, Hungary, Netherlands, Spain and Belgium have 3 different centers/associations, members of BEDA. This data shows that the number of centers is not necessarily related with the demographic size or design companies operating in the country (e. g. UK and Slovenia have the same number of centers). Regarding the timeline in Fig. 1, Hungary, Belgium, Estonia, and

France created centers, sometimes, with less than one year apart. This data already indicates that certain centers/associations are representative of specific cities or regions as opposed to all the territory, providing a more detailed view of design integration within a certain geographical area.

Archetypes. In addition to this chronological analysis, and based on the information available on the website of each center/association, we applied the classification developed by Love (2006, 2007) i.e. promotion, counseling, services, investigation activities. Most European centers - with the exception of 10 cases - show polyvalent functions, fitting in multiple categories of activities (Fig. 1), but mainly focused on Promotion and Counselling activities with 66% and 51% respectively; about one third provides Services; the eight members which have more evident Research activities constitute a much smaller part (17%). Moreover, the only research center which fitted within all the categories is the Design Council (UK).

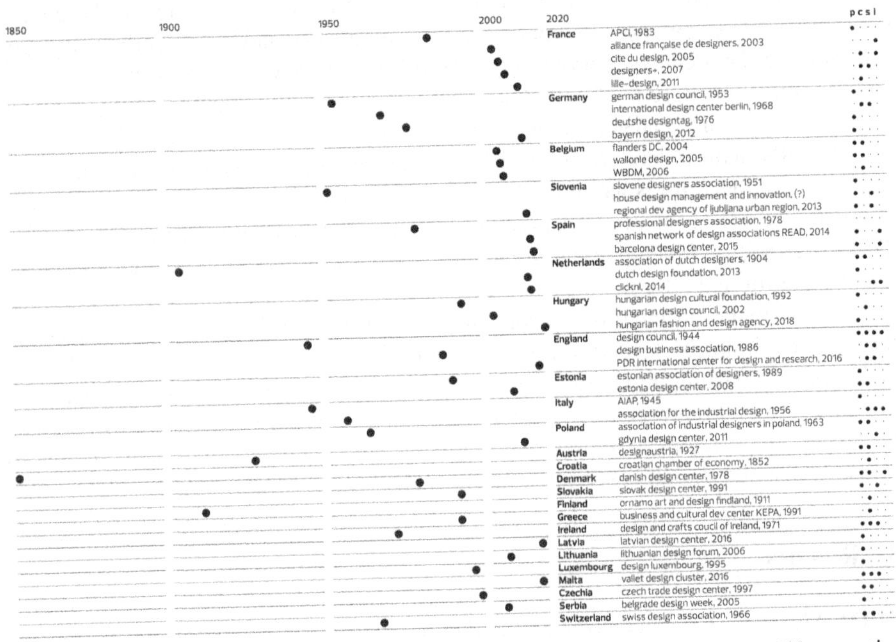

Fig. 1. Year of foundation and classification of BEDA members according to Love [3] promotion (p), counseling (c), services (s), investigation (i) (on the right).

Design Area. Evidence shows that most of the centers are focused on multiple areas of design, going from fashion, interior, industrial and graphic/communication design (74%). A very small portion is focused on one specific design area only, whilst 10% are about Creative Industries as a whole (including communication science). Three members are not design-focused, but rather include design within business innovation and economic activity (Croatia, Greece and Slovenia).

Stakeholders/Beneficiaries. Evidence shows that an overwhelming part of members are focused on design professionals only (53%). Centers which focus on both users and designers constitute 32% of the sample. Most websites focus on displaying best cases of products and services that demonstrate design craft and impact at socio-economic level, winning prizes and announcing contests (ex. DesignAustria). This gives visibility to design work at the national and international level. Associations such as ADI (Italy) regularly update a repository of design professionals in all or specific areas of design knowledge or present new regulations that affect/benefit design professionals (e. g. patents' rights, branding, intellectual property). Centers can also be more focused on users, connecting their needs with certain competencies and companies (ex. Dutch Designers Association). Few websites seem to be government oriented. Most of them do have a repository of professionals, but surprisingly, few present studies and/or encompassing information on the overall parts of the design ecosystem (e.g. education, research, designers, users, support, funding, policies), which could be used to develop public policy. We found some exceptions in Centers with research activities which we analyze below.

Centers with Research Activities. Results show that Centers/associations which undertake research activities develop state of the art design knowledge on topics mostly focused on industry and design profession, including (i) studies about intellectual property legal issues, (ii) case studies which demonstrate the impact of design infusion in multiple industry sectors (iii) state of the art knowledge about the design ecosystem, focused on adopting a critical approach to develop guidelines for improvement of the sector. Table 1 lists examples of topics of research of these centers.

Table 1. Examples of research topics and projects of selected centers/associations.

Center/Associations	Current research activities
UK design council	Series: black creatives, better places, design economy [11], leading women in design, future of design
DK danish design center	Projects: design cities, future welfare, design startups, danish design (DNA); cases: circular consumption, tech-focused solutions, urban-mobility [12]
FR alliance française de designers	Studies: intellectual property, designers rights and competencies, impact of covid in design profession
FR cite du design	Exploring the role of design within contemporary societies and the relationship between arts/crafts and design
NH clicknl	Projects: video games, social cohesion, home for the elerly, event experience (…); topics: energy transition and sustainability, agriculture, water and food, healthcare (…)
ES Spanish network of design associations (READ)	Projects: deontological code, design strategy, Spanish design ecosystem [13], design and public administration

The UK design council is one of the leading centers. Its website comprises four main parts: (1) presentation and mission of the Center, (2) strategic plan and offers (what we do), (3) calls for action and points of interaction with the general public (events, news, contacts), and (4) research results communicated via reports, interviews, stories, guidelines and recommendations. Although not as systematically, the DDC (DK) shares periodic studies showcasing the impact of design within the industrial sector. Recent projects have focused on understanding how design is accelerating businesses; and exploring the Danish design identity (DNA) in contemporary societies. Initiatives developed by READ (Spain) count with complementary research projects: one focused on creating a national strategy for design in Spain ("somos cultura, hacemos economia"), and another [13], more recent, aiming to collect and map the design resources and demand in the country.

4 Infrastructuring: The Portuguese Case

Building on the insights of the previous section, we provide an analysis of the potential advantages and limitations of embedding existing practices within a territory with no supporting infrastructures. We use Portugal as a case and indicate alternative routes for infrastructuring currently being applied in the DesignOBS project.

Synergies and Experiences. Creating partnerships or collaborations with international centers/associations can lever the project, providing guidelines, sharing experiences and giving some visibility to its initiatives. Following these guidelines, we explored new connections with other research international centers, including the DDC and the Cardiff Metropolitan University for its role in the development of the Design Ecosystem Model [14] which has been applied in diverse EU countries. DDC's collaboration and lessons learned emphasized the need to improve communication of design impact in multiple sectors, via case studies; using existing statistical data as well as social media information more efficiently; and lobbying the discipline at the government-level. Although structurally limited, these objectives were partially implemented or served as a guideline in our actions. A case study about design doctorates [15] demonstrated that the community needed to be more involved in data collection and curation – aspect which we embed in the development new design-focused databases through the involvement of REDE [16] – the National design school meeting, with 42 different professors/researchers, from 30 schools. The information that we currently have available is still not sufficient to have lobbying power at the government level but was so far sufficient to propose new practices regarding design research [17].

Instruments for Inquiry. From the studies we had access to, existing mechanisms of data collection about design - either education, research, professionals, users etc. rely on statistical data collected by governmental-led entities (i. e. public databases); surveys addressing one part of the ecosystem; invitations for partnerships in design-related topics. Latest initiatives use workshops with multiple stakeholders (users, professionals, policy makers) to create an encompassing, simplified map of the design ecosystem - using it as a support to guide policy making for the discipline [14]. In Portugal, these processes are still being developed. In the first instance, our efforts are focused on collecting secondary data and building participatory instruments to enable the co-design of a first map of the ecosystem and making a compelling case about Design. The approach, model and instruments are evolving objects of design, co-created with/by the community whose use depends on the feedback of multiple actors involved in the network.

Distributed and Participatory Network. One of the key differences between the Centers/Associations mentioned in Table 1 and Portugal, is the lack of a formal design infrastructure. To overcome this limitation, we adopted an alternative data collection approach partially based on a distributed network of actors/informants [15, 17] - the Design schools. Schools are currently the only infrastructure built with territorial reach and proximity to local actors and institutions; they do not heavily rely on governmental changes nor on intermittent funds that shifts every four years. Moreover, their involvement with the local systems can enrich design representation, create ownership of the data collected and bring forth issues which would go missing with a formal top-down approach. Knowledge transfer is a core mission of Schools, however, as entangled as it may be, the rules, roles, norms, advantages and tasks of informants within the observation-action loop are subject of continuous negotiation and inquiry via yearly meetings and an online digital and participatory platform. This aspect of infrastructuring and value creation for the actors involved in their multiple contexts and realities, is a key concern of the project as is the infusion of new practices of observation.

5 Conclusions

This study maps the design infrastructures currently available in Europe based on BEDA members, and explores how their best practices can be adopted/adapted in territories with lower maturation of design culture. The study's results show most centers are focused on promotion and counseling activities, with few oriented to design research/investigation, which are key to support the development of public policies. The question as to why this is so, given the increasing discussion about design and policy, should be further analyzed.

Additionally, research centers/associations do show a certain pattern of action, which we partially embed in the Portuguese case. Other structures, however, are harder to replicate. To overcome these issues, we propose distributed networks of observation and enabling participatory mechanisms of inquiry. This modus-operandi can be further replicated and expanded in countries with similar conditions.

Acknowledgments. This article is a result of the project Design Obs. Towards a design Observatory in Portugal: models, instruments, representation and strategies supported by Lisbon Regional Operational Program (LISBOA 2020) and the Competitiveness and Internationalization Operational Program (POCI-01-0145-FEDER-032445), under the PORTUGAL 2020 Partnership Agreement, through the European Regional Development Fund (ERDF) and FCT – Foundation for Science and Technology.

References

1. NESTA: The Innovation Index: Measuring the UK's Investment in Innovation and its Effects, London (2009)
2. Whicher, A.: Design ecosystems and innovation policy in Europe. Strateg. Des. Res. J. **10**(2), 117–125 (2017)
3. Love, T.: Design centres as elements of design infrastructure. SEE Des. Bull. **44**(2), 3–5 (2006)
4. Love, T.: Design infrastructures: the key to design - driven socio - economic. Int. Assoc. Scieties Des. Res. (2007)
5. Branco, V., et al.: Towards a Portuguese design observatory: models, instruments, representation and strategies (project description) (2019). http://designobs.pt/. Accessed 07 Nov 2019
6. Agid, S.: 'Dismantle, change, build': designing abolition at the intersections of local, large-scale, and imagined infrastructures. Des. Stud. **59**, 95–116 (2018)
7. Vink, J., Koskela-Huotari, K., Tronvoll, B., Edvardsson, B., Wetter-Edman, K.: Service ecosystem design: propositions, process model, and future research agenda. J. Serv. Res. **24**(2), 168–186 (2020)
8. Bødker, S., Dindler, C., Iversen, O.S.: Tying knots: participatory infrastructuring at work. Comput. Support. Coop. Work (CSCW) **26**(1–2), 245–273 (2017). https://doi.org/10.1007/s10606-017-9268-y
9. Whicher, A., Cawood, G., Walters, A.: Research and practice in design and innovation policy in Europe. In: Leading Innovation Through Design. International Design Management Research Conference, pp. 1–19 (2012)
10. Miles, M.B., Huberman, M.A.: Qualitative Data Analysis: AN Expanded Sourcebook. Sage, Thousand Oaks (1994)
11. Design Council: The design economy 2018: the state of design in the UK (2018)
12. Danish Design Center: Shaping the Next (2019)
13. Ecosistema del Diseno Espanhol (2019). https://xn--ecosistemadeldiseo-30b.es/
14. Whicher, A., Swiatek, P., Ward, J.: Design4Innovation policy booklet 1: mapping design ecosystems (2018)
15. Costa, N., et al.: Towards a design observatory: the case of scholarly design research in Portugal. In: Proceedings of the Design Society: Design Conference, vol. 1, pp. 827–836 (2020)
16. Borges, A., Silva, A.C., Modesto, A., Cunca, R., Costa, R.C., Branco, V.: REDE#01: Reunião de Escolas de Design, Aveiro, Portugal (2018)
17. Costa, N., et al.: Mapping the research thread of PhDs in design: a PhD citation analysis of the Portuguese doctorates. In: Chakrabarti, A., Poovaiah, R., Bokil, P., Kant, V. (eds.) Design for Tomorrow—Volume 2: Proceedings of ICoRD 2021, pp. 203–216. Springer, Singapore (2021). https://doi.org/10.1007/978-981-16-0119-4_17

Psychosocial Toxicology: Emotional Work and Mental Health in Security Guards

Olga Piñeros(✉) and Carlos Marín

Occupational Health Administration Program, Corporación Universitaria Minuto de Dios – Campus – UVD, Bogotá, DC, Colombia
olga.pineros@uniminuto.edu

Abstract. Mental health is decisive in workers with surveillance service activities. The activity includes dynamics of treatment and emotionality of users who interact with them, determining physical, cognitive and emotional overexertion.

The World Health Organization (WHO), recognizes it, and requests actions for psychological, fiscal and social well-being.

Qualitative-quantitative, descriptive study of emotional conditions and health disorders. 162 workers, 34 residential buildings in Bogotá-Colombia. Non-probabilistic sample of volunteer participants. Informed consent signature. Instruments "Battery of Instruments for the Evaluation of Psychosocial Risk Factors" with intra-labor reliability levels 0.957; and stress 0.83.

78% report monotony in work development and 82% due to verbal abuse; 32% affected by work stress with physiological and behavioral symptoms, depression and a sense of isolation, physiological gastrointestinal disorders and sleep disorders.

Emotional dissonance and conflict in the role, alienation and estrangement from the self; non-self-recognition and when they act for their role.

Keywords: Toxicology-psychosocial · Work-emotional · Psychology · Ergonomics · Management

1 Introduction

Mental health in workers who perform surveillance service activities is decisive in their performance. The activity is directly influenced by the dynamics of treatment and emotionality of some users who arrive and interact with these workers, determining an effort, not only physical or cognitive, but also emotional.

The aforementioned dynamics means that security guards must control feelings and emotions according to the behavioral protocols determined by their organization, considering this task as an integral part of the work and as a requirement to keep the job.

It is of great importance to emphasize that government bodies acknowledge these situations and adopt measures to outline actions to mitigate this risk, as is the case of the call made by the World Health Organization (WHO) towards psychological well-being, treasury and social.

D. Raposo et al. (Eds.): AHFE 2021, LNNS 277, pp. 135–142, 2021.
https://doi.org/10.1007/978-3-030-80415-2_17

For all the above, it is necessary that the psychosocial factor due to emotional work should be evaluated by the companies, in order to prevent negative consequences that, in the long term, deteriorate the mental health of the worker, increasing the probability of the occurrence of derived pathologies from job stress.

Now, the affectation by stress triggered by environmental situations, determines in the affected individuals, behavioral changes after a critical event to which they are subjected, triggering general malaise, and disinterest in pleasant activities that does not allow them to enjoy the situations that life presents [1]. Discouragement and anhedonia are the prevalent symptoms of stress reactions that lead to a depressive pathology in the individual. However, this symptomatology is controlled by a response of the humoral cell pathway of the immune system, which on many occasions, fails to regulate it, and consequently, triggers depression and the appearance of multiple diseases in the individual [2].

It is necessary to specify that the nervous system and the immune system have parallel functions in the recognition of elements that surround an individual's environment, valuing them as strange, known or not dangerous, and that they allow an adaptive response in a simple or quick [3].

The nervous system shows its reaction through the "reflex arc" and the immune system through "the inflammatory reflex", in order to detect dangerous invaders present in the body [4].

When there is a reaction of the immune system, the reflex of this, leads to an inflammation in the individual that prepares the body for an immediate-innate and rapid response of basic defense, with its action being limited in time.

Likewise, the immune reflex has a slower but more specific adaptive reaction and recognizes specific antigens against a good number of pathogens that attack it[4].

It is necessary to emphasize that inflammatory and anti-inflammatory reflexes regulate the cardiac and digestive system in accordance with the central nervous system and have a direct relationship with the individual's mood [4, 5].

That is why when an individual reacts to a situation derived from external non-biological or viral agents, they will have an identical reaction of protection to the individual as if it were biological or viral.

It should be noted that according to Sung Ja Rhie, et al., establishes evidence in the appearance of a neuroinflammation by inflammatory cytosines, derived from disorders of the psychological, neuroendocrine and nervous system.

Thus, the metabolism of neurotransmitters changes, in addition; it alters the hypothalamic pituitary-adrenal axis, due to a pathological activation of microglial cells.

The foregoing showing an alteration in neuroplasticity with structural brain changes, intervening in cognition and emotional behavior, and in the appearance of anxiety and depression [6].

2 Method

Qualitative-quantitative, descriptive study of emotional conditions, in the performance of emotional work functions, in centers that serve internal and external clients, and whose functions are focused on private surveillance activities.

Qualitative, due to the fact that workplace conditions are analyzed using an open version strategy where each worker was asked 5 questions that were answered in a free report.

This study addresses the specific routine task, aimed at fulfilling emotional management functions in customer service; towards the identification of situations that alter workers, in order to outline actions to improve mental health and well-being conditions for the population.

Quantitative, with application of "The battery of instruments for Psychosocial Risk Factors", developed for Colombia by the Ministry of Social Protection. It has a methodology of assessment, for the approach and qualification, triangulating and correlating the data collected from the situations raised in the questionnaire. They have liker-type scales with 5 frequency response options.

In addition, a review of the occupational medical history of workers with risk levels was carried out; tall and very tall, in addition, semi-structured interview.

Then, the process, activity, functions and their relationship with the internal and external client were verified; In addition, the types of interaction that were had with each of them, in such a way that the over-effort or protective factor of the interrelation with these clients was verified, determining the triggers of their psycho-pathological conditions reported in the format of stress.

A population of 162 private security guards who carry out their work activities in 34 residential buildings in different locations and socioeconomic strata of Bogotá-Colombia. In the application of the instruments, no supervisors or heads of these personnel were included.

Non-probabilistic sample of voluntary participants. Carrying out an invitation campaign to participate in the study with the signing of the informed consent.

A participation agreement was made with the general management that grants permission to the worker of the times for the development of the test, in addition, the interaction by individual videoconference with those who scored with risk levels; high and very high, this activity carried out by the psychologist of the research team. In addition, the company's occupational physician facilitates the review of the occupational medical history.

2.1 Inventory of Instruments Used

The instruments used "The Battery of Instruments for the Evaluation of Psychosocial Risk Factors" with intra-labor reliability levels 0.957; and stress 0.83

a. The informed consent format, which confirms information to the worker on the use of their data in the improvement of health and safety conditions at work, in accordance with Colombian law, and where they express their acceptance of participation.

b. General data sheet or sociodemographic profile, consisting of 19 items that inquire about personal data, way of life, other companies where he has worked, seniority in the position developed, clarity of the location of his position in the organizational structure, hours of work and type of contract.
c. The intra-work questionnaire made up of 97 questions that address the dimensions of:

- Leadership characteristics,
- Social relationships at work,
- Performance feedback,
- Recognition and compensation,
- Clarity of the role,
- Environmental demands and physical effort,
- Participation and management of change
- Demands of the working day,
- Rewards derived from belonging to the organization and the work carried out,
- Quantitative demands, Influence of work on the non-work environment,
- Opportunities for the use and development of skills and knowledge,
- Training,
- Control and autonomy over work,
- Emotional demands,
- Mental burden lawsuits.

d. The stress questionnaire, made up of 35 items that analyzes the symptoms:

- Physiological,
- Of social behavior,
- Intellectual and labor,
- Psychoemotional.

2.2 Inclusion Criteria for Workers in the Study

Those who voluntarily and after the awareness campaign agreed to participate in the study by signing the informed consent.

Personnel older than 6 months after being hired.

Personnel with operational surveillance charge.

2.3 Exclusion Criteria for Participation in the Study

Workers diagnosed with mental illness, in the status of general illness, not work.

Personnel in charge of leadership.

3 Results

3.1 Individual Conditions

The study found (Table 1):

Table 1. General data sheet

General data	n	%
Complete baccalaureate	105	65%
Male gender	162	100%
Free Union	121	75%
Worker's residence Bogotá	162	100%
Socio-economic stratum predominate: 2	132	82%
Type of home you live in: rent	118	73%
Number of people financially dependent: 3	121	75%
Length of service in the company: 1 to 3 years	73	45%
Length of service: 1 to 3 years	73	45%
9 h of daily work 9 h of work to day 30 years of average age in the daily population	162	100,00%

The population of this study is:

Male. Average age of 30 years. With completed high school studies. Belonging to socioeconomic stratum level 2.

73% of them live in leased locations. A seniority in the position related to seniority in the company. A total working hours of 9 h a day are reported with rotating shifts; of 2 consecutive shifts in the day, 2 in the afternoon, 2 at night and 2 breaks.

3.2 Intra-employment Conditions

Low quantitative and environmental demands and physical effort; Main risks found monotony in the development of work in 78%.

High emotional demands, evidence of verbal abuse by users in 82%.

The demands of responsibility in the position have a high indicator because it has to respond to the entrance to residents of the buildings and visitors, expressed by 83%.

High demands of the working day in 100% of the population since they must cover rotating shifts in the morning, afternoon and night, with coverage on weekends, involving night shifts.

Respecto al a consistencia del rol, en el 100% de la población son claras sus funciones en el lugar de trabajo.

The influence of work on the extra-labor environment, reports 49% of workers with expression of affectation due to night and weekend shifts.

Control and autonomy over work has a high influence, because despite knowing their functions, on many occasions the building administrators issue orders contrary to those of their supervisor, this in 15% of them.

Regarding the opportunities for the use and development of skills and knowledge, they report that they do not see the possibility of carrying out a different activity, due to the specificity of their work, this for 100%.

100% state that their role is clear.

Regarding recognition and compensation, 100% refer that the salary level is low and it forces them on many occasions to cover another colleague, in their rest times.

3.3 Stress Conditions

32% (17 Workers) affected by work stress with physiological symptoms of muscle tension, neck and back. In addition, sleep disorders in 26% (42 workers) of them.

32% of affected by behavioral symptoms of social behavior, framed in the desire not to want to meet any coworker.

Psycho-emotional symptoms with reports of depressive symptoms and a feeling of isolation in 24% (39 workers).

Physiological of gastrointestinal disorders 69% due to peptic ulcers, irritable bowel and diarrhea.

4 Discussion

Private security workers have been considered a population with high exposure to environmental agents derived from psychosocial factors, due to high work demands that cause an interrelation between work results, physical, mental and emotional conditions [7]. Further: the environment in which they work, the conditions of the work centers where they carry out the work with the interaction of many people and the responsibility with all of them.

It is necessary to highlight that in Colombia those who work in this activity have a precarious remuneration that does not exceed the minimum wage. Situation that worsens the condition, due to the fact that the work days that exceed the hours established by Colombian law, and with rotating shifts in the week, do not offer an opportunity for them to carry out an alternative activity that contributes to their monthly income [8].

5 Conclusions

Workers with work situations that differ from their own feelings because of actions they face at work that trigger an emotional dissonance leading them to a conflict situation in their role, in addition to causing, in some cases, alienation and estrangement from the me by not distinguishing when they are being themselves and when they act for their role.

This fact leads to the worker facing alterations derived from the environment, according to the results obtained, they coincide with the alterations or symptoms reported.

The worker faces alterations derived from the environment, according to the results obtained, which coincide with the alterations or symptoms reported.

The worker faces alterations derived from the environment, according to the results obtained, which coincide with the alterations or symptoms reported.

We determine a direct relationship with the treatment schemes they receive in their jobs, from the internal client and from the external client.

By causing a "reflex arc" with reports of feelings of isolation, sadness, anguish and depression, as well as immunosuppression and evidenced, in reports of permanent flu and respiratory disorders. They also refer to alterations of the cardiovascular system due to palpitations and alterations in the digestive system caused by peptic ulcers among other alterations of the system [9].

The emotional work in security guards establishes the need to review intra-work conditions, and project the study in the verification of symptoms associated with work stress, caused by alterations resulting from this work.

In order to identify the processes and target cases that merit direct intervention [8].

The verification of the production processes, their conditions, identification of their leaders and the activities that are developed allows an organization to establish necessary actions within the improvement of its organizational culture, and that this allows the improvement of the conditions of the workers [7].

The discipline of safety and health at work establishes the need to open spaces that promote the identification and improvement of working conditions. The continuous improvement cycle requires it, in such a way that the institutions must include in their action plans, activities that allow them to be vigilant and guarantors of the health and well-being of their collaborators, in addition to having a better knowledge of who day to day.

References

1. Ramírez, L.A., Pérez-Padilla, E.A., García-Oscos, F., Salgado, H., Atzori, M., Pineda, J.C.: Nueva teoría sobre la depresión: un equilibrio del ánimo entre el sistema nervioso y el inmunológico, con regulación de la serotonina-quinurenina y el eje hipotálamo-hipófiso-suprarrenal. Biomedica **38**(3), 437–450 (2018). https://doi.org/10.7705/biomedica.v38i3.3688
2. Dantzer, R., O'Connor, J.C., Lawson, M.A., Kelley, K.W.: Inflammation-associated depression: from serotonin to kynurenine. Psychoneuroendocrinology **36**(3), 426–436 (2011)
3. Sankowski, R., Mader, S., Valdés-Ferrer, S.I.: Systemic inflammation and the brain: novel roles of genetic, molecular, and environmental cues as drivers of neurodegeneration. Front. Cell. Neurosci. **9**, 28 (2015)
4. Medzhitov, R., Janeway, C.A.: Innate immunity: the virtues of a nonclonal system of recognition. Cell **91**(3), 295–298 (1997). https://doi.org/10.1016/s0092-8674(00)80412-2
5. Rosas-Ballina, M., et al.: Acetylcholine-synthesizing T cells relay neural signals in a vagus nerve circuit. Science **334**, 98–101 (2011). https://doi.org/10.1126/science.1209985
6. Rhie, S.J., Jung, E.-Y., Shim, I.: The role of neuroinflammation on pathogenesis of affective disorders. Soc. Coreana Rehabil. Ejerc. (2020). https://doi.org/10.12965/jer.2040016.008
7. Piñeros, O., Marín, C.: Psychosocial toxicity in colombian service companies. In: Goossens, R. (ed.) AHFE 2018. AISC, vol. 792, pp. 421–429. Springer, Cham (2019). https://doi.org/10.1007/978-3-319-94000-7_42

8. Marín, C., Piñeros, O.: Organizational management, human resources and mobbing. Findings in Colombia. In: Arezes, P.. (ed.) AHFE. AISC, vol. 791, pp. 110–115. Springer, Cham (2019). https://doi.org/10.1007/978-3-319-94589-7_11
9. Piñeros, O., Marín, C.: Toxicología psicosocial. Disruptores y predictores. Una mirada a docentes Colombianos. ORP 2017. Psicosociología (2017).

Traje à Vianesa – A Study on Historical Costume to Inform Contemporary Design Projects

Lídia Araújo and Gabriela Forman(✉)

CIAUD, Lisbon School of Architecture, Universidade de Lisboa, Rua Sá Nogueira, 1349-063 Lisboa, Portugal

Abstract. This paper investigates the *Traje à Vianesa*, a Portuguese traditional costume, focused on the abundance of textile craftsmanship. The study aims to discuss the preservation of technical knowledge through the documentation of related data. A qualitative methodology - relevant literature review, observation, *in situ*, and interviews to experts -, was used. Certain books, specifically the costume accreditation book approach the garment concerning its preservation in terms of original typology. Results suggest that, despite the existent bibliography, there is still comprehensive information to be compiled and documented (e.g., pattern making and technical know-how). This data should contribute to the local community and to inform contemporary projects as researchers/designers occasionally look into historical objects to investigate and gain perspective on methods and processes. This new understanding should help, not only the systematization of techniques refined through the ages but, also, to create awareness related to identity and cultural heritage.

Keywords: Historical costume · *Traje à Vianesa* · Sustainable design · Strategies for circularity

1 Introduction

1.1 Context and Aim of Investigation

The *Traje à Vianesa* is an emblematic traditional costume from the North Portuguese Region of Minho, that was defined and enriched throughout the 19th century [1]. The relevance of selecting this garment is based on its abundance of textile craftsmanship. From the raw materials to its manufacture, it used to be made locally by the artisans of the region. The study aims to discuss the preservation of that technical knowledge through the documentation of related data. It is focused on the original techniques and the respective materials. This should contribute to the local community (both cultural and economically) and, also, assist professionals as a tool able to be used during the creative process of varied contemporary projects.

Designers occasionally resource to strategies (e.g., *TED's TEN*) [2] or inspiration that look into textile practices from history or habits from a specific culture in a traditional

Traje means costume.

D. Raposo et al. (Eds.): AHFE 2021, LNNS 277, pp. 143–149, 2021.
https://doi.org/10.1007/978-3-030-80415-2_18

folk costume to gain fresh perspective on processes and methods [3]. This is equally the case if designers are interested in learning specific techniques to apply in projects or to support community, social engagement or cultural identity continuity.

The ecological, economic and social impact upon fast fashion production created concern about what, how, where and why things are made in the minds of designers, manufacturers and citizens. According to these issues, the *TED Research Group* from *University of the Arts, London* developed a set of *TEN* strategies for the design [2].

The proposal of these strategies is to contribute to the future of sustainable textile products [2]. The *Traje à Vianesa* content fits in the *TED's TEN* strategies 6th card – Design that Takes Models from Nature & History [4]. The present study can elucidate designers and researchers to look at this historical garment and the way it was made to rediscover techniques for contemporary sustainable fashion design [4] (Fig. 1).

Fig. 1. Earley & Politowicz's The TEN: design strategy cards [3].

Certain books, specifically the costume accreditation book *Traje à Vianesa – Caderno de Especificações para a Certificação* [1], approach this garment concerning its preservation in terms of original typology. However, authors and experts agree that the book needs further improvement in terms of data on its primary raw materials and eventual motifs that were changed or lost throughout the times. Fiber composition deviations, blends (instead of 100% wool) or replacements to metal sequins, metallic thread, natural dyes, started since the industrial revolution, following the invention of synthetic materials which might have had influence the materialisation of the design.

Other studies expose the increasing loss of information and appeal for the documentation of the knowledge that still remains, underlining the importance of valuing mainly the quality rather than the quantity [5].

Results suggest that, despite the existent bibliography, several details are still to be explored and there is still comprehensive information to be compiled and documented (mainly on pattern making and accurate technical know-how) thus making an extensive data collection improvement pertinent.

1.2 Traje à Vianesa - Techniques and Materials

Regarding the *Traje à Vianesa*, in 1930, Cláudio Basto [6] standardized the various costumes from different places around the main city, Viana do Castelo. Aside colors and ornaments, the general attire usually includes:

- **Shirt** – white, long-sleeved;
- **Vest** – waist level;
- **Skirt** – until the ankle, vertical stripes, pleated waistband, wide bar at the bottom;
- **Apron** – pleated waistband;
- **Pouch** (*algibeira*) – heart-shaped waist bag, between the skirt and the apron;
- **Socks** – white;
- **Clogs**;
- **Scarf** – crossing the chest and tight behind at waist level (sometimes it is used half scarf, replacing the whole scarf folded diagonally);
- **Head Scarf** – tied on the top of the head (Figs. 2 and 3).

Fig. 2. *Traje à Vianesa* [1].

Fig. 3. Front view with traditional gold jewelry [1].

Currently, there is a document that certifies the *Traje à Vianesa* [1], describing approved general characteristics. This is an established standard outfit regulation that unifies the costume and all its variations, created to avoid eventual deviations from the traditional typology (once well-defined and noticeable in each locality around Viana do Castelo).

According to the accreditation book [1], presently, the costume is comprised of several pieces of handcrafted origin, excluding the scarves (that were imported) and fabrics used for shirts, vests, skirts linings and pouches.

In the garments, raw materials such as linen and wool for weaving, cotton, wool or silk threads (the latter practically not used), glass beads, metal sequins (originally) to embroidery and others ornamental goods (e.g., metallic thread, lace, decorative stripes) are applied. Some fabrics of industrial manufacture are also used, such as cotton, linen, velvet, cotton flannels and wool cloth.

The craftsmanship know-how is still necessary to the manufacture of skirts and aprons (manual weaved), to embroidery shirts, skirts bars, vests and pouches, to produce socks laces, to make the clogs and to sew skirts, aprons, shirts, vests and pouches.

The following images illustrates the pouch (*algibeira*) details (Fig. 4) and the varied ornaments of the bottom part of the garment (Fig. 5).

Fig. 4. Pouch (*algibeira*) [1].

Fig. 5. *Traje à Vianesa* skirt and apron embroidery detail [1].

2 Methodology

A qualitative methodology - relevant literature review, observation, and interviews to experts -, was used.

The literature review focuses on two main subjects, the design circular strategies and the studied traditional costume. Some books about the *Traje à Vianesa* were read and the information was intersected (from the oldest to the most recent one) to present the garments and each technique and related materials, according to the costume original typology.

To complement and to enhance understanding on how costumes are currently made, certified artisans were observed, *in situ*, while working at their studio. It was then possible to collect fabric samples and to photograph costume details. Gaps and uncertainties from the literature review were illuminated through formal semi-structured conducted interviews (complementing data gathered thus far). During these interviews and through demonstrations, the accounts by a history expert and certified artisans made possible to observe how the whole attire is correctly dressed.

3 Results and Conclusions

The materials and techniques bellow were photographed to better expose the Table 1 content (Fig. 6).

Fig. 6. A, B, C, D, E, F, G, H - detailed images referring to the *Traje à Vianesa* techniques, also down below in Table 1 (photographs by the authors).

The Table 1 compiles and synthesizes the *Traje à Vianesa* costume techniques and materials, executed accordingly to its genuine elements (despite the existence of mentioned deviated designs, which may use fiber blends or different resources).

This new understanding should help, not only the systematization of techniques refined through the ages (developed with local and natural raw materials until the beginning of the 20th century) but, also, to create awareness related to identity and cultural heritage. This data is also of importance to inform contemporary projects as researchers/designers occasionally look into historical objects to investigate and gain perspective on methods and processes [2–4].

Table 1. Synthesis of the *Traje à Vianesa* techniques and materials.

Garments	Techniques	Materials
Shirt	- Manual weaving - Embroidery [A] - Smocking [A]	- 100% linen or linen/cotton blend - Mercerized cotton thread (nº 8, *perlé*) - Lace
Vest	- Embroidery [B]	- Wool Cloth (*fazenda*) - Cotton velvet - Embroidery: Mercerized cotton (*perlé*), wool or silk thread; Glass beads; Metal sequins; Metallic thread (*palheto*); Decorative stripes; Lace
Skirt	- Manual weaving (textured patterns – *puxados*) [E] - Embroidery [E] - Smocking (waistband)	- 100% wool or blends (manual weaving) - Wool cloth (*fazenda*) - Cotton fabric (lining) - Embroidery: Cotton or wool thread; Glass beads; Metal sequins
Apron	- Manual weaving (textured patterns – *puxados*) [F] [G] - Embroidery [F] - Smocking (waistband) [F]	- 100% wool or blends (manual weaving) - Embroidery: cotton or wool thread; Glass beads; Metal sequins
Pouch (*algibeira*)	- Embroidery [C]	- Wool Cloth - *fazenda* (red, blue, green or black) - Black velvet (for the pocket interior) - Embroidery: Mercerized cotton (nº 8, *perlé*), wool or silk thread; Glass beads; Metal sequins; Metallic thread (*palheto*); Decorative Stripes; Lace
Socks	- Manual lace [D]	- Cotton thread
Clogs	- Handmade manufacture	- Wooden soles - Hide
Scarf	- Stamping [H] - Wool fringes [H]	- Fine wool fabric - Wool thread

Additional research is needed to further explore accuracy in production and quality. It is crucial a system that may prevent knowledge from declining, technically and aesthetically.

Acknowledgments. The authors gratefully acknowledge support from FCT and CIAUD, Lisbon School of Architecture, Universidade de Lisboa.

References

1. Ramos, G., Pires, A.: Traje à Vianesa – Caderno de Especificações para a Certificação. Câmara Municipal de Viana do Castelo, Viana do Castelo (2017)
2. Earley, R.: The TEN: a tool for narrative prototypes. In: SHARE Handbook for Artistic Research Education, pp. 94–96 (2010)
3. Earley, R., Goldsworthy, K.: Playing for time: seven practice-led workshop tools for making design decisions to extend the life of fashion textile materials and products. In: PLATE: Product Lifetimes and the Environment. Research in Design Series, pp. 127–132. IOS Press (2017). http://ebooks.iospress.nl/volumearticle/47856
4. Earley, R.: Sustainable design inspiration for H&M – 100 great ideas. Presented by Professor Rebecca Earley. Textile Toolbox (2013)
5. Oliveira, J.L.: Folclore – Artesanato. Centro de Estudos Regionais - Boletim Cultural, pp. 82–91 (1985)
6. Basto, C.: Traje à Vianesa. Edições Apolino, Gaia (1930)

Kalokagathìa, Made in Italy and Cultural Heritage in Campania Region

Rosa Maria Giusto[1(✉)] and Mario Buono[2]

[1] National Research Council Italy (CNR), Institute for Research on Innovation and Services for Development (IRISS), Via G. Sanfelice 8, 80134 Napoli, Italy
r.giusto@iriss.cnr.it

[2] Università degli Studi della Campania "Luigi Vanvitelli", Via Roma 9, 81031 Aversa, CE, Italy
mario.buono@unicampania.it

Abstract. The paper is focused on the relationship between artistic craftsmanship, Made in Italy and cultural heritage as distinctive elements of the Italian "product".

"To understand Italian culture, way of being and beauty, the way forward is precisely that groove, that imprint left by style. The Italian style (…) is the form that explains the substance. There is perhaps no people in the world more than the Italian one that can be understood through its external forms, which are appearances full of meaning" [1].

Interest in culture and beauty can foster a new interpretation of the assets themselves, inserting you into artistic, architectural and museum contexts in which new vocations and peculiarities are revealed. To this end, the activities promoted by two institutions of excellence in Campania region: the MANN – National Archaeological Museum of Naples – and the Archaeological Park of Pompeii, were analyzed.

Keyword: Beautiful and well done · Italian style · Widespread museum · Enhancement · Fruition

1 Introduction

Rereading the cultural heritage, both tangible and intangible, in the light of a renewed interpretation of the concept of Made in Italy, means tracing the principal and identifying acronym that makes the Italian product an artefact of high ethical and aesthetic quality. It is a question of knowing how to combine aesthetic appearance and production reliability – beautiful and well made – art and craftsmanship, design and large-scale production, identifying them as multipliers of productivity and excellence [2].

Of course, it is not enough to recognize "beautiful and well-made" products if one fails to place them in relational networks of use and reciprocity. Interest in culture and beauty can foster a new interpretation of the assets themselves, inserting you into artistic, architectural and museum contexts in which new vocations and peculiarities are revealed.

A fashion show, as well as a commercial and marketing event, is a cultural event capable of bringing together different knowledge through which to convey and promote

D. Raposo et al. (Eds.): AHFE 2021, LNNS 277, pp. 150–157, 2021.
https://doi.org/10.1007/978-3-030-80415-2_19

artistic craftsmanship, attention to detail, the value of history, traditions, customs – from wealth and the quality of the fabrics, to the manufacturing, the models that reinterpret and inherit themes of art, the choice of places.

All these aspects help to understand how the real cultural revolution taking place in recent years has consisted and will consist in contaminating places and knowledge of Italian excellence – among the leading sectors in terms of GDP – opening art to fashion, design, tourism in a progressive interweaving of themes and values destined to entertain and educate new audiences, significantly affecting territories and cities "so that the cultural and artistic heritage, incorporated in Made in Italy products, becomes an incremental value perceived by the national and international consumer" [3].

The recent orientations of cultural centres and institutions go in this direction, first of all museums, increasingly interested in favoring and promoting educational and participatory processes in which the enhancement of their specific identity – historical-artistic, cultural, etc. – opens up to the city and its inhabitants in a process of continuous transmission and co-creation of new cultural contents.

In this logic, opening the museum to citizens, enriching it with an enlarged, flexible and dynamic cultural offer, also means intercepting and promoting new professionalisms, fueling the development of a real "beauty and culture market" that is all the more effective and incisive as the more the proposed "cultural product" is broad, recognizable and shared.

2 "Think Locally, Act Globally"

If it is true that the economic and health crisis of the last year has disrupted the economies of the world forcing us to change lifestyles and forms of living, it is precisely in circumstances like these that the *Italian style*, the original and authentic way of crossing and interpreting one's time can make a difference by bringing back to the focus of the debate the meaning and impact that shared and recognized values, life practices and ethically sustainable productions can bring also in economic terms to future scenarios. In the form of nostalgic evocations or of recovery of an aesthetic dimension that is also an ethical dimension of doing and living according to beauty, the *Italian style* translates into the "Italian way of life", high-lighting, if possible, the centrality that the "tradition of beauty" and the culture of doing with quality can take as an antidote and as a remedy for the sudden suspensions of time and meaning that the pandemic forces us to reconsider [4].

It is not a question of designing an "escape route" from reality but of recalibrating ways and rhythms of life to recover that ability to "enjoy one's time" which makes the Italian way of living and producing, a true distinctive feature as well as a "brand" among the most appreciated and recognized in the world. To the point of inducing experts to declare that "if made in Italy were a commercial brand (…) it would be the third best known in the world, after Coca-Cola and Visa" [5].

The whole issue of quality production and artistic craftsmanship that guides and distinguishes the different sectors of Made in Italy revolves around the theme of particularity, or if you want of diversity and uniqueness. It is about practical and millennial knowledge that, in the recovery of trades and knowledge built up over time, have renewed them in processes and products while maintaining a continuity constraint, a "semantic legacy constraint", perfectly identifiable and recognizable, which translates into that concept of "cultural and productive vocation" by which we habitually identify the individual territorial specificities.

It is no coincidence that territorial identity is one of the primary resources capable of generating value: promoting the cultural identity of a place means identifying its cultural heritage as a fundamental strategic resource for the enhancement of competitive sectors of the Made in Italy and Italian know-how, effectively summarized in the slogan *Think locally, act globally* [6].

In this sense, an important role is played by all the actions aimed at strengthening and consolidating the link that has always existed between Made in Italy, cultural heritage and sectoral tourism, aiming to encourage these aspects not only in terms of territorial marketing but as tools to transfer and communicate to the outside the production reliability, the aesthetic value, the know-how of Italian products, revealing their multiple connections with the world of culture, design and history to explore aspects inherent to the relationship between art, territory and production which have only recently joined the active policies adopted by public and private institutions and cultural associations.

Culture is therefore understood as a factor of production, to be used to conceive innovative products and services, but also as a "product" to be promoted, transferred, communicated to generate well-being and social inclusion.

It is not a question of "seducing customers", [7] – to paraphrase the words of Zygmunt Bauman that warns against the dangers arising from the processes of "commodification" of culture in place by many – but rather of investing in forms of education and training in awareness and recognition that living in beauty contexts also entails in terms of product quality. Hence the term Made in Italy with which it is customary to uniquely identify the excellence of Italian production, entrusting the cultural heritage of the place – the "land of Italy", not surprisingly defined as *Belpaese* – with the task to synthesize and certify its values.

Italian products, highly symbolic and evocative, *incorporate* the beauty of places and traditions, transferring it to objects in the form of creativity and "uniqueness in multiplicity", according to that attitude defined by Romano Benini as "doing things for many, but thinking about everyone" [8].

Culture, tourism, cultural and creative industries, then become the main development assets around which to organize the competitive growth of the country so that "we understand (…) the potential that our heritage, on the one hand, and the cultural and the creative industry, on the other hand, can express, finally placing them at the centre of a renewed development policy for our cities and territories" [9].

Speaking of cultural planning, in fact, means dealing with the aspects inherent to the management and enhancement of cultural heritage; integration with local production chains; accessibility and usability of cultural heritage and sites, favoring phenomena of inclusion and social and territorial regeneration [9].

The concept of *supply chain* – of luxury, fashion, craftsmanship, food and wine, art and knowledge – has recently opened up more to that of sectorial, cultural and integrated tourism, adding relational value to the usual way of considering and promote each sector by encouraging cross-sectoral and experiential approach.

3 An Example of Integrated Cultural Enhancement. The Case of Campania Region

Recent initiatives launched in Campania by two excellent cultural institutions are part of this framework: the MANN – National Archaeological Museum of Naples - one of the most important museums in the world for classical art – and the Archaeological Park of Pompeii, a real forge of ancient works and cultural deposit of excellence whose finds and furnishings feed and enrich a large part of the collections exhibited and kept at the MANN.

The interventions promoted aim to underline the importance of museums and cultural sites as "laboratories" for training and education to the beauty of an increasingly wide and diversified public of users and visitors, as well as a research and discussion centre, training and work.

In the strategic plan developed by the MANN for the years 2020–2023, some fundamental interventions are envisaged that highlight the multiple role that the museum of the future will be called upon to play: that of an incubator of knowledge and techniques; of an institution for the study and enhancement of the history and culture of the Mediterranean; of a city centre for the exchange, recognition and promotion of participatory processes aimed at empowering and including the inhabitants of the most disadvantaged neighborhoods, and in general of the city, in programs of mutual collaboration and co-creation of cultural and creative contents.

In other words, the model proposed is that of an institution that opens to the city to become an incubator of ideas and projects, activator of initiatives and discussions, the promoter of start-up companies and partnerships.

This context includes: the creation of the future *District of Mediterranean culture*, the main fulcrum of an *insula* that will gather around itself the places of culture and knowledge (the museum as a permanent institution and as a Palazzo degli Studi); places of creation and research (laboratories and repositories open to the city and to researchers with collaborations with interested cultural institutes - universities, research centres, foundations); the places of crafts and trades – the *ExtraMANN* – made up of a network of small shops and historic shops (30) grouped around the museum that will coordinate the activities and initiatives from below [10]. Finally, the idea of physically opening the building to the city through its atrium which will become a hybrid space where the boundary between inside and outside will be overcome in favor of a new promiscuity that will make every separation imperceptible, "mending" the *space of the urban identities* (based in the overlooking Galleria Principe di Napoli, taken to itself in an extensive interpretation of the concept of museum as a "civic" space), with the area of the UNESCO historic centre to combine knowledge, creativity and culture in a very broad, flexible and diversified cultural and educational offer.

To fully encourage this *osmosis* between places of culture and living spaces, it will not only be the city that will *enter* the museum by "appropriating" spaces once destined for a select few: it will also be art that will *come out* of the exhibition halls to pour into the squares and alleys of the city where, from the most famous monuments to the stairs of the buildings and the workshops of the artisans, you can walk immersed in history and its millenary suggestions (Fig. 1).

Such operation has already been partly initiated by the Municipality of Naples on the occasion of the creation of the *Stazioni dell'Arte* inaugurated in 2000 under the artistic direction of Achille Bonito Oliva when, with the concept of a *mandatory* and *widespread* museum, one of the most fruitful and stimulating cultural seasons in the city was launched. This was possible by placing in the newly built subway stations works of art – some of which are reproductions of classic works kept at the MANN – intended to educate and entertain the "involuntary" and "unaware" public of travellers, reinforcing the identity spirit of neighborhoods that had hitherto been peripheral and marginalized and returned to be part of the new urban image.

Fig. 1. MANN. Statue of the Farnese collection "escaped" in the historic workshop of a watch-maker (Frame taken from *Fuga dal museo*, photographic exhibition by Dario Assisi and Riccardo Maria Cipolla, MANN, December 2019–February 2020).

MANN's will to encourage and make new forms of dialogue between the museum, citizens and "insiders" dates back to 2017 with the conception and creation of the *Father and Son* videogame.

Through the new technological and digital tools of game design and with a storydoing approach, an active knowledge of history was initiated outside the exhibition halls, making it available to a potentially infinite public of international and foreign users who can retrace it every time co-creating one's own "itinerary" to move between the spaces and the identifying artefacts of the material and immaterial culture of the city.

Even the choice to translate the video game in almost all languages: from Russian, to Chinese, to Portuguese, passing through English, French and Spanish, to include the version in Neapolitan dialect, highlights the desire to open up to every audience – young and old, Italian and foreign, real and virtual – to educate them and introduce them to the living traditions of the place through one of the most evocative and powerful tools of Neapolitan culture: its *language*.

The plot of the video game begins in Pompeii in the hours preceding the devastating eruption of Vesuvius in 79 AD. C. and ends with a today's tourist intent on visiting its remains. Through the graphic reconstructions of the places and the narrative dimension of the texts, the participants are induced to constantly confront history in order to reunite the threads of an uninterrupted dialogue between past and present, territory and city that sees the Museum as the interpreter and main promoter of a highly aware and inclusive cultural mediation operation. Thus, "The focus shifts from the protection of the cultural asset itself, to the protection of the right that the community has to enjoy this capital that characterizes our country. The places of culture transcend (…) the elitist dimension that has distinguished them for decades to become devices for inclusion and reception, a business card for our companies" [11].

Similarly, the recent increase in the public and resources collected by the archaeological park of Pompeii, one of the most important archaeological sites in the world, also derives from having made the scientific results deriving from the renewed excavation campaigns accessible, understandable and popular, favoring the recognition and sharing of cultural itineraries – full of meanings, identifying history, traditions, ways of life – in a word of the "made in Italy" of a civilization whose peculiarities are illustrated. With the help of narrative voices lent by writers, researchers and interpreters linked to the city and its imaginary, the six-episode podcast entitled *Pompei la città viva* tackles the themes of: *The Living Museum in a contemporary key*; *Living in Pompeii: from art to street food*; *Fifty thousand times Hiroshima*; *The faces of research*; *The city of love*; *From the Grand Tour to Lonely Planet*, highlighting the relevance of a human and cultural event which, while belonging to the dimension of history, "lives in the present and speaks to the future" [12].

The combination of the material culture of the places, everyday objects, art and craftsmanship transports the visitor to a reality where ancient and contemporary show their points of contact, revealing their surprising *proximity*. A true forge of crafts and knowledge, as well as a historical document of excellence, the discovery of Pompeii represented a formidable opportunity to get closer "to the ways and customs of the ancients (…) and to penetrate into all the details of their domestic life" [13].

From the "skeleton" of the ancient city found under the lava and mud, to the architecture and their classical archetypes, to the statues, to the frescoes, to the mosaics, to the fabrics, to the jewels, to the furnishings and to the lifestyles documented by an original collection of finds from the daily life of the unfortunate inhabitants of those mighty remains of a past considered by many to be unsurpassable, campaigns of studies and surveys were born and nurtured which involved the widespread diffusion and imitation of that "repertoire" of forms in the most different sectors of art and quality craftsmanship, but also the awareness of a surprisingly modern and revealing continuity of values and customs.

This is what happens to Mrs. Ashton J. Yates when, visiting Pompeii in the middle of the nineteenth century, she notes: "In the centre of a room we saw a glass-covered table, on which necklaces, brooches, bracelets, earrings were on display (…), made of multicolored stones and finely worked gold, all with an absolutely modern look (…) we went to our jeweler to see how far the jewels we have ordered are in strict compliance with the ancient models we examined" [14]. From jewelry, to street food, to the graffiti found on the walls "everything brings Pompeii closer to us in an impressive way" [13], leading us to consider how much the relationship with history and memory is deducible also through the comparison with artifacts and the practices of daily life.

On the other hand, "the attention to objects and their evocative, performative power, to their energy as vehicles of single and collective memories, is a fact of our generation, more than any other invaded by the quantity of objects than by the past remote to the more recent one they incessantly appear in our daily experience" [15].

"To the same extent of a work of art, even if with less power and implications", the objects, become things, "trigger in those who use or contemplate them, a succession of references (...). In the form of technological objects, consumer goods, personal effects, furnishings and elements of the house, the street and the city, or in the most ambiguous form of artistic objects, they widely proliferate in every part of our lives. Being them produced, exchanged or consumed, objects become an integral part of the identity of individuals and communities" [16].

Recognition of the fundamental role assumed by Italy both in the processes of conception and creation of artefacts and works of art – the result of millenary history and the genius of a people who made their own ingenuity and research for new knowledge distinctive feature – as in the creation of products and services of excellence, also on an industrial scale, characteristic of the Made in Italy sector, it is accompanied by the necessary awareness that one of its greatest expressions lies precisely in the huge cultural heritage that is necessary to design, through the tool of design, services "of information and tourist use of excellence, both of a traditional, advanced and technological type"[17]. The education and communication of our heritage must be strongly encouraged so that the cultural value of goods and products is transmitted externally: in this sense, new transdisciplinary professionalism and flexible and adaptive information tools are needed that reveal aspects related to the craftsmanship of the "product", its identity value, to the interaction with the world of culture and history through the use of a design that supports and amplifies the Made in Italy that intervenes through innovative communication and transmission devices. "One of the most important aspects of the last decade sees the affirmation of design as a working methodology and not just as a productive attitude. In this way, creative approaches, innovative strategies, continuous invasions of the field, have crossed the disciplinary limits to become current practices in many areas of work. From this point of view, the current transformations of sectors far from the influences of traditional design (food, consumer technologies, sports, ceramics and coating materials) owe a lot to the culture of design" [18] which has become one of the most current and incisive tools to "make the city", actively participating in the conception and co-creation of places and contents with a high cultural and creative capital. Cultural dimension, unprecedented value, belonging to a defined historical and territorial reality constitute some of the most incisive declinations of heritage understood as a *dynamic cultural investment* where knowledge and know-how coexist in a cultural and creative process that finds in the union between Kalokagathìa, Made in Italy and cultural heritage its qualifying distinctive trait.

References

1. Benini, R.: Lo stile italiano: Storia, economia e cultura del Made in Italy. Donzelli, Roma, (2018), 12–13
2. Cfr. Cerquetti, M., Montella, M.: Paesaggio e patrimonio culturale come fattori di vantaggio competitivo per le imprese di prodotti tipici della regione Marche. In: Il territorio come giacimento di vitalità per l'impresa, XXIV Convegno annuale di Sinergie. Università del Salento, Lecce, Referred Electronic Conference Proceeding, pp. 549–562 (2012). ISBN 978-88-907394-0-8
3. Cioppi, M.: Review to Napolitano, M.R., Marino, V.: Cultural Heritage e Made in Italy. Casi ed esperienze di marketing internazionale. Editoriale Scientifica, Napoli (2016). Il Capitale culturale, 15 (2017), 328
4. Cfr. Anselmi, P.: Come ci vedono. Note sulla percezione all'estero degli italiani e del Made in Italy. In: The Italian Way. I valori degli Italiani e del made in Italy. Annual Seminar GfK Eurisko, Milano, 10 luglio 2014. https://docplayer.it/4360648-The-italian-way-i-valori-degli-italiani-e-del-made-in-italy.html
5. Benini, R.: Op. cit., 198–199
6. Cfr. Morace, F., Santoro, B.: Italian factor: Moltiplicare il valore di un paese. Egea, Milano (2014)
7. Cfr. Bauman, Z.: Per tutti i gusti. La cultura nell'età dei consumi. Laterza, Roma-Bari (2018)
8. Benini, R.: Op. cit., 197
9. Made with the contribution of Fusetti, A., Filippini, A.: Patrimonio storico-artistico e reti del contemporaneo. In: L'Italia che verrà. Industria culturale, made in Italy e territori. Rapporto 2012. I Quaderni di Symbola, 200, febbraio 2021. https://www.symbola.net/ricerca/litalia-che-verra-rapporto-2012/
10. Cfr. Presentation of the 2020/2023 Strategic Plan - Annual Report. http://www.museoarcheologiconapoli.it/wp-content/uploads/2020/10/PIANO-STRATegico-2020-2023.pdf
11. Bizjak, D.: Cultural heritage e made in Italy. In: Economia della cultura, 28 maggio, 2016. https://wordsinfreedom.com/cultural-heritage-e-made-in-italy/. febbraio 2021
12. Il museo vivente. In: Pompei la città viva, Piano P in collaboration with Electa (2021)
13. Osanna, M.: Pompei: la prossimità del passato. In: Osanna, M., Viliani, A. (eds.) Pompei@Madre. Materia archeologica. Electa, Milano, (2017), 91
14. Yates, Mrs. Ashton J.: Winter in Italy in a Series of Letters to a Friend. London (1844), cit. in: Osanna, M.: Pompei: la prossimità del passato, 94–95
15. Osanna, M.: Op. cit., 97. see also Osanna, M.: Pompei. Il tempo ritrovato. Le nuove scoperte. Rizzoli, Milano (2019)
16. Bodei, R.: La vita delle cose. Ebook, Laterza, Roma-Bari, (2014), 231, 242–244
17. Danesi, S.: Il patrimonio culturale quale fattore trainante del made in Italy. In: XXXIII Conference Aisre: Istituzioni, Reti Territoriali e Sistema Paese: la governance delle relazioni locali nazionali, Roma (2012), Cit. in Buono, M., Giusto, R. M.: Giacimenti culturali Made in Italy. Design e tecnologie per la conoscenza del patrimonio italiano. MDJ, 9 (2020), 211. https://aisre.it/images/old_papers/Danesi1.pdf
18. Made with the contribution of Fusetti, A., Filippini, A.: Design: tra heritage e cultura del territorio. In: L'Italia che verrà. Industria culturale, made in Italy e territori. Rapporto 2012. I Quaderni di Symbola, cit., 129, febbraio 2021. https://www.symbola.net/ricerca/litalia-che-verra-rapporto-2012/

Author Index

D. Raposo et al. (Eds.): AHFE 2021, LNNS 277, pp. 159–160, 2021.
https://doi.org/10.1007/978-3-030-80415-2

The manufacturer's authorised representative in the EU is Springer Nature Customer Service Centre GmbH, Europaplatz 3, 69115 Heidelberg, Germany. If you have any concerns regarding our products, please contact ProductSafety@springernature.com

Printed and bound by CPI Group (UK) Ltd, Croydon, CR0 4YY
30/09/2026
02225261-0018